Focus on Fundamentals of Programming with C

Eighth Edition

Richard L. Stegman

Focus on Fundamentals of Programming with C

Eighth Edition

1001-10-00010011-1000-11000010-11000001-11111111

ISBN: 9781720106821

Cover photo by: sdecoret/shutterstock.com

Table of Contents

Chapter 1. Algorithms

Introduction to Algorithms
Stepwise Refinement – Part 1
Stepwise Refinement – Part 2

An introduction to Algorithms

An algorithm is a step-by-step process for solving a problem. There are typically three important features of an algorithm:

1. The algorithm must have a finite number of instructions or steps.

2. Each instruction in the algorithm is well defined (not ambiguous).

3. The algorithm eventually halts.

For example, let's explore an algorithm for driving a car. Here are the steps:

```
Open the car door.
Enter the car.
Close the door.
Put on your seat belt.
Put the key in the ignition and turn on the ignition.
Put the car in drive.
Step on the gas.
```

Did we omit any steps?

Greatest Common Divisor

Sometimes an algorithm can be more mathematical in nature. Actually the oldest known arithmetic algorithm was reported around 300 B.C. by Euclid and is a method for computing the greatest common divisor of two whole numbers. The greatest common divisor is the largest whole number that divides both numbers without remainders.

If the two numbers are A and B, Euclid's algorithm is as follows:

```
1. Compute the remainder of the division of A and B.

2. Replace A by B.

3. Replace B by the remainder computed in step 1.

4. Repeat steps 1 - 3 until B is zero.

5. The greatest common divisor is the final value of A.
```

For example, find the greatest common divisor of A = 24 and B = 9:

```
1. The remainder of 24 / 9 = 6.
2. A = 9.
3. B = 6.
4. Repeat steps 1 - 3.

1. The remainder of 9 / 6 = 3.
2. A = 6.
3. B = 3.
4. Repeat steps 1 - 3.

1. The remainder of 6 / 3 = 0.
2. A = 3.
3. B = 0.
5. The greatest common divisor is 3.
```

A computer program is also an example of an algorithm. In fact, here's a program written in C to compute the greatest common divisor of two numbers following Euclid's algorithm:

```c
// gcd.c
// Program to calculate the greatest common divisor of two numbers

#include <stdio.h>

int main(void) {
    int A, B, remainder;

    printf("Enter two positive integers: ");
    scanf_s("%d%d", &A, &B);
    while (B != 0) {
        remainder = A % B;
        A = B;
        B = remainder;
    }
    printf("The greatest common divisor = %d\n", A);
    return 0;
}
```

Stepwise Refinement – Part 1

To show you an example of top-down design or stepwise refinement, we'll take the act of making scrambled eggs. Starting from the top we have the task to:

```
// eggs1

• Make scrambled eggs
```

But saying that by itself isn't enough to actually make any scrambled eggs, so we need to break the task down:

```
// eggs2

• Make some scrambled eggs
        1. Organize the kitchen
        2. Make scrambled eggs
        3. Serve the scrambled eggs
```

Each of these tasks can then be broken down further:

```
// eggs3

1. Organize the kitchen
        1. Clean surfaces
        2. Get out mixing bowl, whisk, spoon
        3. Get out eggs, salt, milk, and butter
        4. Put on apron

2. Make scrambled eggs
        1. Break eggs into bowl
        2. Whisk the eggs
        3. Add water and milk to the bowl
        4. Whisk
        7. Cook the scrambled eggs

3. Serve the scrambled eggs
```

And each of these tasks can be broken down further, let us take a look at the Cook the scrambled eggs component:

```
// eggs4

• Cook the scrambled eggs
        1. Get the frying pan to correct temperature
        2. Add the scrambled eggs mixture
        3. Keep stirring the eggs
        4. When scrambled eggs are firm the cooking is completed
```

Stepwise Refinement – Part 2

Finding the longest sub-sequence, a description of the problem.
Our goal is to locate the largest adjacent sub-sequence of increasing numbers contained in a larger sequence of numbers. The sequence of numbers is ended with a zero. We don't want to remember the sub-sequence itself, only the number of elements in the largest sub-sequence.

For example, given the sequence of numbers:

```
12, 22, 9, 8, 1, 4, 7, 2, 8, 9, 11, 12, 0
```

The largest number of elements in an increasing sequence is 5.

Designing an algorithm by successive refinement.
How do you start? Well, think of the problem as a series of smaller problems. You must break it down. Then you will break down the smaller problems into still smaller ones. You should continue this process until you have a series of precise steps, each one well defined, which will always yield a solution. This is called designing an algorithm by *stepwise refinement*.

The first try.
At the top level, the algorithm looks like this:

```
// stepwise1

1. Find the longest increasing sub sequence.

2. Print its length.
```

Try again.
Obviously step 1 must be expanded somehow, but how? Well, now the question comes down to: how do we find the longest increasing sub-sequence? Must we find all the sub-sequences and them compare them?

With a bit of ingenuity you will realize that you only have to remember the length of the longest sub-sequence that you have seen so far. You can compare the GREATEST_LENGTH_SO_FAR with the length of the next sub-sequence that you find and let the longest of the two be called the GREATEST_LENGTH_SO_FAR.

So the next attempt at the algorithm might look like this:

```
// stepwise2

1. Find the longest increasing sub sequence.

    1.1. Find the next increasing sub sequence.

    1.2. Compare the length of it to the GREATEST_LENGTH_SO_FAR.

    1.3. Call the longer of the two the GREATEST_LENGTH_SO_FAR.

    1.4. Repeat step 1.1 through 1.3 until finished.

2. Print the GREATEST_LENGTH_SO_FAR.
```

Some further refinement.

Now, this rather large problem is being described in a series of smaller tasks. However, there is still a lot of room for refinement. Each step is still not spelled out precisely enough. In fact, each step can be further refined into a series of smaller steps. Let's see how to find the next increasing sub-sequence:

```
// stepwise3

1.1 Find the next increasing sub sequence.

    1.1.1. Examine the CURRENT_NUMBER.

    1.1.2. Compare the CURRENT_NUMBER to the PREVIOUS_NUMBER.

    1.1.3. If the CURRENT_NUMBER is greater than the PREVIOUS_NUMBER
           then

               1.1.3.1. Add 1 to the LENGTH_OF_CURRENT_SUB_SEQUENCE.

    1.1.4. Let CURRENT_NUMBER now be called PREVIOUS_NUMBER.

    1.1.5. Let the next number now be the CURRENT_NUMBER.

    1.1.6. Repeat steps 1.1.2 through 1.1.5 until CURRENT_NUMBER is not
               greater than PREVIOUS_NUMBER.
```

Almost finished.

We are almost finished refining our algorithm. Let's put it all together and see how it looks.

```
// stepwise4

1. Find the length of the largest increasing sub sequence.

    1.1 Find the next increasing sub sequence.

        1.1.1. Examine the CURRENT_NUMBER.

        1.1.2. Compare the CURRENT_NUMBER to the PREVIOUS_NUMBER.

        1.1.3.If CURRENT_NUMBER is greater than the PREVIOUS_NUMBER
            then

            1.1.3.1. Add 1 to the LENGTH_OF_CURRENT_SUB_SEQUENCE.

        1.1.4. Let CURRENT_NUMBER now be called PREVIOUS_NUMBER.

        1.1.5. Let the next number now be the CURRENT_NUMBER.

        1.1.6. Repeat steps 1.1.2 through 1.1.5 until CURRENT_NUMBER is
                        not greater than PREVIOUS_NUMBER.

    1.2. Compare the length of it to the GREATEST_LENGTH_SO_FAR.

    1.3. Call the longer of the two the GREATEST_LENGTH_SO_FAR.

    1.4. Repeat step 1.1 through 1.3 until finished.

2. Print the GREATEST_LENGTH_SO_FAR.
```

A few words about variables, counting and initialization.

Don't be put off by unfamiliar names for some relatively simple concepts. A variable is no more than the name of something. It is a way of referring to some value that will vary over the course of an algorithm or program. For example, as we look at one number at a time in original sequence of numbers, whichever number we are looking at right now: we call CURRENT_NUMBER.

CURRENT_NUMBER is the name of the variable that holds the value of the number we are currently looking at. This allows us to create an algorithm that will work for any sequence of numbers that meet the original description, not just one specific sequence of numbers.

A counter is just a variable that counts. In this algorithm we use one counter. We use LENGTH_OF_CURRENT_SUB_SEQUENCE to hold the number of elements in the current sub-sequence. This counter starts out at zero and gets increased by one or incremented every time the CURRENT_NUMBER is greater than the PREVIOUS_NUMBER.

The term *initialize* means to set your counters and variables to the appropriate starting values. For example, what about remembering the GREATEST_LENGTH_SO_FAR? Well, when we begin we haven't seen any sub-sequence, so we can say that at the beginning of execution of the program the GREATEST_LENGTH_SO_FAR is zero.

Another example is the variable PREVIOUS_NUMBER. We can tell that we are looking at an increasing sequence when the CURRENT_NUMBER is greater than the PREVIOUS_NUMBER. What about the first time? There is no PREVIOUS_NUMBER. Well to get around that we initialize PREVIOUS_NUMBER to zero. How do we know what value to initialize different numbers to? By trying the algorithm. Remember, the algorithm should be a precise step-by-step description of the solution to the problem. You must test it by following it through by hand. When you do that you can adjust your algorithm where necessary.

Tying it all together.
So, now let's see what our complete algorithm looks like:

```
// stepwise5

1. Find the length of the largest increasing sub sequence.

    1.0.1. Initialize variables.

        1.0.1.1. Set GREATEST_LENGTH_SO_FAR to 0.

        1.0.1.2. Set the LENGTH_OF_THE_CURRENT_SEQUENCE to 0.

        1.0.1.3. Set the PREVIOUS_NUMBER to 0.

    1.1 Find the next increasing sub sequence.

        1.1.1. Examine the CURRENT_NUMBER.

        1.1.2. Compare the CURRENT_NUMBER to the PREVIOUS_NUMBER.

        1.1.3.If CURRENT_NUMBER is greater than the PREVIOUS_NUMBER
           then

            1.1.3.1. Add 1 to the LENGTH_OF_CURRENT_SUB_SEQUENCE.

        1.1.4. Let CURRENT_NUMBER now be called PREVIOUS_NUMBER.

        1.1.5. Let the next number now be the CURRENT_NUMBER.

        1.1.6. Repeat steps 1.1.2 through 1.1.5 until CURRENT_NUMBER is
                        not greater than PREVIOUS_NUMBER.

    1.2. Compare the length of it to the GREATEST_LENGTH_SO_FAR.

    1.3. Call the longer of the two the GREATEST_LENGTH_SO_FAR.

    1.4. Repeat step 1.1 through 1.3 until finished.

    1.5 Repeat step 1.1 through 1.4 until CURRENT_NUMBER is 0.

2. Print the GREATEST_LENGTH_SO_FAR.
```

Chapter 2. A First Look at C

Sample C Program
Capturing Program Output

Sample C Program

The program below prints the numbers from 1 to 15, their squares, and their cubes. Please work through the following:

• Enter the program shown below exactly as is into your compiler's editor.

• Compile and execute the program.

• See if you can modify the program to work with the numbers from 1 to 30.

• Compile and execute the program.

• See if you can modify the program to show the 4th and 5th power of each number.

• Compile and execute the program.

• See if you can fix anything in the output that might looks strange.

• Compile and execute the program.

• Modify your code to capture the program output into an output file called `csis.txt`.

```
/*****************************************************************
 Program Name:        power.c
 Author:              Richard Stegman
 Date Submitted:      November 10, 2018
 Class                CSCI 112
 Instructor:          Richard Stegman
 Compiler:            Xcode 10
 OS:                  OS X 10.14
 Description:         Program generates a table of squares and cubes
                      for the numbers 1 - 15
 Input Files:         None
 Output Files:        None
 *****************************************************************/

#include <stdio.h>

#define MIN 1
#define MAX 15

int main(void) {
    int i;

    printf("%10s %10s %10s\n", "Value", "Square", "Cube");
    printf("%10s %10s %10s\n", "-----", "------", "----");

    for (i = MIN; i <= MAX; ++i) {
        printf("%10d %10d %10d\n", i, i * i, i * i * i);
    }
    return 0;
}
```

Capturing Program Output

When you submit your computer lab assignments, it will be necessary to include a file that contains the output generated by your program. While you might be tempted to simply copy and paste the output that appears on the screen into a file, often output generated from your program cannot all fit on the screen and usually gets scrolled off the screen. Please follow the instructions below to capture the output of you program into a file called csis.txt.

- Add the following declaration to your C program before main():

```
FILE *fp;
```

In main(), after your variable declarations, add the following statement:

For Visual Studio (Windows):

```
fopen_s(&fp, "csis.txt", "w");
```

For Xcode (Mac):

```
fp = fopen("csis.txt", "w");
```

This will open the csis.txt data file to capture your program output. Don't worry about the syntax for now, as we'll look at the details later.

- Every printf() statement in your program that sends output to the terminal window should have a corresponding fprintf() statement that also sends the output to the csis.txt file.

For example, if your program contains the following type of printf() statement:

```
printf("Hello, world.\n");
```

then the very next line in your program should contain the following statement:

```
fprintf(fp, "Hello, world.\n");
```

Likewise, if your program contains the following type of `printf()` statement:

```
printf("The sum equals %d\n", sum);
```

then the very next line in your program should contain the following statement:

```
fprintf(fp, "The sum equals %d\n", sum);
```

In each case, the `fprintf()` statement will cause the identical output to be sent to the `csis.txt` output file.

- Finally, the statement in `main()` just before the `return` statement should be:

```
fclose(fp);
```

This statement will close the `csis.txt` data file before the program completes execution.

Note that `fopen()` is the traditional ANSI C function used to work with files and is used in a Mac, Linux, or other non-Microsoft environment. However, as most students typically use Microsoft's Visual Studio environment, the text will utilize Microsoft's more secure `fopen_s()` function.

Here's an example of a C program that captures its output into the `csis.txt` data file (note that all code examples in the text will use the Visual Studio syntax):

```c
// test.c - program illustrates capturing output into csis.txt data
file

#include <stdio.h>

FILE *fp;

int main(void) {
    int a, b, sum;

    fopen_s(&fp, "csis.txt", "w");
    a = 3;
    b = 4;
    sum = a + b;
    printf("The sum of %d plus %d equals %d.\n", a, b, sum);
    fprintf(fp, "The sum of %d plus %d equals %d.\n", a, b, sum);
    fclose(fp);
    return 0;
}
```

Please follow these additional instructions if you are using Xcode:

We must now tell Xcode to place our `csis.txt` output file in the project folder.

Select Product | Scheme | Edit Scheme

Select the Options tab and place a checkmark next to Working Directory.

Under Use Custom Working Directory, navigate to your project folder and click OK.

Your program's output file, `csis.txt`, will now appear in the project's folder after the program executes.

Chapter 3. C Program Elements

Program Structure
Compiler Directives and Comments
Variables and Data Types
Printf and Output Formats
Char Data Type
ASCII Table
Constants
Mixing Data Types
scanf_s() Function
C Reserved Keywords
Program Errors
❖ C Program Elements Homework
❖ Speed Lab
❖ Heart Lab
❖ Salary Lab
❖ Temperature Lab

Program Structure

Let's analyze the traditional first C program:

```
// hello1.c - first C program

#include <stdio.h>

int main(void){
    printf("Hello, world.\n");
    return 0;
}
```

The first line of the program:

```
// hello.c - first C program
```

is a comment which provides the name and description of the program. The symbols `//` represent a single-line comment in C and is ignored by the compiler.

The next line:

```
#include <stdio.h>
```

is necessary in any program that uses an the input or output functions `printf()` or `scanf_s()`. Since you will always want to use `printf()` in your programs, you will always need to include this line.

Note the blank lines in the program. These extra blank lines are not necessary but you should add them as they make your programs more readable. Think of your program as a document, part of which executes on a computer.

All C programs begin execution at the start of the `main()` function. Therefore, every C program must include a `main()` function somewhere in the code.

```
int main(void){
```

The `int` before `main()` signifies that the `main()` function will return an integer value when it completes. The `void` in parentheses after `main()` signifies that no information will be passed to the `main()` function.

The left curly brace, `{`, marks the beginning of the function (program), and the right curly brace, `}`, marks the end of the function (program). As you will soon discover, curly braces are used to group together "blocks" of code.

The statement:

```
printf("Hello, world.\n");
```

is a function call which invokes a function called `printf()` with the argument: `"Hello, world.\n"`. `printf()` is a library function which prints output to the terminal window: `Hello, world.`

The program is linked to the I/O library with the preprocessor command:

```
#include <stdio.h>
```

Without this declaration, the compiler would not understand the what the `printf()` function was to do.

The symbols `\n` represents a newline character and causes a linefeed to be generated. Note that it consists of two characters in the source file, but consists as one character within the program itself.

Note that we could have written the program as follows:

```
// hello2.c - first C program

#include <stdio.h>

int main(void) {
    printf("Hello, ");
    printf("world. ");
    printf("\n");
    return 0;
}
```

and would have generated the same output to the terminal window.

- The statement:

```
return 0;
```

indicates that `main()` is returning the value 0 upon completion. More on this later.

C Program Statements

There are three categories of C program statements:

Simple

```
statement;
statement;
```

Compound

```
{
    statement;
    statement;
}
```

Block

```
{
    declarations;

    statement;
    statement;
}
```

Compiler Directives and Comments

Compiler directives are handled by the C preprocessor as it makes its first pass through your program file. The resulting preprocessed file is then compiled in the second pass by the C compiler to generate the object file that is in the machine language code.

The #include Directive

#include includes the contents of another file, commonly called a header file, into your source code file. The line of code where the #include compiler directive occurs is replaced by the contents of the header file.

For example, if the contents of a header file named myinclude.h were:

```
// This is an empty include file with nothing but comments.
// There is no meaningful code in this file.
```

and the program file contained the following lines of code:

```
#include <stdio.h>
#include "myinclude.h"

int main(void) {
    printf ("This is a 1 line program.\n");
}
```

then the preprocessing step would produce the following lines of code:

```
// include1.c
// This is an empty include file with nothing but comments.
// There is no meaningful code in this file.

int main(void) {
    printf ("This is a 1 line program.\n");
}
```

Sometimes a header file will include angle brackets, <>.

```
#include <stdio.h>
```

The angle brackets tell the C preprocessor that the included file is a C Standard Library header file (sometimes called a system file.) The standard input/output library file, stdio.h, contains the declarations (definitions) of all the standard names needed to do input and output in our programs. It must be included, for example, to use the printf() and scanf_s() standard input/output functions.

Note that the C Standard Library (the header and implementation files) come with the C compiler software. There are about 18 such libraries, including stdio.h for input/output, library files for string manipulation functions, math functions, character manipulation functions, etc. Note that you don't have to know where system header files are located, as the C pre-processor knows where to find them.

User-Defined Header Files
User defined header files are header files that you create that may define information specific to your program.

Assume the following statement:

```
#include "myheader.h"
```

The double quotes, " ", tell the C preprocessor that the included file is a user-defined header file as opposed to a C Standard Library header file. The C preprocessor assumes that the file myheader.h is located in the same directory where the program is compiled. If the user defined header file is not located in the same directory where you compile the program, then the information inside the double quotes must contain the path information for the user defined header file. Otherwise, the C preprocessor will not know where to find user defined header files.

The #define Directive

#define defines a macro constant name and value whose name is automatically replaced by the macro constant value throughout the program file. For example, consider the following statement:

```
#define KMS_PER_MILE 1.609
```

The C preprocessor substitutes the macro constant name KMS_PER_MILE with the macro constant value, 1.609, throughout the program file. We would write the C line of code:

```
kms = miles * KMS_PER_MILE;
```

After the C pre-processor step, this line would look like this:

```
kms = miles * 1.609;
```

C Comments

Comments are statements that clarify the meaning and content of your program file. They are a means of documenting your program code so that people can better understand how the program works.

Comments are removed by the C preprocessor before the resulting program code is compiled so the C compiler does not see them. However, the comments can be read by humans looking at the contents of your program file.

Comments start with /* and end with */ and everything between /* and */ is removed by the C preprocessor.

```
/* This is a single comment. */


/*
 * This is also a single comment.
 */
```

Be very careful to terminate your comments correctly or you may get surprising results. The comment on the first line (below) is not terminated which results in the C preprocessor removing the `#include` and `#define` statements that follow it. It is as though these lines were never in the program to begin with.

```
// include2.c
/* Include the standard input and output header file.

#include <stdio.h>

#define KMS_PER_MILE 1.609 /* Kilometer conversion factor */

int main(void) {
    ...
    ...
    return 0;
}
```

This kind of error is very hard to find. Can you see why the additional code:

```
int main(void) {
    ...
    ...
    return 0;
}
```

isn't also "swallowed up" by the preprocessor?

Comments can also start with `//` and anything that follows, through the end of the line, is ignored by the preprocessor.

```
// This is a single comment.
```

Variables and Data Types

Identifiers (Variable Names)

A variable is an object that can assume different values during the execution of a program. Every variable has a *name* and a *value*. The name identifies the variable and the value stores data. There is a limitation on what these names can be. Every variable name in C must start with a letter or an underscore, the rest of the name can consist of letters, digits and underscore characters. C recognizes upper and lower case characters as being different. Finally, you cannot use any of C's keywords like `main`, `while`, `switch` etc. as variable names.

Examples of legal variable names include:

```
x           x1          x2          tempValue       r2d2
result      num         value       outFile         c3po
```

A capital letters is often used as the first letter of the second word when two words are combined into a variable name. The rules governing variable names also apply to the names of functions.

Variables and Data Types

In C, a variable must be declared before it can be used. Most variables are declared at the start of each function. These local variables are created when the function is called, and are destroyed on return from that function.

A declaration begins with the type, followed by the name of one or more variables. For example:

```
int test, min, max;
```

Declarations can be spread out, allowing space for an explanatory comment. Variables can also be initialized when they are declared, this is done by adding an equals sign and the required value after the declaration:

```
int test = 25;          // test value
int min = 10;           // minimum value
int max = 50;           // maximum value
```

C provides a wide range of types. The most common are:

```
int          represents a whole number
float        represents a floating point (real) number
double       represents a floating point (real) number
char         represents a single byte of memory, enough to hold a character
```

There are also several variants on these types:

```
short           represents an integer, possibly of reduced range
long            represents an integer, possible of increased range
unsigned        an integer with no negative range
unsigned long   like unsigned, possible of increased range
```

All of the integer types plus the `char` are called the integral types. `float` and `double` are called the real types.

As said previously, all C program variables must be declared, or associated with a data type, before they are used in a program. This serves four purposes:

Data types define the amount of storage that must be allocated for each variable.

Data types define the interpretation given to each storage location.

Data types define the range of values a variable may take.

Data types define a set of operations that may be performed on the variable.

Integer Data Types

Integers, or `int` in C, can represent whole numbers that do not have a fractional component such as 1, 10, -35, 450, 11232, etc. Commas or blanks are never used to represent integers. Integer variables should be used where the numeric value will not have a fractional component, such as in counting, etc.

The table below indicates the number of bytes allocated for variables of each data type along with the range of values that can be held by a variable of each data type.

Integer Types on a 32-bit Machine

Name	Bytes	Minimum Value	Maximum Value
short int	2	-32,768	32,767
unsigned short int	2	0	65,535
int	4	-2,147,483,648	2,147,483,647
unsigned int	4	0	4,294,967,295
long int	4	-2,147,483,648	2,147,483,647
unsigned long int	4	0	4,294,967,295

Integer Types on a 64-bit Machine

Name	Bytes	Minimum Value	Maximum Value
short int	2	-32,768	32,767
unsigned short int	2	0	65,535
int	4	-2,147,483,648	2,147,483,647
unsigned int	4	0	4,294,967,295
long int	8	-9,223,372,036,854,775,808	9,223,372,036,854,775,807
unsigned long int	8	0	18,446,744,073,709,551,615

`sizeof()` Operator

The operator `sizeof()` is built-in as part of the C language. It returns an integer that represents the number of bytes used to store an object on the host computer. All that is guaranteed by C is that:

```
sizeof(char) = 1
sizeof(short) <= sizeof(int) <= sizeof(long)
sizeof(unsigned) = sizeof(int)
```

Note that problems can occur if the result of an integer operation is assigned to a variable of a shorter data type.

For example:

```
long x = 10000;
long y = 10000;
short answer;

answer = x * y;
```

The calculation of `answer` will correctly evaluate to 100000000. However, the assignment of the `long` result to a `short` produces a value that is too large to be held in the `short` and the `short` will therefore hold an incorrect value.

Note that the integer ranges in the tables above aren't mandated by the C standard and may vary from one compiler to another. All that is guaranteed by C is that a `char` is one byte and that:

```
sizeof(short) <= sizeof(int) <= sizeof(long) <= sizeof(long long)
```

One way to determine the range of integer types for a particular implementation is to check the `<limits.h>` header file, which is part of the standard C library. This header defines macros that represent the smallest and largest values of each integer type.

```c
// limit.c

#include <stdio.h>
#include <limits.h>

int main (void) {
    printf("Data Type\t\t\t\t\tBytes\t\t\t
                        Min Value\t\t\t\t   Max Value\n");
    printf("Short Int\t\t\t\t\t %ld\t\t%20d\t\t%20d\n",
                        sizeof(short), SHRT_MIN, SHRT_MAX);
    printf("Unsigned Short Int\t\t\t %ld\t\t%20d\t\t%20u\n",
                        sizeof(unsigned short), 0, USHRT_MAX);
    printf("Int\t\t\t\t\t\t\t %ld\t\t%20d\t\t%20d\n",
                        sizeof(int), INT_MIN, INT_MAX);
    printf("Unsigned Int\t\t\t\t %ld\t\t%20d\t\t%20u\n",
                        sizeof(unsigned int), 0, UINT_MAX);
    printf("Long int\t\t\t\t\t %ld\t\t%20ld\t\t%20ld\n",
                        sizeof(long int), LONG_MIN, LONG_MAX);
    printf("Unsigned Long int\t\t\t %ld\t\t%20d\t\t%20lu\n",
                        sizeof(unsigned long int), 0, ULONG_MAX);
    printf("Long Long int\t\t\t\t %ld\t\t%20lld\t\t%20lld\n",
                        sizeof(long long int), LONG_LONG_MIN,
                            LONG_LONG_MAX);
    printf("Unsigned Long Long int\t\t %ld\t\t%20d\t\t%20llu\n",
                        sizeof(unsigned long long int), 0,
                            ULONG_LONG_MAX);
    return 0;
}
```

Depending upon your computer system, the program output might look like this:

```
Data Type                Bytes   Min Value               Max Value
Short Int                2       -32768                  32767
Unsigned Short Int       2       0                       65535
Int                      4       -2147483648             2147483647
Unsigned Int             4       0                       4294967295
Long int                 8       -9223372036854775808    9223372036854775807
Unsigned Long int        8       0                       18446744073709551615
Long Long int            8       -9223372036854775808    9223372036854775807
Unsigned Long Long int   8       0                       18446744073709551615
```

Floating Date Types (Floats and Doubles)

Real or floating point numbers can be designated as either float or double. Floats or doubles can represent numbers that have a fractional component such as 1.01, 10.1654, -35.7, 450.333, etc. Note that the fractional component can be zero such as 3.0. Floating point (float or double) variables should be used whenever a numeric value can have a fractional component such as in mathematical operations involving division, etc.

For example, we create a float variable called myFloat which we set equal to 7.2.

```
float myFloat = 7.2f;
```

Note the letter f after the number. Now it would actually work without the f but it's a good rule of thumb that if we want to set a float, we use the little f to be explicit about what we're doing.

The double data type is also floating point, but uses double the storage. A float is 4 bytes, a double is 8 bytes. double is used whenever the accuracy provided by a float is not sufficient.

```
double myDouble = 7.2;
```

Doubles provides double precision versus the single precision of floats. As on any computer system, we can lose precision with floating-point operation simply because of the way the computer stores this information. The representation of floating point numbers is not as accurate as the representation of integers.

Note when we set the `float`, we use the `f`; when we set the `double`, we don't. That's because when we write a literal, including the decimal point, it's always going to take it as a double unless we put the `f` after it. In both of these cases we're just using 7.2, which is a value that will fit in both a float and a double just fine. So it doesn't really matter in this case, but the `f` is good practice.

C provides three floating data types:

```
float              Single-precision floating point
double             Double-precision floating point
long double        Extended-precision floating point
```

The C standard doesn't state how much precision the `float`, `double`, and `long double` provide, since different computers may store floating-point numbers in different ways. All that is guaranteed by C is that:

```
sizeof(float) <= sizeof(double)
```

So depending upon your computer system, the maximum and minimum values for a `float` and a `double` might look like this:

Name	Bytes	Minimum Value	Maximum Value	Precision
float	4	1.17549×10^{-38}	3.40282×10^{38}	6 digits
double	8	2.22507×10^{-308}	1.79769×10^{308}	15 digits

Printf and Output Formats

We've already taken a look at the `printf()` statement that comes as part of the standard C library:

```
printf("Hello, world.\n");
```

Let's take a closer look at its syntax:

```
printf("format_control_string", arguments);
```

The format control string describes how the arguments to the `printf()` function are to be printed. For example:

```
int num = 5;
printf("sum = %d\n", num);
```

prints the value of `num` using the format control string:

```
"%d\n"
```

This prints the output as a decimal (base 10) number (`%d`), and then generates a line feed (`\n`).

```
sum = 5
```

We can add two integers and display the result:

```c
// add.c

#include <stdio.h>

int main(void) {

    int num1, num2, sum;

    num1 = 50;
    num2 = 75;
    sum = num1 + num2;
    printf("The sum of %d and %d is %d.\n", num1, num2, sum);
    return 0;
}
```

The output is:

```
The sum of 50 and 75 is 125.
```

Shown below is a table of control string formats:

%d	integer or decimal (base 10) format	%u	unsigned decimal
%ld	long decimal format	%lu	unsigned long decimal format
%f	floating point format	%e	scientific notation format
%lf	double format	%o	octal format
%c	character format	%x	hexadecimal format
%s	character string format		

Consider the following C program:

```
// format1.c

#include <stdio.h>

int main (void) {

    int i = 65;
    char c = 'A';

    printf("Decimal = %d    Char = %c\n", i, i);
    printf("Decimal = %d    Char = %c\n", c, c);
    return 0;
}
```

The output is:

```
Decimal = 65    Char = A
Decimal = 65    Char = A
```

Note that the same variable can be printed using several different formats. The choice of output format is given entirely by the format string, not by the type of the variable being printed!

The following C program gives additional specification of printing width and justification:

```c
// format2.c

#include <stdio.h>

int main(void) {
    int num = 123;
    float value = 123.456;

    printf("<%d> is not justified.\n", num);
    printf("<%10d> is right justified.\n", num);
    printf("<%-10d> is left justified.\n", num);
    printf("\n");
    printf("<%f> is not justified.\n", value);
    printf("<%10.3f> is right justified.\n", value);
    printf("<%-10.3f> is left justified.\n", value);
    return 0;
}
```

The output is:

```
<123> is not justified.
<       123> is right justified.
<123       > is left-justified.

<123.456001> is not justified.
<   123.456> is right justified.
<123.456   > is left justified.
```

Without the width specification, C takes only as many positions as are needed to output the data. Note that the use of angle brackets in the code above is just to show how the output will appear. They are not used for justification purposes in your program.

Char Data Type

Each character is stored in 1 byte (8-bits) according to its ASCII code and is considered to have the corresponding integer value $(0 - 255)$. Characters are written between single quotes and can be:

- uppercase letters: $('A' \ldots 'Z')$
- lowercase letters: $('a' \ldots 'z')$
- digits: $('0' \ldots '9')$
- punctuation: $('. ', '! ', '; ', \text{etc.})$
- special characters $('*', '+', '\%')$
- white space characters (blank, tab, newline)

C is best described as a somewhat weakly-typed language and thus can blur the distinction among data types. For example, we can add characters as if they were integers:

```
printf("%5d", 'A' + 'B' + 'C');
```

This outputs the sum of the ASCII values as 198.

Here's a program to print all the characters in a machine's character set, showing the decimal, hexadecimal, and character values. Note that the character sequence \t represents a tab. Please enter this code into your C compiler and execute the program:

```
// ascii.c

#include <stdio.h>

int main(void) {
    int i;

    for (i = 0; i < 128; i++) {
        printf("%4d\t  %4x\t %4c\n", i, i, i);
    }
    return 0;
}
```

Escape Characters

Some non-printing and hard to print characters require an escape sequence. The newline character, `'\n'`, is a good example. Even though it is described by the two characters \ and n, it represents a single ASCII character. The backslash, \, is called the *escape character* and is used to escape the usual meaning of the character that follows it.

Escape characters can be used in character and string constants to represent characters that would be awkward or impossible to enter in the source program directly. There are both *character escapes* and *numeric escapes*:

• Character escapes can be used to represent some particular formatting as well as special characters.

• Numeric escapes allow a character to be specified by its numeric coding.

Character Escape Codes

Character escape codes are used to represent some common special characters in a fashion that is independent of the target computer character set:

Escape Characters	Written in C	ASCII Value
null	`'\0'`	0
backspace	`'\b'`	8
horizontal tab	`'\t'`	9
vertical tab	`'\v'`	11
newline	`'\n'`	10
form feed	`'\f'`	12
carriage return	`'\r'`	13
double quote	`'\"'`	34
single quote	`'\''`	39
backslash	`'\\'`	92
arbitrary bit pattern (contains 1-3 octal digits)	`'\ddd'`	
arbitrary bit pattern (contains 1-2 hez digits)	`'\xdd'`	

Below are some examples.

Display tabbed output:

```
printf("%d\t    %d\t    %d\n", a, b, c);
```

Include the backslash character itself in a character string:

```
printf("\\t is the horizontal tab character.\n");
```

Include double quotes inside the character string:

```
printf("\"hello, \" he said.\n");
```

The output looks like:

```
"Hello, " he said.
```

Here's a program that counts the number of lines in the input. Type in the program and execute it. You will need to enter some input during program execution. To end the program input, type in a control-z sequence, ^z, or a control-d sequence, ^d. Although we haven't yet looked at all the details of the syntax, see if you can figure out how the program works!

```
// countLines.c

#include <stdio.h>

int main(void) {
    int nextChar;
    int numLines = 0;

    while ((nextChar = getchar()) != EOF) {
        if (nextChar == '\n') {
            ++numLines;
        }
    }
    printf("%d lines read.\n", numLines);
    return 0;
}
```

Here's the program output:

```
The
sky
is
blue
4 lines read.
```

Numeric Escape Codes

Numeric escape codes allow any character to be expressed by writing that character as its octal (base 8) encoding in the target character set. From 1 – 3 octal digits may be used to express the value of the character.

For example:

```
'a' may be written as '\141'

'?' may be written as '\77'
```

The null character, which is used to terminate strings, is represented as: '\0'.

Numeric escape codes enables characters that may not be directly available from the keyboard to be coded into a character string. For example, we can sound three bells and display a message with:

```
printf("\7\07\007 Attention!!\n");
```

Note that the numeric escape characters are only considered a single character inside a string. Thus, the character string:

```
"\007\"Hello\"\n"
```

actually consists of 9 characters.

Finally, we must be cautious when using numeric escape codes as a numeric escape code terminates when either 3 octal digits have been used or when the first character that is not an octal digit is encountered.

For example, the string:

```
'\0111"
```

consists of two characters:

```
'\011' and '1'
```

The string:

```
"\080"
```

consists of three characters:

```
'\0' and '8' and '0'.
```

ASCII Table

Dec	Binary	Hex	Char	Dec	Binary	Hex	Char	Dec	Binary	Hex	Char
0	00000000	0		43	00101011	2b	+	86	01010110	56	V
1	00000001	1		44	00101100	2c	,	87	01010111	57	W
2	00000010	2		45	00101101	2d	-	88	01011000	58	X
3	00000011	3		46	00101110	2e	.	89	01011001	59	Y
4	00000100	4		47	00101111	2f	/	90	01011010	5a	Z
5	00000101	5		48	00110000	30	0	91	01011011	5b	[
6	00000110	6		49	00110001	31	1	92	01011100	5c	\
7	00000111	7		50	00110010	32	2	93	01011101	5d	]
8	00001000	8		51	00110011	33	3	94	01011110	5e	^
9	00001001	9		52	00110100	34	4	95	01011111	5f	_
10	00001010	a		53	00110101	35	5	96	01100000	60	`
11	00001011	b		54	00110110	36	6	97	01100001	61	a
12	00001100	c		55	00110111	37	7	98	01100010	62	b
13	00001101	d		56	00111000	38	8	99	01100011	63	c
14	00001110	e		57	00111001	39	9	100	01100100	64	d
15	00001111	f		58	00111010	3a	:	101	01100101	65	e
16	00010000	10		59	00111011	3b	;	102	01100110	66	f
17	00010001	11		60	00111100	3c	<	103	01100111	67	g
18	00010010	12		61	00111101	3d	=	104	01101000	68	h
19	00010011	13		62	00111110	3e	>	105	01101001	69	i
20	00010100	14		63	00111111	3f	?	106	01101010	6a	j
21	00010101	15		64	01000000	40	@	107	01101011	6b	k
22	00010110	16		65	01000001	41	A	108	01101100	6c	l
23	00010111	17		66	01000010	42	B	109	01101101	6d	m
24	00011000	18		67	01000011	43	C	110	01101110	6e	n
25	00011001	19		68	01000100	44	D	111	01101111	6f	o
26	00011010	1a		69	01000101	45	E	112	01110000	70	p
27	00011011	1b		70	01000110	46	F	113	01110001	71	q
28	00011100	1c		71	01000111	47	G	114	01110010	72	r
29	00011101	1d		72	01001000	48	H	115	01110011	73	s
30	00011110	1e		73	01001001	49	I	116	01110100	74	t
31	00011111	1f		74	01001010	4a	J	117	01110101	75	u
32	00100000	20		75	01001011	4b	K	118	01110110	76	v
33	00100001	21	!	76	01001100	4c	L	119	01110111	77	w
34	00100010	22	"	77	01001101	4d	M	120	01111000	78	x
35	00100011	23	#	78	01001110	4e	N	121	01111001	79	y
36	00100100	24	$	79	01001111	4f	O	122	01111010	7a	z
37	00100101	25	%	80	01010000	50	P	123	01111011	7b	{
38	00100110	26	&	81	01010001	51	Q	124	01111100	7c		
39	01000111	27	'	82	01010010	52	R	125	01111101	7d	}
40	00101000	28	(	83	01010011	53	S	126	01111110	7e	~
41	00101001	29	)	84	01010100	54	T	127	01111111	7f	
42	500101010	2a	*	85	01010101	55	U				

The ASCII Codes are ordered and can be compared to each other in the same way that other numeric values can be compared to each other.

Character: 'A' < 'B' < 'C' < 'D' < ...
ASCII Code: 65 < 66 < 67 < 68 < ...

Character: 'a' < 'b' < 'c' < 'd' < ...
ASCII Code: 97 < 98 < 99 < 100 < ...

Character: '1' < '2' < '3' < '4' < ...
ASCII Code: 49 < 50 < 51 < 52 < ...

The ordering of the ASCII codes from lowest to highest is called a *collating sequence* and allows character comparisons for things like alphabetic ordering.

Constants

Constants are values that cannot be modified during the execution of a program. A constant can be a number, character, or character string.

Numeric Constants

Decimal constants are written as a non-empty sequence of digits, the first of which is not zero.

```
234
9032
```

Octal constants are written with a leading zero followed by digits 0-7:

```
032
0266
```

Hexadecimal constants are written with a leading 0x followed by 0-9, A-F, a-f:

```
0x42
0x1AF
0xAB9D
```

Character Constants

Character constants are usually just the character enclosed in single quotes:

```
'A'
'a'
'$'
'5'
'\n'
'\t'
'\0'
```

Character constants have the type `int` whose values are the integer encodings of the characters in the target character set (ASCII – Unicode). For example:

```
'A'   = 65
'a'   = 97
'$'   = 36
'5'   = 53
'\n'  = 10
'\t'  = 9
'\0'  = 0
```

String Constants

String constants are a (possibly empty) sequence of characters enclosed in double quotes:

```
"Carol"
"William"
"Yellow"
""
```

Note that string constants, unlike other constants, actually have a location in memory. For each string constant of N characters, there will be at run-time a statically allocated block of n+1 characters whose first n characters are initialized with the characters from the string and whose last character is the null character, '\0'. The null character is used so programs can conveniently find the end of a string.

We can now see why the character 'a' is not the same as the string "a". The character 'a' represents a single ASCII character, while the string "a" contains an array of two characters that contains the ASCII character 'a' along with the null character '\0'.

The shortest string is the null string and is represented as "". It is stored in memory as the single null character '\0'.

Mixing Data Types

Numerical data types can be converted from one type to another. For example:

* `int` can be converted to `double` or `float`

* `int` can be converted to `char` (may cause some loss of information)

* `char` can be converted to `int`

* `float` can be converted to `double`

* `double` can be converted to `float` (may cause some loss of accuracy)

* `double` or `float` can be converted to `int` (but fractional values will be truncated)

Implicit (automatic) Conversions

Whenever different data types are used in an assignment expression, the data type on the right side of the expression is converted to the data type on the left side. For example:

```
int num;
char c;
:
num = c;
```

Here, `c` is converted to an `int` and then assigned to `num`. Because a `char` data type needs fewer bits than an `int`, `c` is normally zero-filled on the left during conversion.

However, when you make the assignment:

```
c = num;
```

the integer `num` is assigned to a `char` and any excess bits in `num` are discarded before assignment to `c`. In fact, the most significant bits are discarded so information will be lost!

Performing Binary Operations on Mixed Data Types

If you perform binary operation on two different data types, the compiler will convert the data type that requires the fewer number of bits to the data type that requires the greatest number of bits for internal storage.

For example, if an int and a double are multiplied, the int is converted to a double before the multiplication because the double requires a larger number of bits for its internal representation than does an int. The result returned from the operation is converted to the data type that requires the largest number of bits for its representation, in this case a double.

See if you can figure out the output produced from the following program:

```c
// mixed.c

#include <stdio.h>

int main(void) {
    float f1 = 123.125, f2;
    int i1, i2 = 150;
    char c = 'a';

    // float to int conversion
    i1 = f1;
    printf("%d\n", i1);

    // int to float conversion
    f1 = i2;
    printf("%f\n", f1);

    // int divided by int
    f1 = i2 / 100;
    printf("%f\n", f1);

    // int divided by float
    f2 = i2 / 100.0;
    printf("%f\n", f2);
    return 0;
}
```

Here's the output:

```
123
150.000000
1.000000
1.500000
```

Can you see why?

Note that integer division truncates towards zero:

```
int a, b;
:
a = 1/3;      // produces 0
b = 6/7;      // produces 0
```

However, if either operand of the division is a `float`, both operands are converted to `float`:

```
float w, x, y, z;
:
w = 1.0 / 3.0;           // 0.333333
x = 1.0 / 3;             // 0.333333
y = 6.0 / 7.0;           // 0.857143
z = 6 / 7.0;             // 0.857143
```

Explicit (automatic) Conversions
The *cast operator* converts (casts) the value of a variable into a type that is different from the original type of the variable. The cast is specified by giving the cast type in parentheses followed by the expression to be cast:

```
(cast-type) expression
```

For example::

```
int x;
float y;
:
:
y = (float) x;
```

This converts the integer value of x to its corresponding `float` value and assigns that value to y. Note that the conversion does not change the value or the type of x. The conversion is held in temporary storage.

We normally cast a variable to ensure that the arithmetic is carried out with the type of the left-hand side:

```
a = (int) 17.7 * 2;
```

The result is:

```
a = 34;
```

We can round a variable to an integer by first adding 0.5 and then casting to an `int`:

```
a = (int) (val + 0.5);
```

A typical use of cast is in forcing division to return a real number when both operands are integers:

```
average = (float) sum / num;
```

Without the cast, truncated integer division is performed, since both sum and num are integers.

scanf_s() Function

`scanf_s()` is a function standard library which allows you to input values into a program from standard input (keyboard). It's usually used to input numerical data using formats similar to the `printf()` statement.

Note that `scanf()` is the traditional ANSI C function used to capture user input and is used in a Mac, Linux, or other non-Microsoft environment. However, as most students typically use Microsoft's Visual Studio, the text will utilize Microsoft's more secure `scanf_s()` function.

Like `printf()`, `scanf_s()` has a control string, followed by the list of items to be read. However `scanf_s()` wants to know the *addresses* of the items to be read, since it is a function which will change those values. Therefore the names of variables are preceded by the `&` sign. Note that character strings are an exception to this. Since a string is already a character pointer, we give the names of string variables unmodified by a leading `&` (more on strings later).

In the expression:

```
scanf_s("%d %d", &x, &y);
```

the arguments `&x` and `&y` tell `scanf_s()` where to store the data that it reads. `&` is an operator in C which gives the address of its operand, i.e., `&x` gives the address of `x`. Note that the arguments to the `scanf_s()` function MUST be pointers to the locations in memory (addresses) where the input is to be stored.

Here are `scanf_s()` fomat codes:

```
Code        Meaning
%c          read a character
%d          read a decimal integer
%ld         reads a long decimal integer
%f          read a floating point number
%lf         reads a double
%h          read a short integer
%x          read a hexadecimal number
%s          read a string
```

Here's an example of the use of `scanf_s()`:

```
// scanf_s.c

#include <stdio.h>

int main(void) {
    int i;
    double d;

    printf("Enter an integer and a double: ");
    scanf_s("%d %lf", &i, &d);
    return 0;
}
```

Input line:

```
250    123.45
```

The two input fields may be separated by as many blanks, tabs, and newlines (whitespace characters) as desired. `scanf_s()` skips any leading whitespace characters in the input (except when using the `%c` format specifier).

Any non-format characters specified in the format string of `scanf_s()` is to be expected on the input. For example, to enter the current time from terminal we can use:

```
scanf_s("%d:%d:%d", &hour, &min, &sec);
```

The `:` specifies that colons are expected as separators between the three integer values.

Strings, characters, and scanf_s()
Microsoft has determined that any format string of the form `"%s"` is dangerous because it doesn't prevent buffer overflow (a security concern). This is why Microsoft uses the more secure `scanf_s()` function. In fact, if you are using Visual Studio and just use `scanf()`, the compiler will produce a warning message during the build phase.

So unlike `scanf()`, `scanf_s()` requires the buffer size to be specified for all input parameters of type `c` or `s`. The buffer size is passed as an additional parameter immediately following the variable name. For example, if reading a string, the buffer size, 10, for that string is passed as follows:

```
char name[10];

scanf_s("%9s", name, 10);   // or scanf_s("%9s", name, sizeof(name);
```

The buffer size, 10, includes the terminating null character. A width specification field, 9, may be used to ensure that the token read in will fit into the buffer. If no width specification field is used, and the token read is too big to fit in the buffer, nothing will be written to that buffer, preventing a buffer oveflow. Security!

In the case of characters, one may read a single character as follows:

```
char c;

scanf_s("%c", &c, 1);
```

When reading multiple characters for non-null terminated strings, integers are used as the width specification and the buffer size.

```
char c[4];

scanf_s("%4c", &c, 4);      // not null terminated
```

But plain-old `scanf()` is the ANSI standard, and it is not deprecated by anyone but Microsoft. Just make sure there is always a number between `%` and `s` in your format strings.

Note: If you want to strictly use ANSI C and not Microsoft C without getting the warning messages, add the following line of code **before** you include any header files:

```
#define _CRT_SECURE_NO_WARNINGS
```

More on the %s Specifier

When the `%s` specifier is used, the value to be read is a sequence of characters that begins with the first non-whitespace character and is terminated by the first whitespace character. The corresponding argument is a pointer to a character array, which must contain enough locations to contain all the characters that are read plus the null character that is added to the end of the string automatically by the function.

The `scanf_s()` function can also take an optional modifier between the `%` and the format character that determines the field-width number used to indicate the maximum number of positions or digits to expect in an argument (or that a field occupies). For example:

```
scanf_s("%4d %10s", &num, buf, 10);

Input: 1234hello        Output: 1234      hello
Input: 123456hello      Output: 1234      56hello
```

If a field-width modifier is supplied, the specified number of characters is read, unless a whitespace character is encountered first.

Note that when `scanf_s()` reads in a particular value, reading of the value will terminate as soon as a character that is not valid for the value being read is encountered (or as soon as the number of characters specified by the field width is reached, if specified).

White space characters inside a format string match an arbitrary number of whitespace characters on the input:

```
scanf_s("%d%c", &i, &c, 1);

input:
29   w

assign:
29 to i
space to c
```

To correctly read the input, we must therefore use:

```
scanf_s("%d %c", &i, &c, 1);

input:
29  w

assign:
29 to i
'w' to c
```

This works since the blank space in format string causes `scanf_s()` to ignore any leading whitespace characters after 29 has been read.

Note when `scanf_s()` searches input for value to be reads, all leading whitespace characters are skipped, except when using `%c`, which reads the next character from input, no matter what it is.

For character strings read in with `%s`, any non-whitespace character is valid. For `&c`, any character is valid.

When a value is read that does not match a value expected by `scanf_s()`, then `scanf_s()` does not read any further items from input and returns to the calling program with the number of items that were successfully read. This value can be tested to determine if any errors occurred in the input. For example,

```
scanf_s("%d %f %d", &i, &f, &n);
```

will return the value 3 given the input:

```
-300, 12.34, 23
```

since the 3 values of `i`, `f`, and `n` would successfully get assigned.

If the input were:

```
-300, x, 17.8, 27
```

then 1 would be returned.

We could use this test in the calling program as follows:

```
if (scanf_s("%d %f %d", &i, &f, &n) == 3) {
    :
}
```

C Reserved Keywords

The following words are reserved keywords in C, and may not be used as identifiers:

auto	double	int	switch
_Bool	else	long	typedef
break	enum	register	union
case	extern	restrict	unsigned
char	float	return	void
_Complex	for	short	volatile
const	goto	signed	while
continue	if	sizeof	
default	_Imaginary	static	
do	inline	struct	

Program Errors

There are three basic types of programming errors: syntax errors, semantic (logic) errors, and run-time errors.

Syntactic Errors

Syntax errors are errors in the programming language syntax. They are errors made with the "grammatical rules" of C and are diagnosed by the compiler at *compile time*. For example, the following code fragment is not syntactically correct. Can you see what the problem is?

```
printf("Enter the distance traveled in miles: );
```

The program will not compile successfully until all syntax errors have been corrected. The following code fragment has been corrected and is now syntactically correct.

```
printf("Enter the distance traveled in miles: ");
```

Semantic (Logic) Errors

Semantic, or logic errors, are errors in the meaning or implementation of the program. The program may compile and run successfully but the results may be incorrect. The following code fragment is not semantically correct as the formula for calculating kilometers is incorrect. Can you see why?

```
kilometers = miles / 1.609;
```

You should be multiplying miles by 1.609, not dividing. The following code fragment has been corrected and is now semantically correct.

```
kilometers = miles * 1.609;
```

The only way you can locate errors such as these is to use carefully constructed tests to verify that the program is semantically correct. But you have to know what answers are expected for each test case, or you have no way of evaluating each test.

Run-Time Errors

Run-time errors are errors that occur when the computer attempts to perform an illegal operation or instruction. The program may compile and run but, due to a run-time error, might stop unexpectedly or "crash."

For example, if the user enters a value of 0 for milesPerGallon:

```
gasolineUsed = miles / milesPerGallon;
```

the resulting calculation would attempt to divide the number of miles traveled by 0. Dividing a number by zero is mathematically undefined and is an illegal operation on the computer. It will cause your program to terminate (we sometimes say "crash", or abort) with a run-time "divide by 0 error" or a run-time "nan" (not a number) error.

Program Testing

Program testing can be used to verify that the program does not produce run-time errors. The goal is to test the program for several representative cases and ensure that the appropriate output is generated in each case.

First calculate the results you expect the program to produce for each of the test cases. Then compare the results you expect to see with the actual results that the program produces to verify that the program is working correctly. If the results the program produces do not match the results you expect to see, then you must "debug" the program to find where the program code is incorrect.

You should always verify that you are using the proper variables in your formulas and output statements and that the variables you are using have the correct values when used in formulas and output statements. In particular, you always need to check to ensure you have entered correct values for a variable before trying to use the variable in a calculation. Also be sure you are using the correct units in your computations as well.

❖ C Program Elements Homework

1. Write a single C statement to accomplish each of the following tasks.

   a) Define variables `temp`, `num`, and `total` to be of type `int`, `avg` to be of type `float`, and `value` to be of type `double`.

   b) Initialize variable `temp` to `7665`, variable `num` to `42`, variable `avg` to `123.45`, and variable `value` to `3.14159265`.

   c) Add variable `num` to variable `temp` and assign the result to variable `total`.

   d) Multiply variable `temp` by `num` and assign the result to `temp`.

   e) Increment variable `temp` by `5`.

   f) Calculate the product of the three integers contained in `int` variables `x`, `y` and `z`, and assign the result to the `int` variable `product`.

2. Which of the following are not legal C identifiers:

   a) `hello_world`   c) `purpleRain`

   b) `_4_out_of_7`   d) `12345`

3. What is the value of each of the following expressions?

   a) `6 + 2 * 4 - 1`

   b) `8 * 2 - 3 * 2 + 8 * 4`

   c) `3 * 4 * 2 - 5 + 20 / 2 / 2`

   d) `4 * ( 2 * ( 4 - 1 ) ) - 5`

4. Which of the following are not legal data types in C?

    a) `short int`   c) `long long`

    b) `long float`   d) `unsigned long`

5. If `c` is a variable of type `char`, which one of the following statements is illegal?

    a) `putchar(c);`   c) `c = 'c';`   e) `c = 50;`

    b) `printf(c);`   d) `c = '5';`   f) `c = 3 + c * 2;`

6. Suppose that `i` is a variable of type `int`, `j` is a variable of type `long`, and `k` is a variable of type `unsigned int`. What is the type of the expression:

    `(long) i + (int) j * k`

7. Suppose that `i` is a variable of type `int`, `f` is a variable of type `float`, and `d` is a variable of type `double`. What is the type of the expression:

    `i * f / d`

8. Suppose that `value` is a variable of type `float`, `num` is a variable of type `long`, and `sum` is a variable of type `int`. Explain what conversions take place during the execution of the following statement:

    `sum = value + num;`

9. Write a single C statement that performs each of the following tasks:

    a) Display each of the words below on a separate line:

        `All you need is love.`

    b) Output the value of `double` variable `temp` using `printf()`.

c) Read three doubles from the keyboard and store the value entered into doule variables `value1, value2, value3.`

d) Print the double `123.456789` with 2 digits of precision. What value is printed?

e) Print the floating-point value `3.14159f` with 3 digits to the right of the decimal point. What value is printed?

f) Print `"The sum equals: "` followed by the integer value of variable `sum.`

10. What output is produced for each of the following statements?

a) `printf("%5d, %6d", 123, 1234);`

b) `printf("%10.2e", 12.345);`

c) `printf("%.5f", 12.345);`

❖ Speed Lab

Write a C program, `speed.c`, which performs the following operations (be sure to give all numeric output to two decimal places):

Assigns a value (275.5) representing the distance in miles traveled by a car

Assigns a value (8.5) representing the number of hours taken to travel that distance

Computes the speed of the car in miles/hour (speed = distance / time)

Computes the speed of the car in meters/second (use 1 mile = 1600 meters)

Note: Do not perform your own calculations and have your program output the results. All of the calculations for the lab should be performed within your program. Use the following guidelines to develop your program:

Declare your variables with appropriate data types.

Assign values to your variables.

Perform your calculations.

Generate appropriate output.

Points to Remember:
Make sure you are creating a C program and not a C++ program. The `.c` suffix to your source code will invoke the C compiler while the `.cpp` suffix will invoke the C++ compiler. As this is a class in C and not C++, please make sure your source code uses the `.c` suffix. You should not be using any global variables in your program. A global variable is a variable declared outside of `main()`.

Output from your program should be sent to the terminal window (your screen) as well as the requested `csis.txt` output file. Be sure to read the document on Capturing Program Output. Your full name must appear as a comment in the source file that contains `main()`. Be sure to include the `csis.txt` output file in your zip archive.

❖ Heart Lab

Assume a human heart beats on the average of once per second. Write a C program, `heart.c`, which calculates how many times the heart beats in 50 years. You may use 365 for days in a year. Do not use floats or doubles for this lab and do not worry about leap yrars.

Note: Do not perform your own calculations and have your program output the results. All of the calculations for the lab should be performed within your program.

Use the following guidelines to develop your program:

Declare your variables with appropriate data types.

Assign values to your variables.

Perform your calculations.

Generate appropriate output.

Points to Remember:

Make sure you are creating a C program and not a C++ program. The `.c` suffix to your source code will invoke the C compiler while the `.cpp` suffix will invoke the C++ compiler. As this is a class in C and not C++, please make sure your source code uses the `.c` suffix. You should not be using any global variables in your program. A global variable is a variable declared outside of `main()`.

Output from your program should be sent to the terminal window (your screen) as well as the requested `csis.txt` output file. Be sure to read the document on Capturing Program Output. Your full name must appear as a comment in the source file that contains `main()`. Be sure to include the `csis.txt` output file in your zip archive.

❖ Salary Lab

Write a C program, `salary.c`, which performs the following operations (be sure to give all numeric output to two decimal places):

Assigns a value (38.5) representing the number of hours worked

Assigns a value (18.50) representing the hourly payrate of an employee

Computes the wages earned by the employee (wages = hours * payrate)

Note: Do not perform your own calculations and have your program output the results. All of the calculations for the lab should be performed within your program. Use the following guidelines to develop your program:

Declare your variables with appropriate data types.

Assign values to your variables.

Perform your calculations.

Generate appropriate output.

Points to Remember:

Make sure you are creating a C program and not a C++ program. The `.c` suffix to your source code will invoke the C compiler while the `.cpp` suffix will invoke the C++ compiler. As this is a class in C and not C++, please make sure your source code uses the `.c` suffix. You should not be using any global variables in your program. A global variable is a variable declared outside of `main()`.

Output from your program should be sent to the terminal window (your screen) as well as the requested `csis.txt` output file. Be sure to read the document on Capturing Program Output. Your full name must appear as a comment in the source file that contains `main()`. Be sure to include the `csis.txt` output file in your zip archive.

❖ Temperature Lab

Write a C program, `temp.c`, which performs the following operations:

Assigns a value (72) representing the temperature in degrees Farenheit.

Converts the temperature to degrees Celsius. Converting from Farenheit to Celsius requires subtracting 32 from the Farenheit temperature and then dividing the difference by 1.8. Be sure to give all numeric output to one decimal place.

Converts the Celsius temperature to degrees Kelvin. Converting from Celsius to Kelvin requires adding 273 to the Celsius temperature. Be sure to give all numeric output to one decimal place.

Note: Do not perform your own calculations and have your program output the results. All of the calculations for the lab should be performed within your program. Use the following guidelines to develop your program:

Declare your variables with appropriate data types.

Assign values to your variables.

Perform your calculations.

Generate appropriate output.

Points to Remember:

Make sure you are creating a C program and not a C++ program. The `.c` suffix to your source code will invoke the C compiler while the `.cpp` suffix will invoke the C++ compiler. As this is a class in C and not C++, please make sure your source code uses the `.c` suffix. You should not be using any global variables in your program. A global variable is a variable declared outside of `main()`.

Output from your program should be sent to the terminal window (your screen) as well as the requested `csis.txt` output file. Be sure to read the document on Capturing Program Output. Your full name must appear as a comment in the source file that contains `main()`. Be sure to include the `csis.txt` output file in your zip archive.

Chapter 4. Operators

Assignment Operators
Arithmetic Operators
Relational Operators
Logical Operators
Combining Logical and Relational Operators
Character Type Tests
Increment and Decrement Operators
Precedence of Operators
❖ Operators Homework
❖ Weight Lab
❖ Character Constant Lab
❖ Change Lab
❖ Days Lab

Assignment Operator

One reason for the power of C is its wide range of useful operators. An operator is a function that is applied to values to give a result. You should be familiar with operators such as =, +, -, *, /.

Assignment and arithmetic operators are the most common. Other operators are used for comparison of values, combination of logical states, and manipulation of individual binary digits. The operators of C provide the programmer with really all the capabilities that are available in assembler language without limiting the program to one specific hardware.

The assignment operator, =, assigns the value of the operand on the right hand side to the operator on the left hand side.

```
num = 7;
```

assigns the value of 7 to num. The value 7 becomes the value of the assignment expression as a whole, i.e., the assignment statement actually returns the assigned value.

Another example:

```
x = (y = 5) + (z = 7);
```

Here, the value of 5 is assigned to y, and the value of 7 is assigned to z. But 5 is returned from the first assignment statement is added to the 7 that is returned by the second assignment statement, and the value of 12 is assigned to x. The code below has the same effect:

```
y = 5;
z = 7;
x = y + z;
```

The assignment operator actually associates right to left so the following code:

```
x = y = z = 0;
```

actually is interpreted as;

```
x = (y = (z = 0));
```

which assigns 0 to z, then y, then x.

The assignment operator is even more flexible. For example:

```
x = x + 2
```

can be written as:

```
x += 2;
```

The assignment += is a combination of the add (+) and assignment (=) operators. All arithmetic operators have combined forms like this:

```
x += n;        // add n to x
x -= n;        // subtract n from x
x *= n;        // multiply x by n
x /= n;        // divide x by n
x %= n;        // x gets the remainder of dividing x by n
```

Note that:

```
x *= y + 1;
```

is equivalent to:

```
x = x * (y + 1);
```

and not:

```
x = x * y + 1;
```

Arithmetic Operators

Operators and values are combined to form expressions. The values produced by these expressions can be stored in variables, or used as a part of even larger expressions.

```
+       addition
-       subtraction
*       multiplication
/       integer division
%       modulus (only defined for ints)
-       unary minus (negates the operand)
```

Operators `*`, `/`, `%` will be performed before `+` or `-` in any expression. Brackets can be used to force a different order of evaluation to this. Where division is performed between two integers, the result will be an integer, with remainder discarded. For example:

```
7 / 3 = 2
8 / 4 = 2
3 / 3 = 1
4 / 7 = 0
0 / 7 = 0
7 / 0 = error
```

Note that if a program is ever required to divide a number by zero, this will cause an error, usually causing the program to crash.

The modulus operator, `(%)`, is only meaningful between integers and returns the remainder of a division and ignores the quotient. For example:

```
7 % 3 = 1
8 % 3 = 2
4 % 2 = 0
2 % 5 = 2
```

The modulus operator turns out to be surprisingly useful. For example, we could check whether one number is divisible by another:

```
If x % y is zero, then x is divisible by y.
```

We can also use the modulus operator to extract the rightmost digit or digits of a number:

```
x % 10 yields the rightmost digit of x

x % 100 yields the rightmost two digits of x
```

Hand trace the value of the variables in the following two programs and see if you can match the output:

```
// trace1.c

#include <stdio.h>

int main(void) {
    int a, b, c;

    b = 1;
    c = 5;
    a = b + c;
    b = a + b + c;
    c = a % b;
    b = c / a;
    printf("%d   %d   %d\n", a, b, c);
    return 0;
}
```

Here's the output that's produced:

```
6    1    6
```

```
// trace2.c

#include <stdio.h>

int main(void) {
    int a, b;

    a = 1;
    b = -1;
    printf("a = %d    b = %d\n", a, b);
    a = a + b;
    b = a - b;
    a = a - b;
    printf("a = %d    b = %d\n", a, b);
    return 0;
}
```

Here's the output that's produced:

```
a = 1     b = -1
a = -1    b = 1
```

Extracting Digits

Assume that num refers to a three-digit integer. Which of the following evaluates to the middle digit of num? For example, if num referred to 456, we want an expression with the value 5.

a) (num / 10) % 10

b) (num % 100) / 10

c) (num % 10) / 10

d) more than one of the above

e) none of the above

Relational Operators

A relational operator is a comparison symbol showing a relationship between two expressions. Each relational operator takes two operands and produce a numerical (not Boolean) result which is either 0 (false) or non-zero (true). This is called *semi-boolean* logic.

```
>     greater than
>=    greater than or equal to
<     less than
<=    less than or equal to
==    equal to
!=    not equal to
```

Precedence of Relational Operators

```
>   >=  <   <=
==  !=
```

The precedence of the relational operators is just below that of the arithmetic operators. Therefore,

```
a + b < c + d
```

would be a valid C expression. What would be the output of the program below?

```
// precedence.c

#include <stdio.h>

int main(void) {              a) some non-zero value
    int a, b;                 b) 0
                              c) 3
    a = 3;                    d) syntax error
    b = a == 3;               e) true
    printf("%d\n", b);        f) false
    return 0;
}
```

Logical Operators

Quite often we express conditions based upon the truthhood and/or falsehood of more than one condition. For example:

You will receive an A in the class if you do well on the exams AND if you do well on the programming assignments.

C provides logical operators that allow us to express such compound conditions. The three logical operators in C are:

```
&& - and

|| - or

!  - not (unary negation operator)
```

Logical statement can be analyzed using a truth table that lists all possible values for the conditions (variables):

Truth Table: Logical And Operator (&&)

p	q	p && q
True	True	True
True	False	False
False	True	False
False	False	False

Truth Table: Logical Or Operator (||)

p	q	p || q
True	True	True
True	False	True
False	True	True
False	False	False

Truth Table: Logical Negation Operator (!)

p	! p
True	False
False	True

In C, logical operators are frequently used to combine relational operators to build larger expressions:

```
if (x < 20 && x >= 10)
```

Expressions using the logical operators are evaluated left to right and evaluation stops as soon as the truth or falsehood of the result is known. In other words, logical expressions evaluate their left hand operand, and then only evaluate the right hand one if this is required.

Note that `false &&` anything is always `false`. `True ||` anything is always `true`. In such cases the second test is not even evaluated. This is referred to as a *short-circuit*. Negation (!) operates on a single logical value and its effect is to reverse its state. Here is an example of its use:

```
if (!acceptable) {
    printf("Not Acceptable!!\n");
}
```

The precedence of logical operators is below that of the relational operators. Therefore, we can write the following code without parenthesis:

```
a < b && c < d
```

The result of any logical expression is either:

```
0        - false
non-zero - true
```

The unary negation operator (!) produces a 1 when the operand is false (zero) and a zero when the operand is true (non-zero):

```
!0 = 1

!1 = 0
```

Note that !a means the same as a==0. Rather than writing code like this:

```
if (a == 0)
```

C programmers like to write code like this:

```
if (!a)
```

Both statements have the same meaning.

Note that the unary negation operator (!) is not the same as the mathematical not operator. In mathematics:

```
not(not(s)) = s
```

while in C:

```
!!5 = 1
```

Why?

```
!!5 = !(!5) = !(0) = 1
```

As mentioned previously, in the evaluation of logical expressions, the evaluation process stops as soon as the outcome, true or false, is known (short circuit.)

For example, if `expr1` is false (0), then in the statement:

```
expr1 && expr2
```

`expr2` will not be evaluated because the value of the logical expression is already determined to be zero.

Likewise, if `expr1` is true (non-zero), then in the statement:

```
expr1 || expr2
```

`expr2` will not be evaluated because the value of the logical expression is already determined to be 1.

De Morgan's Laws

De Morgan's Laws can sometimes make it more convenient for us to express a logical expression. De Morgan's Laws can be expressed mathematically as follows:

```
~(P or Q) = ~P and ~Q

~(P and Q) = ~P or ~Q
```

In C, these laws state that the expression:

```
!(condition1 && condition2)
```

is logically equivalent to the expression:

```
(!condition1 || !condition2)
```

Also, the expression:

```
!(condition1 || condition2)
```

is logically equivalent to the expression:

```
(!condition1 && !condition2)
```

To summarize:

```
!(condition1 && condition2) = (!condition1 || !condition2)

!(condition1 || condition2) = (!condition1 && !condition2)
```

See if you can apply DeMorgan's Law to the following expression:

```
!(x > 5) || !(y > 7)
```

Combining Logical and Relational Operators

We can combine logical and relational operators to test whether a character is a:

• digit
• uppercase letter
• lowercase letter
• printable character

Note that it is typical to place $0x$ in front of a hexadecimal (base 16) digit:

```c
// ascii1.c

#include <stdio.h>

int main(void) {
    unsigned char c;

    for (c = 0; c <= 127; ++c) {
        printf("%3d  0x%03x", c, c);

        // check for printable character
        if (c >= ' ' && c <= '~') {
            printf(" '%c' ", c);
        }

        // check for digit
        if (c >= '0' && c <= '9') {
            printf("digit");
        }

        // check for uppercase
        if (c >= 'A' && c <= 'Z') {
            printf("uppercase");
        }

        // check for lowercase
        if (c >= 'a' && c <= 'z') {
            printf("lowercase");
        }

        printf("\n");
    }
    return 0;
}
```

Here's the program output:

```
 0   0x000
 1   0x001
 2   0x002
 3   0x003
 4   0x004
 5   0x005
 6   0x006
 7   0x007
 8   0x008
 9   0x009
10   0x00a
11   0x00b
12   0x00c
13   0x00d
14   0x00e
15   0x00f
16   0x010
17   0x011
18   0x012
19   0x013
20   0x014
21   0x015
22   0x016
23   0x017
24   0x018
25   0x019
26   0x01a
27   0x01b
28   0x01c
29   0x01d
30   0x01e
31   0x01f
32   0x020 ' '
33   0x021 '!'
34   0x022 '"'
35   0x023 '#'
36   0x024 '$'
37   0x025 '%'
38   0x026 '&'
39   0x027 '''
40   0x028 '('
41   0x029 ')'
42   0x02a '*'
43   0x02b '+'
44   0x02c ','
45   0x02d '-'
46   0x02e '.'
47   0x02f '/'
```

```
48  0x030 '0' digit
49  0x031 '1' digit
50  0x032 '2' digit
51  0x033 '3' digit
52  0x034 '4' digit
53  0x035 '5' digit
54  0x036 '6' digit
55  0x037 '7' digit
56  0x038 '8' digit
57  0x039 '9' digit
58  0x03a ':'
59  0x03b ';'
60  0x03c '<'
61  0x03d '='
62  0x03e '>'
63  0x03f '?'
64  0x040 '@'
65  0x041 'A' uppercase
66  0x042 'B' uppercase
67  0x043 'C' uppercase
68  0x044 'D' uppercase
69  0x045 'E' uppercase
70  0x046 'F' uppercase
71  0x047 'G' uppercase
72  0x048 'H' uppercase
73  0x049 'I' uppercase
74  0x04a 'J' uppercase
75  0x04b 'K' uppercase
76  0x04c 'L' uppercase
77  0x04d 'M' uppercase
78  0x04e 'N' uppercase
79  0x04f 'O' uppercase
80  0x050 'P' uppercase
81  0x051 'Q' uppercase
82  0x052 'R' uppercase
83  0x053 'S' uppercase
84  0x054 'T' uppercase
85  0x055 'U' uppercase
86  0x056 'V' uppercase
87  0x057 'W' uppercase
88  0x058 'X' uppercase
89  0x059 'Y' uppercase
90  0x05a 'Z' uppercase
91  0x05b '['
92  0x05c '\'
93  0x05d ']'
94  0x05e '^'
95  0x05f '_'
96  0x060 '`'
```

```
 97  0x061 'a' lowercase
 98  0x062 'b' lowercase
 99  0x063 'c' lowercase
100  0x064 'd' lowercase
101  0x065 'e' lowercase
102  0x066 'f' lowercase
103  0x067 'g' lowercase
104  0x068 'h' lowercase
105  0x069 'i' lowercase
106  0x06a 'j' lowercase
107  0x06b 'k' lowercase
108  0x06c 'l' lowercase
109  0x06d 'm' lowercase
110  0x06e 'n' lowercase
111  0x06f 'o' lowercase
112  0x070 'p' lowercase
113  0x071 'q' lowercase
114  0x072 'r' lowercase
115  0x073 's' lowercase
116  0x074 't' lowercase
117  0x075 'u' lowercase
118  0x076 'v' lowercase
119  0x077 'w' lowercase
120  0x078 'x' lowercase
121  0x079 'y' lowercase
122  0x07a 'z' lowercase
123  0x07b '{'
124  0x07c '|'
125  0x07d '}'
126  0x07e '~'
127  0x07f
```

Character Type Tests

Character-type tests occur frequently enough in programming that they have been incorporated into the standard C library in a header file called `ctype.h`. Use of this file allows us to say:

```
if(isdigit(c))
```

instead of

```
if (c >= '0' && c <= '9')
```

or

```
if (isupper(c))
```

instead of

```
if (c >= 'A' && c <= 'Z')
```

To use the `ctype.h` header file that would allow us to access this library, we issue the following preprocessor command:

```
#include <ctype.h>
```

This line is a command to the C preprocessor to include some standard definitions into our compilation so that names such as `isdigit()` and `isupper()` will be recognized.

Here is a list of the available library functions:

```
int isalnum(int c);
```
c is an alphanumeric character
returns nonzero if c is a letter (A-Z or a-z) or a digit (0-9)

```
int isalpha(int c);
```
c is a letter
returns nonzero if c is a letter (A-Z or a-z)

```
int isascii(int c);
```
c is an ascii character (code less than 0200 or 128)
returns nonzero if the low order byte of c is in the range 0-127 (0x00-0x7F)

```
int iscntrl(int c);
```
c is a non-printable character (less than ' ')
returns nonzero if c is a delete character or ordinary control character (0x7F or 0x00-0x1F)

```
int isdigit(int c);
```
c is a digit
returns nonzero if c is a digit (0-9)

```
int isgraph(int c);
```
c is a graphics character
returns nonzero if c is a printing character, like isprint(), except that a space character is excluded

```
int islower(int c);
```
c is a lower case letter
returns nonzero if c is a lower case letter

```
int isprint(int c);
```
c is a printable character (including space)
returns nonzero if c is a printing character (0x20-0x7E)

```
int ispunct(int c);
```
c is a punctuation character
returns nonzero if c is a punctuation character (iscntrl() or isspace())

```
int isspace(int c);
```
c is a whitespace character (space, tab, carriage return newline, or form feed
returns nonzero if c is a space, tab, carriage return, new line, vertical tab, or
formfeed (0x09-0x0D, 0x20)

```
int isupper(int c);
```
c is an uppercase letter
returns nonzero if c is an uppercase letter

```
int isxdigit(int c);
```
c is a hex digit
returns nonzero if c is a hexadecimal digit (0-9, A-F, a-f)

```
int toascii(int c);
```
converts integer c to ASCII by clearing all but the lower 7 bits (0-127)
returns the converted value of c

```
int tolower(int c);
```
translates c to lowercase
returns the converted value of c if it is uppercase; it returns all others unchanged

```
int toupper(int c);
```
translates c to uppercase
returns the converted value of c if it is lowercase; it returns all others unchanged

We can rewrite the previous program using the `ctype.h` library:

```
// ascii2.c

#include <stdio.h>
#include <ctype.h>

int main(void) {
    unsigned char c;

    for (c = 0; c <= 127; ++c) {
        printf("%3d   0x%03x",c, c);
        if (isprint(c)) {
            printf(" '%c'",c);
        }
        if (isdigit(c)) {
            printf(" D");
        }
        if (isupper(c)) {
            printf(" UC");
        }
        if (islower(c)) {
            printf(" LC");
        }
        if (isalpha(c)) {
            printf(" L");
        }
        if (isalnum(c)) {
            printf(" AN");
        }
        if (isspace(c)) {
            printf(" S");
        }
        if (ispunct(c)) {
            printf(" P");
        }
        if (iscntrl(c)) {
            printf(" C");
        }
        printf("\n");
    }
    return 0;
}
```

Here's the program output:

```
0    0x000 C
1    0x001 C
2    0x002 C
3    0x003 C
4    0x004 C
5    0x005 C
6    0x006 C
7    0x007 C
8    0x008 C
9    0x009 S C
10   0x00a S C
11   0x00b S C
12   0x00c S C
13   0x00d S C
14   0x00e C
15   0x00f C
16   0x010 C
17   0x011 C
18   0x012 C
19   0x013 C
20   0x014 C
21   0x015 C
22   0x016 C
23   0x017 C
24   0x018 C
25   0x019 C
26   0x01a C
27   0x01b C
28   0x01c C
29   0x01d C
30   0x01e C
31   0x01f C
32   0x020 ' ' S
33   0x021 '!' P
34   0x022 '"' P
35   0x023 '#' P
36   0x024 '$' P
37   0x025 '%' P
38   0x026 '&' P
39   0x027 ''' P
40   0x028 '(' P
41   0x029 ')' P
42   0x02a '*' P
43   0x02b '+' P
44   0x02c ',' P
45   0x02d '-' P
46   0x02e '.' P
47   0x02f '/' P
```

```
48   0x030 '0'  D AN
49   0x031 '1'  D AN
50   0x032 '2'  D AN
51   0x033 '3'  D AN
52   0x034 '4'  D AN
53   0x035 '5'  D AN
54   0x036 '6'  D AN
55   0x037 '7'  D AN
56   0x038 '8'  D AN
57   0x039 '9'  D AN
58   0x03a ':'  P
59   0x03b ';'  P
60   0x03c '<'  P
61   0x03d '='  P
62   0x03e '>'  P
63   0x03f '?'  P
64   0x040 '@'  P
65   0x041 'A'  UC L AN
66   0x042 'B'  UC L AN
67   0x043 'C'  UC L AN
68   0x044 'D'  UC L AN
69   0x045 'E'  UC L AN
70   0x046 'F'  UC L AN
71   0x047 'G'  UC L AN
72   0x048 'H'  UC L AN
73   0x049 'I'  UC L AN
74   0x04a 'J'  UC L AN
75   0x04b 'K'  UC L AN
76   0x04c 'L'  UC L AN
77   0x04d 'M'  UC L AN
78   0x04e 'N'  UC L AN
79   0x04f 'O'  UC L AN
80   0x050 'P'  UC L AN
81   0x051 'Q'  UC L AN
82   0x052 'R'  UC L AN
83   0x053 'S'  UC L AN
84   0x054 'T'  UC L AN
85   0x055 'U'  UC L AN
86   0x056 'V'  UC L AN
87   0x057 'W'  UC L AN
88   0x058 'X'  UC L AN
89   0x059 'Y'  UC L AN
90   0x05a 'Z'  UC L AN
```

```
 91    0x05b  '['  P
 92    0x05c  '\'  P
 93    0x05d  ']'  P
 94    0x05e  '^'  P
 95    0x05f  '_'  P
 96    0x060  '`'  P
 97    0x061  'a'  LC  L  AN
 98    0x062  'b'  LC  L  AN
 99    0x063  'c'  LC  L  AN
100    0x064  'd'  LC  L  AN
101    0x065  'e'  LC  L  AN
102    0x066  'f'  LC  L  AN
103    0x067  'g'  LC  L  AN
104    0x068  'h'  LC  L  AN
105    0x069  'i'  LC  L  AN
106    0x06a  'j'  LC  L  AN
107    0x06b  'k'  LC  L  AN
108    0x06c  'l'  LC  L  AN
109    0x06d  'm'  LC  L  AN
110    0x06e  'n'  LC  L  AN
111    0x06f  'o'  LC  L  AN
112    0x070  'p'  LC  L  AN
113    0x071  'q'  LC  L  AN
114    0x072  'r'  LC  L  AN
115    0x073  's'  LC  L  AN
116    0x074  't'  LC  L  AN
117    0x075  'u'  LC  L  AN
118    0x076  'v'  LC  L  AN
119    0x077  'w'  LC  L  AN
120    0x078  'x'  LC  L  AN
121    0x079  'y'  LC  L  AN
122    0x07a  'z'  LC  L  AN
123    0x07b  '{'  P
124    0x07c  '|'  P
125    0x07d  '}'  P
126    0x07e  '~'  P
127    0x07f  C
```

Increment and Decrement Operators

The increment and decrement are unary operators (i.e., require only one operand):

```
++      adds one to its operand

--      subtracts one from its operand
```

The statements:

```
++num;

num++;
```

both increment the value of `num` by 1 and have the same effect as the statement:

```
num = num + 1;
```

The statements:

```
--num;

num--;
```

both decrement the value of `num` by 1 and have the same effect as the statement:

```
num = num - 1;
```

Note that when the `++` or `--` operator is used to the left of the operand:

```
++num;

--num;
```

it is referred to as the *prefix* form of the operator. When the ++ or -- operator is used to the right of the operand, it is referred to as the *postfix* form of the operator.

When the increment or decrement operators are simply used on an operand, there is no difference between the prefix and the postfix form of the expression. However, when the increment or decrement operator is used within the context of a larger expression, using the prefix or postfix form of the operator might very well give different results.

For example, examine the use of the prefix increment operator:

```
y = 10;
x = ++y;
```

Initially, the variable y is initialized to 10. In the second statement we use the prefix form of the increment operator. First, the value of y is incremented to 11, and then that new value of y is used in the remaining portion of the expression, i.e., the new value of y (11) is then assigned to x. So after the two statements are executed, both x and y are equal to 11.

Now let's examine the use of the postfix increment operator:

```
y = 10;
x = y++;
```

Here, the initial value if y is also 10. But in the second statement, before y gets incremented, it's current value (10) is used in the expression, i.e., x is assigned the value of 10. Then the value of y is incremented to 11. So after these two statements are executed, x has the value of 10, and y has the value of 11!

The example below:

```
x = y + z++;
```

is actually equivalent to:

```
x = y + z;
++z;
```

Note that increment and decrement operators can only be applied to variables and not to constants or expressions. So the statements:

```
x = (y + z)++;
++5;
```

would not be valid.

These operators are used quite often as the step expression of a for loop:

```
for (i = 0; i < 10; ++i)
```

We must be careful using the auto increment and auto decrement operators. For example the expression below is very ambiguous and will probably not return the value you are looking for:

```
a = ++num + num;
```

Here, num is incremented before it is used, but this changes the value of the other num in the expression. On the other hand, some compilers will take the current value of num and add it to the incremented value of num. Therefore, evaluation is machine dependent and is therefore very poor programming style. If the intent is to increment num before the addition, use the following code:

```
a = 2 * (++num);
```

See if you can calculate the output of the following C program before looking at the answers:

```c
// incDecOperators.c

#include <stdio.h>

int main(void) {
    int a, b, c;

    a = 0;
    b = 0;
    c = 0;

    a = ++b + ++c;
    printf("%d  %d  %d\n", a, b, c);

    a = b++ + c++;
    printf("%d  %d  %d\n", a, b, c);

    a = ++b + c++;
    printf("%d  %d  %d\n", a, b, c);

    a = b-- + --c;
    printf("%d  %d  %d\n", a, b, c);

    return 0;
}
```

Here's the program output:

```
2  1  1
2  2  2
5  3  3
5  2  2
```

Can you see why?

Precedence of Operators

In the following table of operator precedence, C operators are divided into 15 categories. The #1 category has the highest precedence, category #2 (Unary operators) takes second precedence, and so on to the Comma operator, which has lowest precedence. The operators within each category have equal precedence. The Unary (category #2), Conditional (category#13), and Assignment (category #14) operators associate right-to-left; all other operators associate left-to-right.

#	Category	Oper	What it is (or does)
1.	Highest		
		()	Function call
		[]	Array subscript
		->	Indirect component selector
		.	Direct component selector
2.	Unary		
		!	Logical negation (NOT)
		~	Bitwise (1's) complement
		+	Unary plus
		-	Unary minus
		++	Preincrement or postincrement
		--	Predecrement or postdecrement
		&	Address of
		*	Indirection
		sizeof	returns size of operand, in bytes
3.	Multiplicative		
		*	Multiply
		/	Divide
		%	Remainder (modulus)
4.	Additive		
		+	Binary plus
		-	Binary minus
5.	Shift		
		<<	Shift left
		>>	Shift right

6.	Relational		
		<	Less than
		<=	Less than or equal to
		>	Greater than
		>=	Greater than or equal to
7.	Equality		
		==	Equal to
		!=	Not equal to
8.		&	Bitwise AND
9.		^	Bitwise XOR
10.		|	Bitwise OR
11.		&&	Logical AND
12.		||	Logical OR
13.	Conditional		
		?:	
14.	Assignment		
		=	Simple assignment
		*=	Assign product
		/=	Assign quotient
		%=	Assign remainder (modulus)
		+=	Assign sum
		-=	Assign difference
		&=	Assign bitwise AND
		^=	Assign bitwise XOR
		|=	Assign bitwise OR
		<<=	Assign left shift
		>>=	Assign right shift
15.	Comma		
		,	Evaluate

❖ Operators Homework

1. Write a single C statement to accomplish each of the following tasks:

a) Assign the sum of `x` and `y` to `z` and decrement the value of `y` by 1 after the calculation.

b) Multiply `num` by 3 using the `*=` operator.

c) Increment variable `x` by 1, then subtract it from variable `value`.

d) Add variable `x` to variable `total`, then increment `x` by 1.

2. Show the output produced by each of the following program fragments. Assume that `i`, `j`, `k` are `int` variables.

a)
```
i = 7; j = 2;
printf("%d %d", i / j, i % j);
```

b)
```
i = 4; j = 3;
printf("%d", (i + 10) % j);
```

c)
```
i = 7; j = 8; k = 9;
printf("%d", (i + 10) % k / j);
```


3. Show the output produced by each of the following program fragments. Assume that `i`, `j`, `k` are `int` variables.

a)
```
i = 7; j = 8;
i *= j + 3;
printf("%d %d", i, j);
```

b)
```
i = j = k = 1;
i *= j *= k;
printf("%d %d %d", i, j, k);
```

4. Show the output produced by each of the following program fragments.
Assume that `i`, `j`, `k` are `int` variables.

a)
```
i = 4;
j = ++i * 3 - 2;
printf("%d %d", i, j);
```

b)
```
i = 3;
j = 3 - 2 * i++;
printf("%d %d", i, j);
```

c)
```
i = 2; j = 5;
printf("%d ", i++ - ++j);
printf("%d %d", i, j);
```

5. Supply parentheses to show how a C compiler would interpret each of the following expressions.

a)   `a * b - c * d + e`

b)   `a / b % c / d`

6. Give the values of `i` and `j` after each of the following expression statements has been executed. Assume that `i` has the value 1 initially and `j` has the value 2.

a)   `i += j;`   c)   `i * j / i;`

b)   `i--;`   d)   `i % ++j;`

7. Use De Morgan's Laws to write equivalent expressions for each of the following:

a) `! ( x < 8 ) && ! ( y >= 3 )`

b) `! ( x == y ) || ! ( z != 2 )`

c) `! ( ( x <= 3 ) && ( y > 7 ) )`

d) `! ( ( x > 2 ) || ( y <= 4 ) )`

❖ Weight Lab

Our weight on different planets in the solar system will differ due to the varying size and mass of each of the planets. Write a C program, `weight.c`, to compute the weight of a 200 pound person on the following planets, based on the data below:

```
Planet              Percent of Earth Weigh
------              ----------------------
Mercury                    37.8%
Venus                      90.7%
Mars                       37.7%
Jupiter                   236.0%
Saturn                     91.6%
Uranus                     88.9%
Neptune                   112.0%
```

The program should generate the following outputs:

```
Mercury: xxx.x
  Venus: xxx.x
   Mars: xxx.x
Jupiter: xxx.x
 Saturn: xxx.x
 Uranus: xxx.x
Neptune: xxx.x
```

Your program should right-justify the planet names and present the output to one decimal place as shown above. Be sure to line up the decimal points. Use the following guidelines to develop your program:

Declare your variables with appropriate data types.

Assign values to your variables.

Perform your calculations.

Generate appropriate output.

Points to Remember:

Make sure you are creating a C program and not a C++ program. The .c suffix to your source code will invoke the C compiler while the .cpp suffix will invoke the C++ compiler. As this is a class in C and not C++, please make sure your source code uses the .c suffix.

You should not be using any global variables in your program. A global variable is a variable declared outside of main().

Output your calculations to one decimal place.

Output from your program should be sent to the terminal window (your screen) as well as the requested csis.txt output file. Be sure to read the document on Capturing Program Output. Your full name must appear as a comment in the source file that contains main(). Be sure to include the csis.txt output file in your zip archive.

❖ Character Constant Lab

Write a C program, `char.c`, which prints the numerical value of the special character constants given below. Don't just look up the codes and print them directly from your program. You should have your program output the values of the character constants by using them as string literals within your `printf()` statements.

Your output should be presented in a neat, orderly, tabular format as shown below:

```
Char Constant    Description                        Value
     '\n'        newline
     '\t'        horizontal tab
     '\v'        vertical tab
     '\b'        backspace
     '\r'        carriage return
     '\f'        form feed
     '\\'        backslash
     '\''        single quote (apostrophe)
     '\"'        double quote
     '\0'        null
```

Use the following guidelines to develop your program:

Declare your variables with appropriate data types.

Assign values to your variables.

Perform your calculations.

Generate appropriate output.

Points to Remember:

Make sure you are creating a C program and not a C++ program. The .c suffix to your source code will invoke the C compiler while the .cpp suffix will invoke the C++ compiler. As this is a class in C and not C++, please make sure your source code uses the .c suffix.

You should not be using any global variables in your program. A global variable is a variable declared outside of `main()`.

Output from your program should be sent to the terminal window (your screen) as well as the requested `csis.txt` output file. Be sure to read the document on Capturing Program Output. Your full name must appear as a comment in the source file that contains `main()`. Be sure to include the `csis.txt` output file in your zip archive.

❖ Change Lab

Construct a C program, `change.c`, which computes the minimum number of bills and coins needed to make change for a particular purchase. The cost of the item is $21.17 and the amount tendered is $100.00. These values should be built into your program using assignment statements rather than input into the program during program runtime. Your program should indicate how many bills and coins of each denomination are needed for the change. You should make use of the following denominations:

Bills: twenty, ten, five, one

Coins: quarter, dime, nickel, penny

Your program should make use of integer division as well as the modulus operator (`%`). Do not use subtraction in place of the modulus operator! Note that it will be easier to convert the cost and amount tendered into pennies so you can work with integers rather than doubles.

Use the following guidelines to develop your program:

Declare your variables with appropriate data types.

Assign values to your variables.

Perform your calculations.

Generate appropriate output.

Points to Remember:

Make sure you are creating a C program and not a C++ program. The `.c` suffix to your source code will invoke the C compiler while the `.cpp` suffix will invoke the C++ compiler. As this is a class in C and not C++, please make sure your source code uses the `.c` suffix.

You should not be using any global variables in your program. A global variable is a variable declared outside of `main()`.

Output from your program should be sent to the terminal window (your screen) as well as the requested `csis.txt` output file. Be sure to read the document on Capturing Program Output. Your full name must appear as a comment in the source file that contains `main()`. Be sure to include the `csis.txt` output file in your zip archive.

❖ Days Lab

Construct a C program, days.c, which prompts the user to enter a number of days (2347) and computes the number of years, months, weeks, and days in the entered number. You may assume that a year contains of 365 days and a month contains 30 days.

For example, if the user enters 997 days, your program perform the necessary calculations and generate the following output:

years: 2
months: 8
weeks 3
days: 6

Make sure you are creating a C program and not a C++ program. The .c suffix to your source code will invoke the C compiler while the .cpp suffix will invoke the C++ compiler. As this is a class in C and not C++, please make sure your source code uses the .c suffix.

You should not be using any global variables in your program. A global variable is a variable declared outside of main().

Output from your program should be sent to the terminal window (your screen) as well as the requested csis.txt output file. Be sure to read the document on Capturing Program Output. Your full name must appear as a comment in the source file that contains main(). Be sure to include the csis.txt output file in your zip archive.

Chapter 5. Number Systems

Decimal: Base 10
Binary: Base 2
Hexadecimal: Base 16
Negative Numbers
❖ Number Systems Homework
❖ Base Conversion Lab

Decimal: Base 10

A decimal base 10 integer uses 10 digits (0, 1, 2, 3, 4, 5, 6, 7, 8, 9) to represent values. But what does it **mean** to represent a decimal base 10 integer as, say, 739? Remember, in a base 10 integer each digit represents a unique power of 10. The rightmost digit represents 10^0, moving left one position the digit represents 10^1, then 10^2, etc.

```
10⁰  =    1
10¹  =   10
10²  =  100
```

To understand the value represented by 739, we can break it down into its components:

```
9 * 10⁰  =  9 *   1  =    9
3 * 10¹  =  3 *  10  =   30
7 * 10²  =  7 * 100  =  700
---------------------------------
                          739
```

Binary: Base 2

Just as we use 10 digits to represent decimal base 10 integers, we use 2 digits (0, 1) to represent binary base 2 values. However, in a binary number, each digit represents a unique power of 2. The rightmost digit represents 2^0, moving left one position the digit represents 2^1, then 2^2, then 2^3, etc.

```
2⁰  =   1
2¹  =   2
2²  =   4
2³  =   8
2⁴  =  16
2⁵  =  32
2⁶  =  64
2⁷  = 128
```

Below are the equivalent binary base 2 values of the decimal numbers 0 – 15.

Decimal	Binary
0	0000
1	0001
2	0010
3	0011
4	0100
5	0101
6	0110
7	0111
8	1000
9	1001
10	1010
11	1011
12	1100
13	1101
14	1110
15	1111

Note that we can represent the numbers from 0 to 15 in binary using only 4 bits.

Binary to Decimal Conversion

In order to determine what the 8-bit binary number below represents in decimal base 10, it's simply a matter of adding the appropriate powers of two:

```
Binary Number:        1    1    1    0    1    0    1    1
                      |    |    |    |    |    |    |    |
                      |    |    |    |    |    |    |    |
                      |    |    |    |    |    |    |    |
Power of Two:         2⁷   2⁶   2⁵   2⁴   2³   2²   2¹   2⁰
                      |    |    |    |    |    |    |    |
                      |    |    |    |    |    |    |    |
                      |    |    |    |    |    |    |    |
Decimal Equivalent:  128   64   32   16   8    4    2    1
```

```
1 * 2⁰ = 1 *   1 =   1
1 * 2¹ = 1 *   2 =   2
0 * 2² = 0 *   4 =   0
1 * 2³ = 1 *   8 =   8
0 * 2⁴ = 0 *  16 =   0
1 * 2⁵ = 1 *  32 =  32
1 * 2⁶ = 1 *  64 =  64
1 * 2⁷ = 1 * 128 = 128
----------------------
                   235
```

So binary `11101011` is equivalent to `235` decimal.

Decimal to Binary Conversion

Conversion of a decimal number into binary requires the following simple algorithm:

```
while num != 0
      divide num by 2
      store the remainder
      assign the quotient to num
output the remainders in reverse order
```

For example, we can convert the decimal integer `147` into binary:

```
147 / 2 = 73      remainder = 1
 73 / 2 = 36      remainder = 1
 36 / 2 = 18      remainder = 0
 18 / 2 = 9       remainder = 0
  9 / 2 = 4       remainder = 1
  4 / 2 = 2       remainder = 0
  2 / 2 = 1       remainder = 0
  1 / 2 = 0       remainder = 1
```

So `147` decimal is equivalent to `10010011` binary.

Hexadecimal: Base 16

Hexadecimal notation uses 16 digits (0 - 9, A, B, C, D, E, F) to represent base 16 values. Each digit in a 'hex' number represents a unique power of 16. The rightmost digit represents 16^0, moving left one position the digit represents 16^1, then 16^2, etc.

```
16⁰  =     1
16¹  =    16
16²  =   256
16³  =  4096
```

Below are the equivalent hexadecimal base 16 values of the decimal and binary numbers 0 – 15.

Decimal	Binary	Hexadecimal
0	0000	0
1	0001	1
2	0010	2
3	0011	3
4	0100	4
5	0101	5
6	0110	6
7	0111	7
8	1000	8
9	1001	9
10	1010	A
11	1011	B
12	1100	C
13	1101	D
14	1110	E
15	1111	F

Hexadecimal to Decimal Conversion

It's now a matter of adding the appropriate powers of 16 to convert a hexadecimal value into a decimal value:

```
Hexadecimal Number:    1    A    F
                       |    |    |
                       |    |    |
                       |    |    |
Power of 16:          16²  16¹  16⁰
                       |    |    |
                       |    |    |
                       |    |    |
Decimal Equivalent:   256  160   15
```

```
F * 16⁰ = 15 *   1 =   15
A * 16¹ = 10 *  16 =  160
1 * 16² =  1 * 256 =  256
-------------------------
                      431
```

So hexadecimal `1AF` is equivalent to `431` decimal.

Decimal to Hexadecimal Conversion

We use a similar algorithm to convert a decimal value into a hexadecimal value as we used to convert a decimal value into a binary value:

```
while num != 0
      divide num by 16
      store the remainder
      assign the quotient to num
output the remainders in reverse order
```

We can convert decimal `431` into hexadecimal:

```
431 / 16 = 26     remainder = F
 26 / 16 =  1     remainder = A
  1 / 16 =  0     remainder = 1
```

So `431` decimal is equivalent to `1AF` hexadecimal.

Binary to Hexadecimal Conversion

Conversion of a binary number into hexadecimal is simply a matter of converting each nibble (4 bits) of the binary number into its hex equivalent. For example, let's convert the binary number `0011010111111100` into its hexadecimal equivalent:

```
Binary:            0011    0101    1111    1100
                    |       |       |       |
                    |       |       |       |
                    |       |       |       |
Hex Equivalent:     3       5       F       C
```

So `0011010111111100` binary is equivalent to `35FC` hexadecimal.

Hexadecimal to Binary Conversion

To convert a hexadecimal number into its binary equivalent, we simply convert each hex digit in the number into its decimal equivalent. For example, let's convert hexadecimal `B72E` into binary:

```
Hexadecimal:          B       7       2       E
                      |       |       |       |
                      |       |       |       |
                      |       |       |       |
Binary Equivalent:  1011    0111    0010    1110
```

So `B72E` hexadecimal is equivalent to `1011011100101110` binary.

Note that a single hexadecimal digit can be used to represent 4 bits in a binary number. As a result, it becomes more convenient to represent 16-, 32-, or 64-bit memory addresses in hex notation rather than binary!

Negative Numbers

So far, we've only explored how positive numbers are represented internally in the computer's memory. It's now time to explore how negative numbers can also be represented. For example, if the value 6 is represented in memory as:

```
00000110
```

then how is -6 represented? One common suggestion is to make the high-order bit 1 and leave all other bits unchanged, producing:

```
10000110
```

Unfortunately, this is incorrect. This can be shown by adding the two numbers together (6 + -6) which should produce 0.

```
  00000110  =    6
+ 10000110  =   -6
  10001100  =  -12
```

According to this scheme, the sum of 6 + -6 equals –12, and not 0! We must find another representation for negative numbers.

Two's Complement Notation

The technique that computers use to represent negative numbers is called *two's complement notation*. Given any positive number, we can determine its negative internal representation by calculating or taking its two's complement. We do this in two steps:

• flip all bits

• add 1

For example, we can determine the internal representation of -6 by taking the two's complement of 6:

```
00000110     = 6

11111001     flip all bits
+       1    add 1

11111010     = -6
```

According to this scheme, -6 is represented as:

```
11111010
```

We can test this by adding 6 and -6:

```
00000110     =  6
11111010     = -6
00000000     =  0
```

Note that we are only doing 8-bit arithmetic, so any final carry can be ignored. As another example, let's determine how -25 is represented:

```
00011001     = 25

11100110     flip all bits
+       1    add 1
11100111     = -25
```

Once again we can test this by adding together 25 and −25 and see if it produces zero:

```
00011001    =    25
11100111    =   -25
00000000    =     0
```

Suppose we were given the 8-bit binary number:

```
11010001
```

and were asked to determine its decimal equivalent. We would not be able to do so unless we were told whether the number represented a **signed** or an **unsigned** value. If the number represents an unsigned value, then we use our simple algorithm to convert from binary to decimal by adding each of the appropriate powers of two:

```
1 + 16 + 64 + 128 = 209
```

If the number is representing a signed value, then we look at the leftmost high-order bit. If it is a 0, then the number is a positive number and we use the algorithm just mentioned and add each of the appropriate powers of two:

```
1 + 16 + 64 + 128 = 209
```

However, if the number represents a signed value and the leftmost high-order bit is a 1, then the number is a negative number being represented in its two's complement notation. To determine what the negative number is, we must take its two's complement by flipping the bits and adding 1:

```
11010001     original number

00101110     flip all bits
+        1   add 1
00101111     two's complement
```

So, the two's complement of `11010001` is `00101111` which equals `47`:

```
1 + 2 + 4 + 8 + 32  = 47
```

Therefore if the two's complement of our original number is `47`, then our original number must equal `-47`.

❖ Number Systems Homework

1. Give the 8-bit binary equivalent of the following decimal integers:

a) 63   b) 180

2. Give the unsigned decimal equivalent of the following 8-bit binary integers:

a) 10010110   b) 01110101

3. Give the signed decimal equivalent of the following 8-bit binary integers:

a) 10010110   b) 01110101

4. Translate the following binary digits into hexadecimal notation:

a) 10101000   b) 00101001

5. Convert the following decimal numbers into hexadecimal:

a) 427   b) 231

6. Convert the following hexadecimal numbers into decimal:

a) 0x74   b) 0xABC

7. Convert the following hexadecimal numbers into binary:

a) 0x4312   b) 0xEF51

8. Give the two's complement of the following binary numbers:

a) 01111110   d) 00000000
b) 11100110   e) 10000000
c) 10000001

❖ Base Conversion Lab

Write a C program, base.c, which prompts the user for a base 10 integer (961) and converts the integer into binary (base 2) and hexadecimal (base 16).

Note: Do not perform your own calculations and have your program output the results. All of the calculations for the lab should be performed within your program. Use the following guidelines to develop your program:

Declare your variables with appropriate data types.

Assign values to your variables.

Perform your calculations.

Generate appropriate output.

Points to Remember:

Make sure you are creating a C program and not a C++ program. The .c suffix to your source code will invoke the C compiler while the .cpp suffix will invoke the C++ compiler. As this is a class in C and not C++, please make sure your source code uses the .c suffix. You should not be using any global variables in your program. A global variable is a variable declared outside of main().

Output from your program should be sent to the terminal window (your screen) as well as the requested csis.txt output file. Be sure to read the document on Capturing Program Output. Your full name must appear as a comment in the source file that contains main(). Be sure to include the csis.txt output file in your zip archive.

Chapter 6. Functions

User-Defined Functions
Flow of Program Execution
Scope of Identifiers
Math Functions
Techniques of Problem Solving
❖ Functions Homework

User-Defined Functions

A function is a subprogram that carries out a particular task. Its purpose is to group together a related set of statements that performs some well-defined step in an algorithm.

We have already seen examples of functions that are built into C such as:

```
printf()           fopen_s()          isdigit()
scanf_s()          fclose()           isupper()
                   fprint()           islower()
                                      toupper()
                                      tolower()
```

But C also gives us the ability to create our own functions. Suppose we wanted to write a program to display different geometric shapes. We could create our own function, drawRect(), to display a rectangle:

```c
// drawRectangle.c
// Displays a rectangle

void drawRectangle() {
    printf("***********\n");
    printf("*         *\n");
    printf("*         *\n");
    printf("*         *\n");
    printf("***********\n");
}
```

We could create our own function, drawTriangle(), to display a triangle:

```c
// drawTriangle.c
// Displays a triangle

void drawTriangle() {
    printf("   *   \n");
    printf("  * *  \n");
    printf(" *   * \n");
    printf("*     *\n");
    printf("*******\n");
}
```

We could create our own function, `drawCircle()`, to display a circle:

```c
// drawCircle.c
// Displays a circle

void drawCircle() {
    printf("  ***  \n");
    printf(" *   * \n");
    printf("*     *\n");
    printf(" *   * \n");
    printf("  ***  \n");
}
```

There are three things we must do to create our own *user-defined* functions.

1. Declare the Function.
We do this with a *function prototype*, which declares the function so that the compiler knows about it. This declaration provides a complete description of the function interface. Function prototypes usually precede `main()` and they tell the compiler, and us, what a function will do, *but not how it will do it*.

2. Write the Function Definition.
The function definition consists of comments, a header and a body. The header is virtually a repeat of the prototype. The body contains the executable statements for the function.

3. Write the Call(s) to the Function.
These calls cause the function to execute and return values (if there are any values to be returned). While there is one prototype and one definition per function, there may be many calls, with different arguments.

Let's look at an example of a function that calculates the area of a rectangle.

1. Declare the Function.
First we declare a function prototype. The prototype is the interface (sometimes called the *signature*) of the function and also declares how the function must be used. It tells the compiler all it needs to know to properly translate the calls to the function. (We will better understand why this is important when we write functions with arguments).

The function prototype specifies the function return type, the function name and the number and type of arguments (formal parameters). The general form of the function prototype is as follows:

```
returnType functionName (formal-argument-list);
```

The function prototype for the function to calculate the area of a rectangle would look like this:

```
int calcRectArea(int length, int width);
```

The function prototype provides the following information:

• The function return value (i.e., the calculated area of the rectangle) will be of data type `int`. If a function returns no value, then the function return type will be declared as `void`.

• The function name is `calcRectArea()`.

• The formal argument list contains two formal parameters, `length` and `width`, each of which is of data type `int`.

Note that the formal parameter list of a function prototype can optionally omit the names of the formal parameters:

```
int calcRectArea(int, int);
```

The function prototype is placed in the code before function `main()` and has a semi-colon at the end of the line.

Note that just as we are not allowed to use an identifier (a variable) without first declaring the variable to be of a particular data type, we are not allowed to use a function without first declaring a function prototype.

2. Write the Function Definition.

The second thing we must do in writing our own function is to provide the function definition or *implementation*. The function definition consists of comments, a header and a body. The general form of the function body is as follows:

```
// Function comments

returnType functionName (formal-argument-list) {
    executable-statements;
    return (return-value);     // the return statement is omitted
                               // if the function return value is void
}
```

The function definition to calculate the area of a rectangle would look like this:

```
// calculateArea.c
// Calculates area of a rectangle given its length and width.
// Returns the area of the rectangle.

int calcRectArea(int length, int width) {
    int area;

    area = length * width;
    return area;
}
```

• The function comments describe what the function accomplishes as well as what the return value (if any) represents. The comments inform us that the function calculates the area of a rectangle given its length and width. The comments also inform us that the function returns an int that represents the area of the rectangle.

• The function returns the calculated area of the rectangle and the return value is of data type int.

• The function name is calcRectArea().

• The function formal argument list consists of an int type in the first position, length, and an int type in the second position, width. This means that the function is expecting two input arguments with the first of type int and the second of type int.

Note that even though the first argument is named `length` and the second argument is named `width`, there is no connection between these names and the names of the actual arguments passed in the call to the function itself! More on this soon.

When the function is invoked, storage for the formal parameters, `length` and `width`, will be allocated and the storage will be initialized to the values that were passed into the function when the function was called.

Note that the arguments, `length` and `width`, are local variables that are "visible" inside the function and can be used within the function but nowhere else in the program.

Note that while the names of the formal parameters are optional in the function prototype, they must be included in the function header.

• The function body contains the statements that will be executed when the function is called or used. The function uses curly braces `{ }` to indicate the beginning and ending of the function body. Note that there is no semi-colon at the end of the function body!

In our function, the executable statements include the declaration of an `int` variable called `area`. The function also performs a calculation of the area of the rectangle. The calculated value of the rectangle's area is assigned to variable `area`.

• The return value is the value returned by the function to the calling program code. Our function returns an `int` to the calling program code.

In summary, our function body declares a variable named `area`, calculates the area using the height and width passed in as arguments and returns the calculated area to the calling program code. Note that the function is placed in the program after the end of the `main()` function.

3. Write the Call(s) to the Function:

The third thing we need to do is call the function whenever we need it.

```
// calcAreaRect.c
// Calculates the area of a rectangle.

#include <stdio.h>

int main(void) {
    int length, width, area;

    length = 8;
    width = 6;
    area = calcRectArea(length, width);
    printf("The area = %d\n", area);

    return 0;
}
```

Here we declare variables `length`, `width` and `area` and assign values to `length` and `width`. A call is made to the function `calcRectArea()`, passing the two parameters, `length` and `width`. The value returned by the function is assigned to `area`, which is then output.

The function call can be used in the program code itself the same way that any other valid C statement can be used. Functions can be called in `main()` or any other function and can be called as often as necessary or not at all. Note that there is always just one function declaration and one implementation (definition), but there can be multiple calls to a given function.

Below is our complete code which include multiple examples of calls to our function to calculate the area of a rectangle:

```c
// calcRectArea.c
// Calculates the areas of various rectangles.

#include <stdio.h>

int calcRectArea(int length, int width);

int main(void) {
    int length, width, area, l, w;

    // Function Call 1
    length = 8;
    width = 6;
    area = calcRectArea(length, width);
    printf("The area = %d\n", area);

    // Function Call 2
    l = 5;
    w = 3;
    area = calcRectArea(l, w);
    printf("The area = %d\n", area);

    // Function Call 3
    printf("The area = %d\n", calcRectArea(4, 8));

    // Function Call 4
    calcRectArea(2, 6);

    return 0;
}

// Calculates area of a rectangle given its length and width.
// Returns the area of a rectangle.

int calcRectArea(int length, int width) {
    int area;

    area = length * width;
    return area;
}
```

Function Call 1:
Values are assigned to variables length and width and the variables are the arguments to the function calcRectArea(). The function returns a calculated value that is assigned to area, which is then output.

Function Call 2:
Values are assigned to variables `l` and `w` and the variables are the arguments to the function `calcRectArea()`. The function returns a calculated value that is assigned to `area`, which is then output.

Note that in this case the names of the arguments that are passed to the function (called the *actual parameters*) do not have the same name as the arguments that are received by the function (called the *formal parameters*). The names do not need to match! C simply passes the first actual parameter to the first formal parameter, the second actual parameter to the second formal parameter, etc.

However, the number of actual parameters must equal the number of formal parameters (i.e., the number of parameters that are passed to a function must be the same as the number of parameters that the function is declared to receive). Additionally, the data type of the first actual parameter must match the data type of the first formal parameter, the data type of the second actual parameter must match the data type of the second formal parameter., etc.

Function Call 3:
The function return value is not assigned to a variable for output as the function call is itself included within the `printf()` statement! Here the return `int` value is substituted into the `printf()` string for the `%d` format specifier and the return value of the function is immediately output.

Function Call 4:
This function call, while technically correct, does not use the value returned by the function because we're calling the function without assigning or using the return value in any way. The returned value is simply ignored! We'll see other examples of function calls in which the returned value goes unused.

Function Advantages
• Programs become more readable.

• Function can be tested and debugged separately from the rest of the program.

• By isolating a logic step in a function, the parts of a program are more independent and the likelihood of errors are reduced.

• The same function can be invoked from different places in a program. Therefore, a commonly used chunk of logic needs to be written only once.

Flow of Program Execution

The flow of execution of a program refers to the order in which the C code is executed. Execution always begins at the first statement in `main()` and statements are executed one after another, from first to last.

For example, consider the following program that swaps the value of two variables:

```c
// flow.c

int main(void) {
    int x, y, temp;      // Statement 1

    x = 5;               // Statement 2
    y = 8;               // Statement 3

    temp = x;            // Statement 4
    x = y;               // Statement 5
    y = temp;            // Statement 6

    return 0;            // Statement 7
}
```

The statements in the program above are executed in the following order:

```
Statement 1
Statement 2
Statement 3
Statement 4
Statement 5
Statement 6
Statement 7
```

Adding function definitions to a program does not alter the flow of execution of the program. However, the statements within the function are not executed until the function is called.

When a function call is made, control of the program jumps to the first statement in the function. All of the statements in the function are executed until either a return statement is reached or a closing brace to the function is reached. Control of the program returns to the location in the program where the function call was made.

Consider the following program:

```c
// geometric.c
// Geometric drawing program

#include <stdio.h>

// Function prototypes
void drawRectangle(void);
void drawTriangle(void);
void drawCircle(void);


// Calls the geometric drawing functions
int main(void) {
    drawCircle();
    drawRectangle();
    drawTriangle();
    drawCircle();
    return 0;
}

// Displays a rectangle.
void drawRectangle(void) {
    printf("***********\n");
    printf("*         *\n");
    printf("*         *\n");
    printf("*         *\n");
    printf("***********\n");
}

// Displays a triangle.
void drawTriangle(void) {
    printf("   *   \n");
    printf("  * *  \n");
    printf(" *   * \n");
    printf("*     *\n");
    printf("*******\n");
}

// Displays a circle.
void drawCircle(void) {
    printf("  ***  \n");
    printf(" *   * \n");
    printf("*     *\n");
    printf(" *   * \n");
    printf("  ***  \n");
}
```

Note that the order in which the function definitions appear in a program is not important. Let's execute the first line of the `main()` function:

```
drawCircle();
```

Execution of this statement transfers control of the program to the `drawCircle()` function. Each of the following statements in the `drawCircle()` function get executed:

```
printf("  ***  \n");
printf(" *   * \n");
printf("*     *\n");
printf(" *   * \n");
printf("  ***  \n");
```

When the closing brace to the `drawCircle()` function is reached, control of the program returns to the statement in `main()` following the call to `drawCircle()`:

```
drawRectangle();
```

Execution of this statement transfers control of the program to the `drawRectangle()` function. Each of the following statements in the `drawRectangle()` function get executed:

```
printf("************\n");
printf("*          *\n");
printf("*          *\n");
printf("*          *\n");
printf("************\n");
```

When the closing brace to the `drawRectangle()` function is reached, control of the program returns to the statement in `main()` following the call to `drawRectangle()`:

```
drawTriangle();
```

Execution of this statement transfers control of the program to the drawTriangle() function. Each of the following statements in the drawTriangle() function get executed:

```
printf("   *   \n");
printf("  * *  \n");
printf(" *   * \n");
printf("*     *\n");
printf("*******\n");
```

When the closing brace to the drawTriangle() function is reached, control of the program returns to the statement in main() following the call to drawTriangle():

```
drawCircle();
```

Execution of this statement transfers control of the program to the drawCircle() function. Each of the following statements in the drawCircle() function get executed once again:

```
printf("  ***  \n");
printf(" *   * \n");
printf("*     *\n");
printf(" *   * \n");
printf("  ***  \n");
```

When the closing brace to the drawCircle() function is reached, control of the program returns to the statement in main() following the call to drawCircle():

```
return 0;
```

This completes the execution of the program and transfers control back to the operating system.

Now, what happens when one function calls another function which calls another function, which calls another function, etc.? Fortunately, C is good at keeping track of all these function calls. Each time a function completes, the program picks up where it left off in the function that called it.

See if you can figure out what the output of the following program will be:

```c
// figureOut.c

#include <stdio.h>

void foo(void);
void faa(void);
void laa(void);

int main (void) {
    printf("main() 1\n");
    foo();
    printf("main()2\n");
    return 0;
}

void foo(void) {
    printf("foo() 1\n");
    faa();
    printf("foo() 2\n");
}

void faa(void) {
    printf("faa() 1\n");
    laa();
    printf("faa() 2\n");
}

void laa(void) {
    printf("laa() 1\n");
}
```

The output generated would looks like this.

```
main() 1
foo() 1
faa() 1
laa() 1
faa() 2
foo() 2
main()2
```

Can you see why?

So when you read a program, you don't always want to read the program from top to bottom. Sometimes it makes more sense if you follow the flow of execution of the program.

Scope of Identifiers

Identifiers are variable or function names that are referred to in the program code. The scope of an identifier determines where that identifier can be referred to in the program code.

For example, consider the following code.

```
// scope.c

double average (double, double);

int globalVariable;

int main(void) {
    int localVariable;
    ...
    ...
}

double average(double grade1, double grade2) {
    return (grade1 + grade2) / 2;
}
```

Here, the identifiers (the function and variable names) `average`, `main`, `globalVariable`, `localVariable`, `grade1`, and `grade2` all have a specific and well-defined scope. We can understand that scope as follows:

• Identifiers that are declared before the `main()` function have a *global scope* and can be referred to anywhere in the program code. Normally, constants, macros, and functions are declared before the `main()` function so that they have a global scope and are "visible" throughout the program code. Variables declared before the `main()` function are referred to as global variables and are generally frowned upon when used in a program.

• Identifiers that are declared within a specific function have a *local scope* and are "visible" only within that specific function. Function parameters are considered local to the function and are not "visible" outside that function. Typically, any variable used in a program should either be declared within a function or passed to a function as a function parameter.

Math Functions

The `math.h` header defines various mathematical functions in the math library. All the functions available in this library take `double` as an argument and return `double` as the result. Be sure to include the `math.h` header file near the top of each C file that will use math functions:

```
#include <math.h>
```

Power Functions
```
double pow(double x, double y);
```
Returns x raised to the power of y.
```
double sqrt(double x);
```
Returns the square root of x.

Absolute Value Functions
```
double fabs(double x);
```
Returns the absolute value of x.

Nearest Integer and Remainder Functions
```
double ceil(double x);
```
Returns the smallest integer value greater than or equal to x. Rounds up to the nearest integer.
```
double floor(double x);
```
Returns the largest integer value less than or equal to x. Rounds down to the nearest integer.
```
double fmod(double x, double y);
```
Returns the remainder of x divided by y.

Exponential and Logarithmic Functions
```
double exp(double x);
```
Returns the value of e raised to power of x.
```
double log(double x);
```
Returns the natural logarithm (base-e) of x.
```
double log10(double x);
```
Returns the common logarithm (base-10) of x.

Trigonometric Functions
```
double cos(double x);
```
Returns the cosine of a radian angle x.
```
double sin(double x);
```
Returns the sine of a radian angle x.
```
double tan(double x);
```
Returns the tangent of a radian angle x.
```
double acos(double x);
```
Returns the arc cosine of x in radians.
```
double asin(double x);
```
Returns the arc sine of x in radians.
```
double atan(double x);
```
Returns the arc tangent of x in radians.

Here are examples of the use of some of the functions in the math library. Assume that `y` is defined to be a `double`:

```
y = pow(3, 4);      // assigns 81.000000 to y

y = sqrt(25);       // assigns 5.000000 to y

y = sqrt(5);        // assigns 2.236068 to y

y = fabs(-9.3);     // assigns 9.300000 to y

y = ceil(4.3);      // assigns 5.000000 to y

y = floor(4.3);     // assigns 4.000000 to y

y = fmod(5, 3);     // assigns 2.000000 to y
```

The `stdlib.h` header also defines a few mathematical functions in the standard library. Be sure to include the `stdlib.h` header file near the top of each C file that will use the included functions:

```
#include <stdlib.h>
```

```
int abs(int x);        Returns the absolute value of int x.

int labs(long x);      Returns the absolute value of a long x.
```

Here are examples of the use of some of the functions in the standard library. Assume that `i` is defined to be an `int` and `j` is defined to be a `long`:

```
i = abs(-8);        // assigns 8 to i

i = abs(3);         // assigns 3 to i
```

```
j = labs(-10000000001); // assigns 1000000000 to j
                        // Note that is an el (for long)
                        // after the last zero in the function argument
```

Quadratic Equation Example

Let's compute the roots of a quadratic equation in x of the form:

```
ax² + bx + c = 0
```

We're going to code the quadratic formula: $x = \dfrac{-b \pm \sqrt{b^2 - 4ac}}{2a}$

```c
// quadratic1.c

#include <stdio.h>
#include <math.h>

int main (void) {
    int a=1, b=3, c=-4, disc;
    double root1, root2;

    disc = b*b-4*a*c;
    root1 = (-b + sqrt(disc)) / (2 * a);
    root2 = (-b - sqrt(disc)) / (2 * a);
    printf("root1 = %5.2lf\n", root1);
    printf("root2 = %5.2lf\n", root2);
    return 0;
}
```

Here's the output:

```
root1 =  1.00
root2 = -4.00
```

Arithmetic Expressions as Arguments to Functions

One of the most useful features of C is its ability to allow a function to take an arithmetic expression as an argument. For example, we could have used an arithmetic expression as an argument to the `sqrt()` function as follows:

```
root1 = (-b + sqrt(b*b-4*a*c)) / (2 * a);
root2 = (-b - sqrt(b*b-4*a*c)) / (2 * a);
```

However, in this example, it's probably better to calculate the discriminate, assign it to a variable, `disc`, and then use `disc` in our code so we don't have to perform the calculations for the discriminate twice.

But what if the discriminate is < 0? Then there are no real roots to the quadratic equation. We can have our program make the appropriate test and only perform the calculations for a discriminate that is >= 0:

```c
// quadratic2.c

#include <stdio.h>
#include <math.h>

int main (void) {
    int a=1, b=3, c=-4, disc;
    double root1, root2;

    disc = b*b-4*a*c;
    if (disc > 0) {
        root1 = (-b + sqrt(disc)) / (2 * a);
        root2 = (-b - sqrt(disc)) / (2 * a);
        printf("root1 = %0.1lf\n", root1);
        printf("root2 = %0.1lf\n", root2);
    }
    return 0;
}
```

If the discriminate $<$ 0 then no calculations are performed. Perhaps it would be appropriate to generate some output if the discriminate $<$ 0:

```c
// quadratic3.c

#include <stdio.h>
#include <math.h>

int main (void) {
    int a, b, c, disc;
    double root1, root2;

    a = 1;
    b = 3;
    c = 44;

    disc = b*b-4*a*c;
    if (disc >= 0) {
        root1 = (-b + sqrt(disc)) / (2 * a);
        root2 = (-b - sqrt(disc)) / (2 * a);
        printf("root1 = %0.1lf\n", root1);
        printf("root2 = %0.1lf\n", root2);
    }
    else {
        printf("The discriminate is < 0. There are no real roots.");
    }
    return 0;
}
```

Here's the output:

```
The discriminate is < 0. There are no real roots.
```

Our use of the above decision statements will be the focus of our next chapter.

Techniques of Problem Solving

We are now ready to examine problems that computers can solve. First we need to know how to solve a problem and then we need to learn how to use a programming language to implement our solution on the computer.

Before looking at problem solving and writing programs for the computer, we should understand that programming can cause a significant amount of frustration because:

1. Planning is a critical issue. First, you must plan to develop instructions to solve your problem and then you should plan to translate those instructions into code before you sit down at the keyboard. You should not attempt to type in code "off the top of your head."

2. Time is a major problem. Writing programs is not like completing other assignments. You cannot expect to complete a programming assignment by staying up late the night before it is due. You must begin early and expect to make several revisions before your final version will be ready.

3. Successful problem solving and programming require extreme precision. Generally, concepts in computer science are not difficult; however, implementation of these concepts allows no room for error. For example, one misplaced semicolon in a 1,000-line program could prevent the program from working.

In other words, you must be prepared to plan well, start early, be patient, handle frustration, and work hard to succeed in computer science. If you cannot do this, you will probably neither enjoy computer science nor be successful at it.

The key to writing a successful program is planning. Good programs do not just happen; they are the result of careful design and patience. Just as an artist commissioned to paint a portrait would not start out by shading in the lips and eyes, a good computer programmer would not attack a problem by immediately trying to write code for a program to solve the problem. Writing a program is like writing an essay: an overall theme is envisioned, an outline of major ideas is developed, each major idea is subdivided into several parts, and each part is developed using individual sentences.

Six Steps to Good Programming Habits

In developing a program to solve a problem, six steps should be followed: analyze the problem, develop an algorithm, write code for the program, run the program, test the results and document the program. These steps will help develop good problem-solving habits and, in turn, solve programming problems correctly. A brief discussion of each of these steps follows:

Step 1. Analyze the Problem.

This is not a trivial task. Before you can do anything, you must know exactly what it is you are to do. You must be able to formulate a clear and precise statement of what is to be done. You should understand completely what data are available and what may be assumed. You should also know exactly what output is desired and the form it should take.

Step 2. Develop an Algorithm.

An algorithm is a finite sequence of effective statements that, when applied to the problem, will solve it. An *effective statement* is a clear, unambiguous instruction that can be carried out. Each algorithm you develop should have a specific beginning; at the completion of one step, have the next step uniquely determined; and have an ending that is reached in a reasonable amount of time.

Step 3. Write Code for the Program.

When the algorithm correctly solves the problem, you can think about translating your algorithm into a high-level language. An effective algorithm will significantly reduce the time you need to complete this step.

Step 4. Run the Program.

After writing the code, you are ready to run the program. This means that, using an editor, you type the program code into the computer, compile the program, and run the program. At this point, you may discover errors that can be as simple as typing errors or that may require a reevaluation of all or parts of your algorithm. The probability of having to make some corrections or changes is quite high.

Step 5. Test the Results.

After your program has run, you need to be sure that the results are correct, that they are in a form you like, and that your program produces the correct solution in all cases. To be sure the results are correct, you must look at them and compare them with what you expect. In the case of using a program with arithmetic operations, this means checking some results with pencil and paper. With complex programs, you will need to thoroughly test the program by running it many times using data that you have carefully selected. Often you will need to make revisions and return to Step 4.

Step 6. Document the Program.

It is very important to completely document a working program. The writer knows how the program works; if others are to modify it, they must know the logic used. As you develop the ability to write programs to solve more complex problems, you will find it helpful to include documentation in Step 3 as you write the code.

Developing Algorithms

Algorithms for solving a problem can be developed by stating the problem and then subdividing the problem into major subtasks. Each subtask can then be subdivided into smaller tasks. Tasks identified at each stage of this process are called modules. This process is repeated until each remaining task is one that is easily solved and trivial to implement in C. This process is known as *topdown design,* and each successive subdivision is referred to as a *stepwise refinement.* This enables us to solve a large problem one step at a time, rather than provide the entire solution at once.

Not only is this technique of stepwise refinement an efficient design method, it also produces a good algorithm in the sense that:

- the algorithm is easier to understand
- subsequent modifications are relatively easy to make

This technique lets you plan a program without actually writing in C:

- It's easier to think in English than computerese
- Tackling a problem from the top puts off the nitty-gritty of encoding for as long as possible

Stepwise refinement of a problem:

1. State the problem simply, decomposing it into its logical subproblems.

2. If you can immediately figure out how to encode any of the subproblems, do so. These will be the main functions of your program.

3. If the subproblems are too complex, refine them into smaller, more basic subproblems, etc.

The relationship between modules can be shown graphically in a *structure chart.* For example, suppose a public library wishes to computerize its operations - a fairly ambitious programming project. The first step in cutting it down to size is a basic problem decomposition:

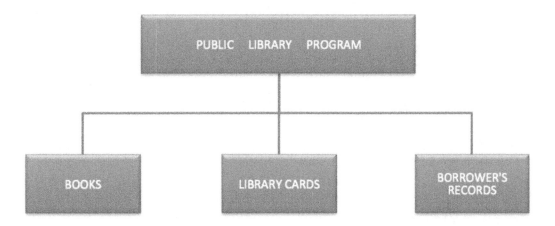

If we've left anything out, we can always backtrack to this step of the refinement. We can now go a stage further and refine each of the first level's subproblems:

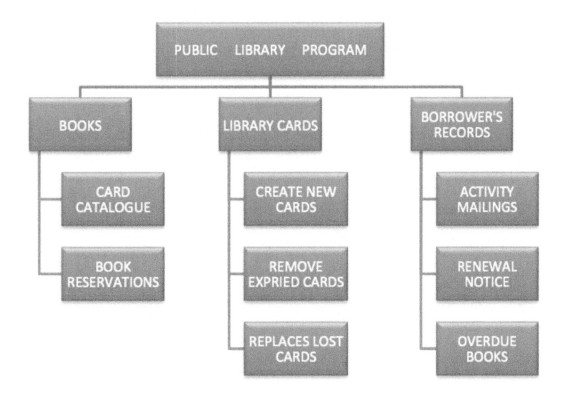

This is still abstract for a programmer so we refine it once more:

Card Catalogue
- Add books to catalogue
- Delete books from catalogue
- Search for books

Book Reservations
- Search for books
- Inform borrower
- Print hold message

Create New Cards
- Print card form
- Get new card information

Remove Expired Cards
- Remove card from permanent file
- Check for outstanding books
- Inform borrower

Replace Lost Cards
- Find old card information
- Print card form

Activity Mailings
- Get activity information
- Inform borrower

Renewal Notice
- Get old card information
- Inform borrower

Overdue Books
- Check for overdue books
- Calculate fine
- Inform borrower

Notice that the refinement starts to pay off as parts of the problem take shape as input / output functions. As an extra bonus, some of this level's refinements (e.g. Inform borrower segments) are similar enough to be written as a single function.

The entire program is still too complicated to encode with C, but some is within reach:

```c
// library.c
// Reads today's date and books due date. Both must be
// in the current month.

#define FinePerDay 0.25

void calculateFines() {
    float totalFine;
    int todaysDate, dueDate, daysLate;

    printf("Enter todays date and books due date.\n");
    scanf_s("%d %d", &todaysDate, &dueDate);
    daysLate = todaysDate - dueDate;
    totalFine = daysLate * FinePerDay;
    printf("The total fine is %5.2f", totalFine);
}
```

1. Give the function header for each of the following functions.

a) Function `areaRectangle` takes two `double` arguments, `length` and `width`, and returns a `double` value.

b) Function `max` takes four integers, `w`, `x`, `y`, `z`, and returns an integer.

c) Function `outputHeaders` does not receive any arguments and does not return a value.

d) Function `getValue` takes an integer argument, `num`, and returns a `char`.

2. Suppose that the function `foo()` has the following definition:

```
int foo (int a, int b, int c) {
    ...
}
```

Which are the following statements are legal? Assume that `i` has type `int` and `x` has type `double`.

```
a)    i = foo (10, 20, 30);

b)    x = foo (10, 20, 30);

c)    i = foo (5.25, 3.45, 7.22);

d)    x = foo (5.25, 3.45, 7.22);

e)    foo (10, 20, 30);

f)    foo (10, 20);
```

3. Which of the following would be valid prototypes for a function that returns nothing and has one `double` parameter?

    a)   `void foo (double x);`

    b)   `void foo (double);`

    c)   `void foo (x);`

    d)   `foo (double x);`

4. mp3s cost $1.25 each, CDs cost $3.25 each, and DVDs cost $12.75 each. Write a function, `buyMusic`, that takes three parameters representing the number of mp3s, CDs, and DVDs, and returns the total dollar cost.

Chapter 7. Selection Statements

If Statement
Switch Statement
Conditional Operator
❖ Selection Homework
❖ Body Mass Index Lab
❖ Large – Small Lab
❖ Wages Lab

If Statements

Decision statements allow programs to follow different courses of action or execute different tasks depending on the data values.

if statement: Single Alternative Decision Statement

The pseudo-code statement below:

```
if x is not equal to zero then
    divide y by x and assign the result to num
```

can be read as follows:

If the condition "x is not equal to zero" is true, divide the value of y by the value of x and assign the result to variable num. Otherwise, the condition "x is not equal to zero" is false. In this case, no alternative action is taken because no alternative actions have been specified if the statement is false.

The syntax of the if statement looks like this:

```
if (expression) {
    statement;
}
```

The if statement uses semi-boolean logic, i.e., zero means false and non-zero means true. Here's what the C code might look like for the above pseudo-code example:

```
if (x != 0) {
    num = y/x;
}
```

Here's a short program that prints the absolute value of a number:

```c
//absoluteValue.c

#include <stdio.h>

int main(void) {
    int num;

    printf("Enter a value: ");
    scanf_s("%d", &num);
    if (num < 0) {
        num = -num;
    }
    printf("The absolute value is %d\n", num);
    return 0;
}
```

Side effects are allowed inside the expression. It's good C style to use them to avoid creating otherwise useless "temporary" variables. Thus,

```c
if (scanf_s("%d", &num) != 1) {
    printf("Bad value.\n");
}
```

is better than

```c
temp = scanf_s("%d", &num);
if (temp != 1) {
    printf("Bad value.\n");
}
```

Due to the fact that an expression will result in a zero (false) or a non-zero value, we would use:

```c
if (expression)
```

instead of

```c
if (expression != 0)
```

`if-else` statement: Double Alternative Decision Statement

The pseudo-code example below:

```
if x is not equal to zero then
    divide y by x and assign the requly to num
else   // otherwise
    display an error message
```

can be read as follows:

If the condition "x is not equal to zero" is true, divide the value of y by the value of x and assign the result to variable num. Otherwise, the condition "x is not equal to zero" is false. In this case, display an error message.

Note that the conditions shown above are logical expressions. When you evaluate them, you get either true or false. These are the only two possible values for a logical expression!

The syntax for the `if-else` statement is as follows:

```
if (expression) {
    statement1;
}
else {
    statement2;
}
```

Here's what the C code might look like for the above pseudo-code example:

```
if (x != 0) {
    num = y / x;
}
else {
    printf ("Divide by zero error condition.");
}
```

Here's a simple program to determine whether or not a number is odd or even:

```c
// oddEven1.c

#include <stdio.h>

int main(void) {
    int num;

    printf("Enter a number: ");
    scanf_s("%d", &num);
    if (num % 2 == 0) {
        printf("The number is even.\n");
    }
    else {
        printf("The number is odd.\n");
    }
    return 0;
}
```

Note that any place C allows a statement in a control structure, the statement can be a compound statement delimited by braces:

```c
// oddEven2.c

#include <stdio.h>

int main(void) {
    int num;

    printf("Enter a number: ");
    scanf_s("%d", &num);
    printf("The number entered is %d.\n", num);
    if (num % 2 == 0)
        printf("The number is even.\n");
    else
        printf("The number is odd.\n");
    }
    return 0;
}
```

Below is a program using the if-else construct to calculate wages based upon a pay rate and the number of hours worked:

```
// calculateWages.c
// Program to Calculate Wages

#include <stdio.h>

int main (void) {
    float payRate, hours, wages;

    printf("Enter hourly salary: ");
    scanf_s("%f", &payRate);

    printf("Enter number of hours worked: ");
    scanf_s("%f", &hours);

    if (hours <= 40)
        wages = hours * payRate;
    else
        wages = (40 * payRate) + (hours - 40) * 1.5 * payRate;

    printf("The employee's weekly wages are $%6.2f\n", wages);
    return 0;
}
```

Nested `if` Statement

Whenever an `if` statement is nested within another `if` statement, put braces around the nested `if` statement. Additionally, an `else` clause is associated with the most recent "un-elsed" `if` statement that is in the same scope:

```
// nesting1.c

// incorrect nesting
if (num > 0)
    if (num % 2 == 0)
        printf("Positive and even.\n");
else
    printf("Not positive.\n");


// correct nesting
if (num > 0) {
    if (num % 2 == 0)
        printf("Positive and even.\n");
}
else
    printf("Not positive. ");
```

`else-if` statement: Multiple Alternative Decision Statement

The pseudo-code example below:

```
if x is less than zero then
    set y equal to -1
else if x is equal to zero then
    set y equal to 0
else
    set y equal to 1
```

can be read as follows:

If the condition "x is less than zero" is true, set the value of y to -1.

Otherwise, the condition "x is less than zero" is a false. So if the condition "x is equal to zero" is true, set the value of y to 0.

Otherwise, the conditions "x is less than zero" and "x is equal to zero" are both false. So we set the value of y to 1.

The else if statement is used whenever an if statement has nesting only inside the else clause. The syntax looks like this:

```
if (expression1) {
    statement1;
}
else if (expression2) {
    statement2;
}
else if (expression3) {
    statement3;
}
else {
    statement4;
}
```

Here's what the C code might look like for the above pseudo-code example:

```
// nesting2.c

if (x < 0) {
    y = -1;
}
else if (x == 0) {
    y = 0;
}
else {
    y = 1;
}
```

Frequently an `else-if` construct can clarify your code. For example, the meaning of this obscure three-way choice:

```
// nesting3.c

if (n > 0) {
    printf("Positive");
}
else {
    if (n == 0) {
        printf("Zero");
    }
    else {
        printf("Negative");
    }
}
```

can be made clearer using the `else-if` construct:

```
// nesting4.c

if (n > 0) {
    printf("Positive");
}
else  if (n == 0) {
    printf("Zero");
}
else {
    printf("Negative");
}
```

Switch Statement

The `switch` statement is another multiple choice control structure.

• It can only be used in certain cases where only one variable is tested. All branches must depend on the value of that variable.

• The variable must be an integral type such as `int`, `long`, `short`, or `char`.

• Each possible value of the variable can control a single branch. A final, catch all, `default` branch may optionally be used to trap all unspecified cases.

Here's a simple calculator program that uses a `switch` statement:

```c
// calculator.c

#include <stdio.h>

int calc(int operand1, int operand2, char operator);

int main(void) {
    int a, b;
    char op;

    printf("Enter two integers and an operator: ");
    scanf_s("%d %d %c", &a, &b, &op);
    calc(a, b, op);
    return 0;
}

int calc(int operand1, int operand2, char operator) {
    switch (operator) {
        case '+' :      printf("%d\n", operand1 + operand2); break;
        case '-' :      printf("%d\n", operand1 - operand2); break;
        case '*' :      printf("%d\n", operand1 * operand2); break;
        case '/' :      printf("%d\n", operand1 / operand2); break;
    }
    return 0;
}
```

Note that at the end of each alternative section of code there should be a `break` statement. The `break` statement prevents any further statements from being executed by leaving the `switch`. Control jumps to the closing brace after the `switch` statement. Actually, the most common way to leave a `switch` statement is with a `break` or a `return` statement.

Conditional Operator

The conditional operator, `? :`, is the only ternary operator in C, i.e. requires 3 operands:

- the expression being tested
- the two alternative outcome expressions

Here's what the syntax of the conditional operator looks like:

```
// conditional1.c

condition ? expr1 : expr2;
```

The condition is a relational expression returning true or false (0 or non-zero). If true, then `expr1` is evaluated, otherwise `expr2` is evaluated. In fact, the conditional operator behaves very much like an `if-else` statement. The following code:

```
// conditional2.c

if (x > y) {
    max = x;
}
else {
    max = y;
}
```

can be rewritten using the conditional operator:

```
// conditional3.c

max = x > y ? x : y;
```

The conditional statement is very useful for shortening programs. We can rewrite the following `if-else` statement:

```
// conditional4.c

if (x > y) {
    printf("%d\n", x);
}
else {
    printf("%d\n", y);
}
```

as

```
// conditional5.c

printf("%d\n", x > y ? x : y);
```

In the following statement:

```
// conditional6.c

num = value > 0 ? ++x : ++y;
```

only one of the expressions, either `++x` or `++y` gets evaluated, but never both!

Two functions are shown below using the conditional operator. Note that they also use functions from the `ctype.h` library:

```
// lowerToUpper.c

// convert lower case to upper case

char toUpper(char c) {
    return isLower(c) ? c - 32 : c);
}

// convert upper case to lower case

char toLower(char c) {
    return isUpper(c) ? c + 32 : c);
}
```

Here's an example from that prints n elements of an array, 10 per line, with each column separated by one blank, and with each line (including the last) terminated by exactly one new line:

```c
// printsArrayElements1.c

// Long Form

for (i = 0; i < n; ++i) {
    printf("%6d", a[i]);
    if (i % 10 == 9 || i == n - 1) {
        printf("%c", '\n');
    }
    else {
        printf("%c", ' ');
    }
}
```

A newline is printed after every 10th element, and after the nth all other elements are followed by one blank.

```c
// printsArrayElements2.c

// Short Form

for (i = 0; i < n; ++i) {
    printf("%6d%c", a[i], (i % 10 == 9 || i == n - 1) ? '\n', : ' ');
}
```

1. Write a single statement to accomplish each of the following:

a) If `value` is not equal to 42, print `"The variable value is not equal to 42."`

b) Test if the value of the variable `num` is greater than or equal to 7. If it is, print `"Num is greater than or equal to 7."`

2. What are the values of the following expressions? Remember that C does not use Boolean logic (true or false), but rather uses semi-boolean logic (zero or non-zero). You may assume all variables are declared to be of type `int`.

a)
```
i = 3;
j = 3;
i - j == 0
```

b)
```
i = 3;
j = 7;
k = 2;
i % j + i < k
```

c)
```
i = 10;
j = 5;
!i < j
```

d)
```
i = 2;
j = 1;
!!i + !j
```

e)
```
i = 5;
j = 0;
k = -5;
i && j || k
```

f)
```
i = 1;
j = 2;
k = 3;
i < j || k
```

3. What are the values of the following expressions. You may assume all variables are declared to be of type `int`.

```
c = 1;
d = -2;
a = 0;
e = 3;
```

a) `(c < d) || a`

b) `2 < !d + d`

c) `!(!(!e))`

4. The following `if` statement is unnecessarily complicated. Simplify it as much as possible. (Hint: The entire statement can be replaced by a single assignment.)

```
if (age >= 13)
if (age <= 19)
     teenager = true;
else
     teenager = false;
else if (age < 13)
     teenager = false;
```

5. The mathematical operation:

```
min(x, y)
```

can be represented by the conditional expression:

```
(x < y) ? x : y
```

In a similar fashion, using only conditional expressions, describe the mathematical operation:

```
min(x, y, z)
```

The BMI, or Body Mass Index, is a measure of one's body fat based upon the individual's height and weight. It can determine whether or not an individual is overweight or obese.

The formula for calculating BMI is as follows:

$$BMI = \frac{weightInPounds \times 703}{heightInInches \times heightInInches}$$

The following table can be used to evaluate a BMI score:

BMI VALUES	
Less than 18.5	Underweight
Between 18.5 and less than 25.0	Normal
Between 25.0 and less than 30.0	Overweight
30.0 or greater	Obese

For this lab you are to construct a C program, bmi.c, which includes a function, calculateBMI(), that prompts the user to input a weight, in pounds, and height, in inches, and then calculates and displays the body mass index. The function should also display whether a person is underweight, normal, overweight, or obese.

Be sure that the user prompts as well as the height and weight values input into the program are displayed in the output file. Note that the resultant BMI values should be displayed to one decimal place. The variables in your function that receive the height and weight values should be declared as double.

Provided below is the `main()` function that I would like you to use for your program.

```
int main (void) {
    int i;

    fopen_s(&fp, "csis.txt", "w");
    for (i = 1; i <= 4; ++i) {
        calculateBMI();
    }
    fclose(fp);
    return 0;
}
```

Please do not modify the `main()` function. It should appear as the first function in the program. Be sure to use function prototypes for each of the functions that are used in your program.

Note that the `for` loop invokes the `calculateBMI()` function four times. Each time the `calculateBMI()` function is invoked, a different weight and height will be entered. Please be sure to use the data shown below:

```
First:   175 70

Second: 120 68

Third:   225 65

Fourth: 140 67
```

Output from your program should be sent to the terminal window (your screen) as well as the requested `csis.txt` output file. Be sure to read the document on Capturing Program Output. Your full name must appear as a comment in the source file that contains `main()`. Be sure to include the `csis.txt` output file in your zip archive.

❖ Large-Small Lab

Write a C program, largeSmall.c, which includes a function, compare(), that prompts the user to input four integers and calculates and displays the largest and smallest of the integers. Be sure that the user prompts as well as the four integers input into the program are displayed in the output file.

Provided below is the main() function that I would like you to use for your program.

```
int main (void) {
    int i;

    fopen_s(&fp, "csis.txt", "w");
    for (i = 1; i <= 4; ++i) {
        compare();
    }
    fclose(fp);
    return 0;
}
```

Please do not modify the main() function. It should appear as the first function in the program. Be sure to use function prototypes for each of the functions that are used in your program.

Note that the for loop invokes the compare() function four times. Each time the compare() function is invoked, a different set of four integers will be entered. Please be sure to use the data shown below:

```
First:    28  44  66  82

Second:    8  14  22   6

Third:    21  38  12  16

Fourth:   98  22  45  63
```

Output from your program should be sent to the terminal window (your screen) as well as the requested `csis.txt` output file. Be sure to read the document on Capturing Program Output. Your full name must appear as a comment in the source file that contains `main()`. Be sure to include the `csis.txt` output file in your zip archive.

Write a C program, `wages.c`, which calculates an employees gross pay, taxes, and net pay. The program should calculate overtime pay, if necessary. Overtime is paid as time and a half for each hour worked over 40 hours.

Here's the formula to calculate a salary that does not contain overtime pay:

```
wages = hours * payrate
```

Here's the formula to calculate a salary that contains overtime pay:

```
wages = (40 * payrate) + (hours - 40) * 1.5 * payrate
```

Taxes are calculated as follows:

20% on the first $200
25% on the next $250
30% on the remaining gross pay

For each run of the program, prompt the user for both hours and payrate.

Run1: hours = 28.5; payrate = 22.75

Run2: hours = 63.75; payrate = 35.25

Note that you should not have to modify your code for a different run of the program. Use an if-else statement to test whether or not overtime pay will need to be calculated. Be sure to give all numeric output to two decimal places. Submit the output file for run1 as csis1.txt and run2 as csis2.txt.

Remember, do not perform your own calculations and have your program output the results. All of the calculations for the lab should be performed within your program.

Your `main()` function should appear as the first function in the program. Be sure to use function prototypes for each of the functions that are used in your program.

Output from your program should be sent to the terminal window (your screen) as well as the requested `csis.txt` output file. Be sure to read the document on Capturing Program Output. Your full name must appear as a comment in the source file that contains `main()`. Be sure to include the `csis.txt` output file in your zip archive.

Chapter 8. Repetition Statements

While Statement
For Statement
Comma Operator
Do-While Loop
Break Statement
Continue Statement
❖ Repetition Homework
❖ Grade Lab
❖ Penny Lab
❖ Fibonacci Lab

A repetition statement allows you to specify that an action is to be repeated while some condition remains true. For example, the statement:

```
while there are more items on my shopping list
    purchase next item and cross it off my list
```

describes the repetition that occurs during a shopping trip. The condition:

```
there are more items on my shopping list
```

may be true or false. If it's true, then the action:

```
purchase next item and cross it off my list
```

is performed. This action will be performed repeatedly while the condition remains true. Eventually, the condition will become false (when the last item on the shopping list has been purchased and crossed off the list). At this point, the repetition terminates, and the first statement after the repetition structure is executed.

So loops provide a means of repeating a series of executable statements (the *loop body*) as long as the condition controlling the loop (usually found in the loop header) evaluates to true. The *loop control condition* is a logical expression that evaluates to either true or false. Often, this expression involves a single variable, called a *loop control variable*.

The loop body is the block of code that contains the series of executable statements associated with the loop condition. Note that the loop body may be a single statement or a compound statement. The loop body will be repeated as long as the loop condition evaluates to true. When the loop condition evaluates to false, the loop will terminate. Each time the loop body is repeated, the loop is said to have gone through an *iteration*.

The syntax of a `while` loop looks like this:

```
// Before the loop construct, initialize any loop control variable,
// i.e., the variable appearing in the condition in the loop header.

while (condition) {     // loop header - test the loop condition
    statement;
}

or

while (condition) {     // loop header - test the loop condition
    statement;
    statement;
    . . .
}
```

Keep in mind that the loop body must contain a statement that updates the loop control variable used in the loop condition. The loop control variable is normally found at the bottom of the loop body.

Note that when a while loop construct has only one statement then the curly braces { } are optional. However, it's always a good idea to use the curly braces even though they're not required.

Example: Powers of 2

As an example, consider a program segment designed to find the first power of 2 larger than 100. We first initialize the integer variable `product` to 2. When the following `while` repetition statement finishes executing, `product` will contain the desired answer:

```
// powersOfTwo.c

product = 2;
while (product <= 100) {
    product = product * 2;     // or we can say:  product *= 2;
}
```

When the `while` statement is entered, the value of `product` is 2. The variable, `product`, is repeatedly multiplied by 2, taking on the values 2, 4, 8, 16, 32, 64 and 128 successively. When `product` becomes 128, the condition in the `while` statement:

```
product <= 100
```

becomes false. This terminates the repetition, and the final value of `product` is 128. Program execution continues with the next statement after the `while` loop.

We can generalize this example and write a function, `findMax()`, that will return the first power of 2 greater than some maximum value:

```c
// findMaxValue1.c

#include <stdio.h>

int findMax(int value);

int main (void) {
    int value, max;

    value = 500;
    max = findMax(value);
    printf("The first power of 2 larger than %d is %d.\n", value, max);
    return 0;
}

int findMax(int value) {
    int product = 2;

    while (product <= value) {
        product *= 2;
    }
    return product;
}
```

Here's the output produced:

```
The first power of 2 larger than 500 is 512.
```

We can generalize this example even further to have the function, `findMax()`, return the first power of `num` greater than some maximum `value`:

```
// findMaxValue2.c

#include <stdio.h>

int findMax(int num, int value);

int main (void) {
    int num, value, max;

    num = 5;
    value = 1000;

    max = findMax(num, value);
    printf("The first power of %d larger than %d is %d.\n", num,
                                                  value, max);
    return 0;
}

int findMax(int num, int value) {
    int product = num;

    while (product <= value) {
        product *= num;
    }
    return product;
}
```

Here's the output produced:

```
The first power of 5 larger than 1000 is 3125.
```

Counter Controlled Loops

A counter controlled loop repeats a series of executable statements a specified number of times using a variable to count the number of loop iterations completed.

• The number of times that the loop body will be repeated **must** be known before checking the loop condition the first time and must **not** be changed within the loop body.

• The counting variable **must** be initialized to a known value before checking the loop condition the first time.

- The counting variable **must** be updated within the loop body or the loop condition will never evaluate to false, creating an infinite loop that will never stop.

- The counting variables can be incremented (increased in value) by any amount or decremented (decreased in value) by any amount.

Example: Celsius to Fahrenheit Conversion Table

Our conversion table will utilize a *counter variable*, ctemp, to control the number of times the while loop executes. In this example, repetition terminates when ctemp becomes < 0.

```
// tempConversion.c

#include <stdio.h>

int main (void) {
    int ctemp;
    float ftemp;

    printf("Celsius\t\tFahrenheit\n");
    ctemp = 100;
    while (ctemp >= 0) {
        ftemp = (9.0/5.0) * (float)ctemp + 32.0;
        printf ("%7d\t\t%10.1f\n", ctemp, ftemp);
        ctemp -= 10;
    }
    return 0;
}
```

Program output is as follows:

```
Celsius         Fahrenheit
    100              212.0
     90              194.0
     80              176.0
     70              158.0
     60              140.0
     50              122.0
     40              104.0
     30               86.0
     20               68.0
     10               50.0
      0               32.0
```

• What would have happened if we were to have written (9/5) instead of (9.0/5.0)?

• What would have happened if we left off the parentheses around (9.0/5.0)?

• Why was it a good idea to write `(float)ctemp` in the above expression rather than just `ctemp`?

Summation Variables

Suppose that we wish to find the sum of the numbers from 1-1000. Not only will we need a counter variable to control the number of times the while loop executes, but we will also need a *summation variable* to accumulate the sum of the numbers that we have seen so far.

```
// summation.c

#include <stdio.h>

int main(void) {
    int count = 1;
    int sum = 0;

    while (count <= 1000) {
        sum += count;
        ++count;
    }
    printf("The sum = %d.\n", sum);
    return 0;
}
```

Program output is as follows:

```
The sum = 500500.
```

Note that variable used to store summations, or totals, should normally be initialized to zero before being used in a program; otherwise the summation variable would include the previous value stored in the summation variable's memory location. This is due to the fact that an uninitialized variable usually contains a "garbage value", i.e., the value last stored in the memory location reserved for that variable.

Sentinel Controlled Loops

Sometimes we do not know in advance how many times we want a loop to iterate. For example, suppose we want to output the square and cube of numbers entered into the program. How can the program determine when to stop the input of numbers? One way to solve this problem is to use a special value called a *sentinel value* to indicate "end of data entry."

The user types in data values, whose squares and cubes will be output, until the sentinel value is entered which indicates that the last data value has been entered. Note that the sentinel value must be chosen so that it cannot be confused with an acceptable input value.

```c
// sentinel.c

#include <stdio.h>

int main(void) {
    int num;

    printf("Enter number, -999 to end: ");
    scanf_s("%d", &num);
    while (num != -999) {
        printf("%5d   %5d   %5d\n", num, num * num, num * num * num);
        printf("Enter number: ");
        scanf_s("%d", &num);
    }
    return 0;
}
```

Program output is as follows:

```
Enter number, -999 to end: 2
    2       4       8
Enter number, -999 to end: 5
    5      25     125
Enter number, -999 to end: 8
    8      64     512
Enter number, -999 to end: -999
```

For Statement

The `for` statement works well where the number of iterations of the loop is known before the loop is entered. The head of the loop consists of three parts separated by semicolons: initialization, test, and update.

```
for (i = 1; i <= 10; i++)
```

The first part is run before the loop is entered. This is usually the *initialization* of the loop control variable.

The second part is a *test* of the loop control variable. The loop is exited when this test is no longer true.

The third part is the *update* of the loop control variable. This is typically a statement that is executed every time the loop body is completed. Usually this is an increment or decrement of the loop control variable.

Here's a look at the syntax of the `for` statement:

```
for (initialExpression; loopCondition; loopExpression) {
    statement;
}
```

- `initialExpression` sets an initial value before the loop begins.

- `loopCondition` specifies condition(s) necessary to continue the loop.

- `loopExpression` executes each time after the body of the loop executes.

Example: Sum the integers from 1 - 100

```c
// sumIntegers1.c

int i, sum = 0;

for (i = 1; i <= 100; ++i) {
    sum += i;
}
```

In our example, variable `i` is the loop control variable and is initialized to 1. If the `loopCondition` is true, `i <= 100,` then the body of the loop will execute once. After the last statement of the loop body executes, the `loopExpression` is executed. In this case, the value of i is incremented by 1. If the `loopCondition` is still true, the body of the `for` loop will execute once again, etc.

Note that any or all of the expressions in a `for` statement can be missing, but the two semicolons must always remain. For example, if the `initialExpression` is missing, then no initialization step is performed as part of the `for` loop:

```c
// sumIntegers2.c
// Compute the sum of integers from 1 - 10.

int i = 1, sum = 0;

for ( ; i <= 10; ++i) {
    sum += i;
}
```

When the `loopCondition` is missing, the rule is that the test is always true. Therefore the `for` loop below is an infinite loop;

```c
// sumIntegers3.c

int i = 1, sum = 0;

for ( ; ; ) {
    sum += i++;
    printf("%d ", sum);
}
```

Note that a `for` statement can always be translated into an equivalent `while` statement, and vice versa:

```
// for loop

for (initialExpression; loopCondition; loopExpression) {
    statement;
}


// while loop

initialExpression;
while (loopCondition) {
    statement;
    loopExpression;
}
```

Be sure not to place a semicolon at the end of the header of the for loop:

```
// sumIntegers4.c

int i, sum = 0;

for (i = 1; i <= 100; ++i);
    sum += i;
```

This will create a problem as the `for` loop will no longer have a body. The controlling aspects of the loop will execute 100 times, in this case, but nothing will be done because the loop body is empty.

Note that when a `for` loop construct has only one statement then the curly braces `{}` are optional. However, it's always a good idea to use the curly braces even though they're not required.

Nested `for` Loops

There are times when we have a need to place a `for` loop within the body of another `for` loop. This is referred to as a nested `for` loop. Can you follow the flow of control of the nested `for` loop below:

```c
// nest.c

#include <stdio.h>

int main(void) {
    int i, j;

    for (i = 1; i <= 4; ++i) {
        for (j = 1; j <= 3; ++j) {
            printf("%d  %d\n", i, j);
        }
    }
    return 0;
}
```

Here's the output that gets produced:

```
1  1
1  2
1  3
2  1
2  2
2  3
3  1
3  2
3  3
4  1
4  2
4  3
```

Comma Operator

Once in a while, you find yourself in a situation in which C expects a single expression, but you have two things you want to say. The most common (and in fact the only common) example is in a `for` loop, specifically the first and third controlling expressions. What if, for example, you want to have a loop in which `i` counts up from 0 to 10 at the same time that `j` is counting down from 10 to 0? You could manipulate `i` in the loop header and `j` ``by hand":

```
// comma1.c

j = 10;
for(i = 0; i < 10; i++) {
    ... rest of loop ...
    j--;
}
```

But here it's harder to see the parallel nature of `i` and `j`, and it also turns out that this won't work right if the loop contains a `continue` statement. (A `continue` would jump back to the top of the loop, and `i` would be incremented but `j` would *not* be decremented.) You could compute `j` in terms of `i`:

```
// comma2.c

for(i = 0; i < 10; i++) {
    j = 10 - i;
    ... rest of loop ...
}
```

but this also makes `j` needlessly subservient. The usual way to write this loop in C would be:

```
// comma3.c

for(i = 0, j = 10; i < 10; i++, j--) {
    ... rest of loop ...
}
```

Here, the first (initialization) expression is:

```
i = 0, j = 10
```

The comma is the *comma operator*, which simply evaluates the first subexpression i = 0, then the second j = 10.

The third controlling expression:

```
i++, j-
```

also contains a comma operator, and again, performs first i++ and then j--.

In this example we initialize both variable i and j to 0 in the for loop.

```
// comma4.c

for (i = 0, j = 0; i < 10; ++i)
```

Precisely stated, the meaning of the comma operator in the general expression:

```
e1 , e2
```

is "evaluate the subexpression e1, then evaluate e2; the value of the expression is the value of e2.'" Therefore, e1 had better involve an assignment or an increment ++ or decrement -- or function call or some other kind of *side effect*, because otherwise it would calculate a value that would be discarded.

There's hardly any reason to use a comma operator anywhere other than in the first and third controlling expressions of a for loop, and in fact most of the commas you see in C programs are *not* comma operators. In particular, the commas between the arguments in a function call are not comma operators; they are just punctuation which separate several argument expressions.

It's pretty easy to see that they cannot be `comma` operators, otherwise in a call like:

```
// comma5.c

printf("Hello, %s!\n", "world");
```

the action would be "evaluate the string `"Hello, %s!\n"`, discard it, and pass only the string `"world"` to `printf()`. This is of course *not* what we want; we expect both strings to be passed to `printf()` as two separate arguments (which is, of course, what happens).

Do While Loop

The do while loop is very similar to the while loop except that the test occurs at the *end* of the loop body. This guarantees that the loop is executed at least once before continuing. Such a setup is frequently used where data is to be read. The test then verifies the data and loops back to read again if the data was unacceptable.

For example, suppose you want to read in a positive integer and you want to insist that the integer is positive:

```c
// positive.c

do {
    printf("Enter a positive value: ");
    scanf_s("%d", &num);
} while (num <= 0);
```

Note the following:

• The condition num <= 0 is tested after execution of the loop body.

• The loop continues as long as the evaluation expression, num <= 0, is true.

• The loop terminates when expression, num <= 0, becomes false.

• The code always executes the body of the loop at least once.

• The semicolon is required after the closing parenthesis at the end of the do-while loop construct.

• The variable(s) used in the loop condition normally should be initialized before the loop is entered, and then updated (in the loop body) before the loop condition is tested at the end of each repetition of the loop body.

Note that when a do-while loop construct has only one statement then the curly braces { } are optional. However, it's always a good idea to use the curly braces even though they're not required.

Break Statement

The `break` statement is available within the `while`, `do while`, `for`, and `switch` statements. It serves in each of these constructs as a jump to the end of the statement. It causes an exit from a loop just as it does from a `switch` statement. After the `break` is executed, program control jumps to the statement following the loop. For example:

```
// break1.c

for (i = 0; i < num; ++i) {
    if (i > 100) {
        break;
    }
    sum += i;
}
```

Note that each time you code a `break` (with the exception of the `switch` statement), you should question whether there is not a straightforward way to express the same logic without the `break`. We can modify the code above without using a `break` as follows:

```
// break2.c

for (i = 0; i < num && i <= 100; ++i) {
    sum += i;
}
```

Here's another example. Suppose we want to look for the first whitespace character (blank, tab, or newline) in a string `s`:

```
// break3.c
// misuse of break

for (i = 0; i < max; ++i) {
    if (s[i] == ' ') {
        break;
    }
    else if (s[i] == '\t') {
        break;
    }
    else if (s[i] == '\n') {
        break;
    }
}
```

A more professional approach is to state the looping condition in the test of the loop:

```
// break4.c
// search for whitespace character

for (i = 0; s[i] != ' ' && s[i] != '\t' && s[i] != '\n'; ++i) {
    ;
}
```

We can also generalize the idea of whitespace:

```
// break5.c

for (i = 0; !isspace(s[i]); ++i) {
    ;
}
```

We'll soon be taking a closer look at strings.

Continue Statement

The `break` statement can be used to immediately take you out of a loop. Sometimes, however, you want to go back to the top of the loop when something unexpected happens.

For example, we can use the `continue` statement to avoid a division by zero error:

```
// reciprocals.c
// calculate reciprocals for -5 to 5

int main(void) {
    int i;

    for (i = -5.0; i <= 5.0; i += 1.0) {
        if (i == 0.0) {
            printf("Divide by zero trap.\n");
            continue;
        }
        printf("%f\n", 1.0 / i);
    }
    return 0;
}
```

Note that in the body of the `for` statement, the `continue` statement jumps to the `loopExpression`, the third expression of the `for` statement. In the `while` and `do while` loops, it jumps to the test.

Like a `break` statement, you should always question the need for a `continue` statement. By simply restructuring the code you can often eliminate the need for a `continue` statement. You are very unlikely to use it.

```
-0.200000
-0.250000
-0.333333
-0.500000
-1.000000
Divide by zero trap.
1.000000
0.500000
0.333333
0.250000
0.200000
```

❖ Repetition Homework

1. What output does the following program fragment produce?

```
i = 4;
while (i <= 128) {
    printf("%d ", i);
    i *= 2;
}
```

2. What output does the following program fragment produce?

```
i = 1234;
do {
    printf("%d ", i);
    i /= 10;
} while (i > 0);
```

3. Show the output of each of the code blocks below:

a)
```
for (i = 5; i < 32; i += 6) {
    printf("%d\n", i);
}
```

b)
```
for (i = 25; i > 0; i -= 5) {
    printf( "%d\n", i);
}
```

4. Write C statements to sum the odd integers from 1 and 100 using a `for` statement. Assume the integer variables `sum` and `count` have been defined, but not initialized, to be of type `int`.

5. Write `for` statements that print the following sequences of values:

a)   10, 20, 30, 40, 50

b)   75, 65, 55, 45, 35

6. Assume that we want to calculate the sum of the integers from 50 down to 1. What is wrong with the code below?

```
sum = 0;
num = 50;
while (num >= 0) {
    sum += num;
}
```

7. See if you can improve the following program segments through reorganization. First analyze the code to determine the function actually being performed. Then recode that function as clearly and simply as possibly (i.e. without the use of break or continue).

a)
```
while(a) {
    if(b) {
        continue;
    }
    c();
}
```

b)
```
do {
    if (!a) {
        continue;
    }
    else {
        b();
        c();
    }
} while (a);
```

Write a C program, `grade.c`, which includes a function, `calculateAverage()`, that can calculate the average of an arbitrary number of test scores. Your program will not know in advance how many test scores will be entered into your function so you will need to use a sentinel value (`-1`) to terminate the `while` loop used to collect the test scores. The test scores are integers in the range 0 to 100 and the test score average should be output to two decimal places. Be sure that the user prompts and grades input into the program are displayed in the output file.

Provided below is the `main()` function that I would like you to use for your program.

```c
int main (void) {
    int i;

    fopen_s(&fp, "csis.txt", "w");
    for (i = 1; i <= 4; ++i) {
        calculateAverage();
    }
    fclose(fp);
    return 0;
}
```

Please do not modify the `main()` function. It should appear as the first function in the program. Be sure to use function prototypes for each of the functions that are used in your program.

Note that the `for` loop invokes the `calculateAverage()` function four times. Each time the `calculateAverage()` function is invoked, a different set of test grades will be entered. Please be sure to use the data shown below:

```
First: 78, 93, 45, 88, 89, -1

Second: 87, 68, 100, -1

Third: 84, 86, 90, 86, 96, 68, 82, -1

Fourth: -1
```

Remember that the `main()` function should appear as the first function in the program. Be sure to use function prototypes for each of the functions that are used in your program.

Output from your program should be sent to the terminal window (your screen) as well as the requested `csis.txt` output file. Be sure to read the document on Capturing Program Output. Your full name must appear as a comment in the source file that contains `main()`. Be sure to include the `csis.txt` output file in your zip archive.

On the first day you deposit a penny in the bank. On the second day you deposit two pennies. On the third day you deposit four pennies. On the fourth day you deposit eight pennies, etc. Assuming that you keep doubling your deposit each day, write a C program, `penny.c`, which determines how many days it will take for you to accumulate at least one million dollars. (Assume that no interest is paid.) Note that the amount to be accumulated must be input at run-time.

For each day your output should include the amount of the deposit for that day as well as the total balance in the bank up to that day. Your output should appear in tabular format as shown below:

```
Please enter the amount of money you want to accumulate: 1000000

        DAY          DEPOSIT           BALANCE
        ---          -------           -------
         1            0.01              0.01
         2            0.02              0.03
         3            0.04              0.07
         4            0.08              0.15
        ...           ...               ...

It took XX days to accumulate at least $1000000.00.
```

Your program should include a `main()` function, a function to output the table header as well as a function to generate the table. The function that generates the table should be passed an input parameter of type `double` that tells how much money you want to accumulate. The function output should line up the columns by decimal place and should provide a return value to `main()` that tells how many days it took to accumulate the funds. This returned value should then be output as shown above.

Remember that the `main()` function should appear as the first function in the program. Be sure to use function prototypes for each of the functions that are used in your program.

Output from your program should be sent to the terminal window (your screen) as well as the requested `csis.txt` output file. Be sure to read the document on Capturing Program Output. Your full name must appear as a comment in the source file that contains `main()`. Be sure to include the `csis.txt` output file in your zip archive.

❖ Fibonacci Lab

The Fibonacci Sequence is the series of numbers:

```
0, 1, 1, 2, 3, 5, 8, 13, 21, …
```

Each additional number in the sequence is found by adding the two previous numbers before it.

Write a program, `fibonacci.c`, that calculates the first `20` Fibonacci numbers. Your program should include a function, `fib()`, that receives an input parameter from `main()` telling the function how many Fibonacci numbers to output.

Remember that the `main()` function should appear as the first function in the program. Be sure to use function prototypes for each of the functions that are used in your program.

Output from your program should be sent to the terminal window (your screen) as well as the requested `csis.txt` output file. Be sure to read the document on Capturing Program Output. Your full name must appear as a comment in the source file that contains `main()`. Be sure to include the `csis.txt` output file in your zip archive.

Chapter 9. Input-Output

Streams
getchar()
putchar()
Text Files
❖ Input-Output Homework

Streams

The C language itself does not have any special statements for performing I/O operations. All I/O operations must be carried out through function calls to the standard I/O library.

```
#include <stdio.h>
```

contains declarations and macro definitions associated with the standard I/O library.

Each program starts its execution with access to three file streams of data: one for input and two for output:

stdin (standard input) – the usual source of input characters (keyboard)

stdout (standard output) – the usual destination for output characters (screen)

stderr (standard error output) – where error messages are send (screen)

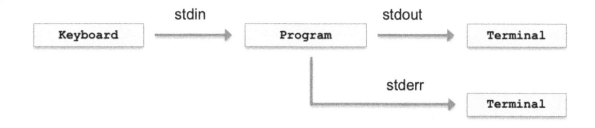

The same program can be made to put its standard output into a file instead of the terminal by adding a redirection request to the command line when you execute the program from the command line:

```
foo > outFile.txt
```

This creates a file containing the output of `foo`. Any values displayed by `printf()` would not be displayed at the terminal but instead would be written into the file called `outFile.txt`. Error messages, if any, will continue to be displayed on the terminal window, instead of being buried inside the output file.

A similar redirection is possible for the standard input. Any call to a function that normally reads data from the terminal, such as `getchar()` and `scanf_s()`, can be made to read its information from a file. For example, we can run program `foo` using data that we have stored in a file called `inFile.txt`:

```
foo < inFile.txt
```

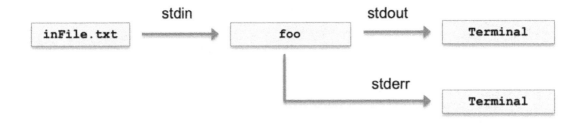

Finally, we can combine both input redirection and output redirection:

```
foo < inFile.txt > outFile.txt
```

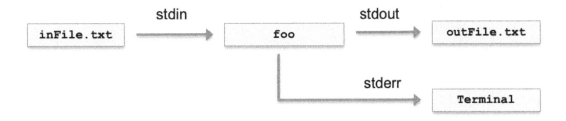

getchar()

I/O is not part of C proper but are basic extensions necessary for writing most programs.

`getchar()` returns the next character from standard input (keyboard) and returns it as a function return value. If there is no more input then `EOF` (end of file) is returned instead. It is therefore usual to compare the value returned by `getchar()` against `EOF` before using it.

At some point during program execution, the user may indicate "no more input" by entering `^z` (control z) (or in some environments `^d`) and `EOF` will be returned from `getchar()`.

`getchar()` and `EOF` are defined in a standard include file named `stdio.h` which we must include in all of our compilations:

```
#include <stdio.h>
```

Certain C expressions become part of our standard vocabulary such as:

```
while ((c = getchar()) != EOF)
```

This expression is used at the beginning of a loop that gets a character at a time from the standard input. Look closely at the expression and note the "extra" pair of parentheses. Can you figure out why are they needed?

Next, think about the difference between:

```
while (c = getchar())

and

while (c == getchar())
```

It can take a long time to see the difference and sometimes even longer to decide which one you really want!

Here's a program to count the number of characters read from an input stream until an EOF is encountered:

```c
// count1.c

#include <stdio.h>

int main(void) {
    int c, count = 0;

    while ((c = getchar()) != EOF) {
        ++count;
    }
    printf("%d\n", count);
    return 0;
}
```

Note that c is declared to be an int rather than a char. This is because EOF is given a defined value of −1. On some machines a char can only be a positive value and therefore to return a −1 we define c to be an int.

We can replace the while statement above with a for statement:

```c
// count2.c

#include <stdio.h>

int main(void) {
    int count;

    for (count = 0; getchar() != EOF; ++count) {
        ;
    }
    printf("%d\n", count);
    return 0;
}
```

We can also count newlines:

```c
// count3.c

#include <stdio.h>

int main(void) {
    int c, count = 0;

    while ((c = getchar()) != EOF) {
        if (c == '\n') {
            ++count;
        }
    }
    printf("%d\n", count);
    return 0;
}
```

Here's a program to map a program's input to lower case:

```c
// map1.c

#include <stdio.h>
#include <ctype.h>

int main(void) {
    int c;

    while ((c = getchar()) != EOF) {
        printf("%c", isupper(c) ? tolower(c) : c);
    }
    return 0;
}
```

Here's an expression that causes blank characters in the input stream to be skipped:

```c
// skipBlanks.c

while ((c = getchar()) == ' ') {
    ;
}
```

Because C contains no built-in function to read an entire line of input, it could be called a rather primitive language. However, this encourages tool building! So let's build a function to read a line of input and package it as a function named getLine() to be used whenever needed.

The following program copies lines of input onto the output. It reads one line at a time into string buf. A null terminator is put at the end of string buf. If the input is at EOF, the value of EOF is returned.

```c
// copyLines1.c

#include <stdio.h>

#define BUFSIZ 81

int getLine(char buf[]);

int main(void) {
    char buf[BUFSIZ];

    while (getLine(buf) != EOF) {
        printf("%s", buf);
    }
    return 0;
}

int getLine(char buf[]) {
    char c;
    int i = 0;

    do {
        c = getchar();
        buf[i++] = c;
    } while(c != '\n');
    buf[i-1] = '\0';
    return i;
}
```

Look how we can rewrite `getLine()` more simply:

```
// copyLines2.c

int getLine(char buf[]) {
    char c;
    int i = 0;

    while ((buf[i++] = getchar()) != '\n') {
        ;
    }
    buf[i] = '\0';
    return i;
}
```

putchar()

`putchar()` outputs a single character to standard output (terminal window). The arguments to `putchar()` should be one individual character, either variable or constant:

```
putchar(c);
putchar('a');
putchar('\n');
```

If you just need to output a single character without format, use `putchar()` instead of `printf()`. Here's a program that copies its input to output:

```
// copy.c

#include <stdio.h>

int main(void) {
    int c;

    while ((c = getchar()) != EOF) {
        putchar(c);
    }
    return 0;
}
```

Note, if this program is applied to a file of 100 bytes, it will call `getchar()` 101 times. The first 100 calls will return a data byte. The 101st call will return the `EOF` value. Therefore the test is evaluated 101 times and the loop body is executed 100 times.

With this program we can write our own command line copy command using I/O redirection:

```
copy < inFile.txt > outFile.txt
```

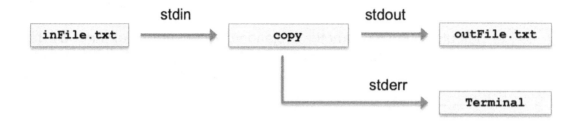

Here's a program to map its input to lower case:

```
// map2.c

#include <stdio.h>
#include <ctype.h>

int main(void) {
    int c;

    while ((c = getchar()) != EOF) {
        putchar(isupper(c) ? tolower(c) : c);
    }
    return 0;
}
```

Finally, let's write some code that reads text of all lower case letters and selectively capitalize the first letter of each word. A letter will be defined as any non-whitespace character.

First an algorithm:

```
// caps1.c

for each whitespace character w
    output w
for each word
    capitalize initial letter
    for each succeeding letter
        output c
    for each whitespace character w
        output w
```

Now some code:

```
// caps2.c

while ((c = getchar()) != EOF) {
    if (isspace(c)) {
        putchar(c);
    }
    else {
        putchar(toupper(c));
        while (!isspace(c = getchar())) {
            putchar(c);
        }
        putchar(c);
    }
}
```

Let's see if we can redesign this algorithm and code:

First the algorithm:

```
// caps3.c

for each input character c
    if c is the first letter of a word
        output capitalized c
    else
        output c
```

Now the code:

```
// caps4.c

for (wasWhite = 1; (c = getchar()) != EOF; wasWhite = isspace(c)) {
    putchar (!isspace(c) && wasWhite ? toupper(c) : c);
}
```

Note that this redesign results in a simpler program.

Text Files

A text file is a sequence of *characters* terminated by an *end-of-file marker*. The length of the file is not specified when the file is defined. The characters in the file are stored on a storage device other than the memory occupied by the program while the program is executing, such as a disk drive.

Note the emphasis on characters. That's all there is in a text file, just characters. Sprinkled among the characters may be newline characters, '\n', or tab '\t' characters. In addition, each data element in the file (words, numeric data) is usually (though not always) separated from the others by blanks.

The advantage of files is that they can exist independently of the program that creates or uses the data in the file. The size of the file is also not a limiting factor as we can increase the file size simply by adding a character to the end of the file.

Accessing Text Files

A text file is accessed via a pointer to a structure that is defined in the standard header file stdio.h as FILE. This structure FILE contains members (fields) that describe the current state of the file.

C communicates with files using a data type called a *file pointer*. This type is defined within stdio.h, and is written as FILE *. A file pointer called fp is declared in a statement like:

```
FILE *fp;
```

Your program must first open a file before it can access the file. This is done using the fopen_s() function, which assigns a value to the required file pointer fp, and opens a file for I/O. fopen_s() is declared as follows:

```
fopen_s(FILE **fp, char *fileName, char *fileMode);
```

fp is the address of a file pointer and both fileName and fileMode are strings. File names may be any valid file name that can exist under the operating system and can include path information:

```
"myfile.txt"
"/users/home/input.txt"
```

If the path information is not specified, then the file location is assumed to be the directory where the program was run from, which is known as the working or project directory.

The file modes are:

```
"r"    read - file to read in data

"w"    write - write data to file

"a"    append - append data to end of file that already contains
                some data
```

The "r" mode opens the named file for reading only from the beginning of the file. The named file must exist in order to be opened successfully. Note that the contents of the file cannot be changed.

The "w" mode opens the named file for writing from the beginning of the file. The named file will be created if it doesn't exist. If it does exist then the original contents of the file will be overwritten regardless of whether any file operations are performed or not.

The "a" mode opens the named file for writing from the end of the file. The named file will be created if it doesn't exist. If it does exist then the original contents of the file will not be changed. All write operations are appended to the end of the file.

To open a file for reading, we might say:

```
FILE *fp;

fopen_s(fp, "infile.txt", "r");
```

If `fileName` cannot be opened for any reason, then the pointer value `NULL` will be assigned to `fp`. We can test this variable against the defined value `NULL`:

```
// file1.c

FILE *fp;

fopen_s(&fp, "infile.txt", "r");
if (fp == NULL) {
    printf("File could not be opened.\n");
    exit(1);
}
```

This will tell us if the open was successful or not. Note that `exit(1)` is a function that requires the `#include <stdlib.h>` header file and will cause the program to immediately abort.

The `fclose()` command can be used to disconnect a file pointer from a file. This is usually done so that the pointer can be used to access a different file. Systems have a limit on the number of files that can be open simultaneously, so it is a good idea to close a file when you have finished using it.

The `fclose()` statement is defined as follows:

```
int fclose(FILE *fp);
```

and is called like this:

```
fclose(fp);
```

`fclose()` empties the buffer and breaks all connections to the indicated file. `EOF` is returned if `fp` is not associated with a file. Note that if you fail to close a file when the program exits, the system will close the file for you. However, it is usually better to close the files properly yourself to ensure that the data in the file is properly saved.

File I/O statements

Having opened a file pointer, you will wish to use it for either input or output. C supplies a set of functions to allow you to do this. All are very similar to input and output functions that you have already seen.

File input and output are performed using the equivalents of `getchar()` and `putchar()` which are called `getc()` and `putc()`. Each takes an extra argument, which identifies the file pointer to be used for input or output.

- `c = getc(fp)`

A macro which retrieves the next character from the file pointed to by `fp`. The value of the character is returned as an `int`. It returns `EOF` if an end of file is encountered or if there is an error. Note that `getchar()` is actually a macro defined as: `getc(stdin)`.

Its function prototype is:
```
int getc(FILE *fp);
```

- `putc(c, fp));`

A macro which places the character value of `c` in the file pointed to by `fp`. It returns the `int` value of the character written. Note that `putchar(c)` is a macro defined as `putc(c, stdout)`.

Its function prototype is:
```
int putc(int c, FILE *fp);
```

- `c = fgetc(fp);`

Similar to `getc(fp)`, but is a function and not a macro.

Its function prototype is:
```
int fgetc(FILE *fp);
```

- `fputc(c, fp);`

Similar to `putc(c, file_ptr)`, but is a function and not a macro.

Its function prototype is:
```
int fputc(int c, FILE *fp);
```

Example: Output the contents of a file to standard output.

```c
// file2.c

#include <stdio.h>
#include <stdlib.h>

int main(void) {
    int c;
    FILE *fp;

    fopen_s(&fp, "infile.txt", "r");
    if (fp == NULL) {
        printf("File could not be opened.\n");
        exit(1);
    }
    while((c = getc(fp)) != EOF) {
        putchar(c);
    }
    fclose(fp);
    return 0;
}
```

Example: Output contents of a file to standard output requesting a filename from user.

```c
// file3.c

#include <stdio.h>
#include <stdlib.h>

int main(void) {
    int c;
    char fileName[32];
    FILE *fp;

    printf("Enter filename: ");
    gets(fileName);
    fopen_s(&fp, fileName, "r");
    if (fp == null) {
        printf("File %s could not be opened.\n", fileName);
        exit(1);
    }
    while((c = getc(fp)) != EOF) {
        putchar(c);
    }
    fclose(fp);
    return 0;
}
```

Example: Copy the contents of one file to a second file and output the contents of the second file.

```c
// file4.c

#include <stdio.h>
#include <stdlib.h>

int main(void) {
    int c;
    FILE *fpIn, *fpOut;

    fopen_s(&fpIn, "infile.txt", "r");
    if (fpIn == NULL) {
        printf("File could not be opened for input.\n");
        exit(1);
    }
    fopen_s(&fpOut, "outfile.txt", "w");
    if (fpOut == NULL) {
        printf("File could not be opened for output.\n");
        exit(1);
    }
    while((c = getc(fpIn)) != EOF) {
        putc(c, fpOut);
    }
    fclose(fpIn);
    fclose(fpOut);
    fopen_s(&fpIn, "outfile.txt", "r");
    if (fpIn == NULL) {
        printf("File could not be opened for input.\n");
        exit(1);
    }
    while((c = getc(fpIn)) != EOF) {
        putchar(c);
    }
    fclose(fpIn);
    return 0;
}
```

Similarly there are equivalents to the functions `printf()` and `scanf_s()` which read or write data to files. These are called `fprintf()` and `fscanf_s()`. The functions are used in the same way, except that the `fprintf()` and `fscanf_s()` take the file pointer as an additional first argument:

- `fprintf(fp, formatSpecifiers, arguments);`

Performs the analogous operations of the `printf()` function on a file. It returns the number of bytes output. In the event of error, it returns `EOF`.

Its function prototype is:
```
int fprintf(FILE *fp, formatSpecifiers, arguments);
```


- `fscanf_s(fp, format_specifiers, arguments);`

Performs the analogous operations of the `scanf_s()` function on a file. It returns the number of arguments that are successfully assigned or the value of `EOF` if the end of file is reached.

Its function prototype is:
```
int fscanf_s(FILE *fp, format_specifiers, arguments);
```


Additionally, there are equivalent functions to `gets()` and `puts()` for file manipulation:

- `fgets(s, N, fp));`

Characters are read from the file pointed to by `fp`, and placed into string `s` until either `N-1` characters have been read or a newline character is read, whichever comes first. Unlike `gets(s)`, if a newline character is read, it is placed in `s`. In both cases, `s` is terminated with a `NULL` character. The value of `s` (pointer to `char`) is returned.

Its function prototype is:
```
char *fgets(char *s, int N, FILE *fp);
```

- `fputs(s, fp));`

The null-terminated string `s` is copied to the file pointed to by `fp`, except that the terminating `NULL` character itself is not copied. Unlike `puts(s)`, a newline character is not appended.

Its function prototype is:
`int fputs(char *s, FILE *fp);`

Finally, we have a function for testing whether or not we are at the end of file `(EOF)`.

- `feof(fp));`

Tests for the end of file. Returns an integer value that is non-zero if all the data from the specified file has been read, and zero otherwise.

Its function prototype is:
`int feof(FILE *fp);`

Example: Output the contents of a file line by line

```c
// file5.c

#include <stdio.h>
#include <stdlib.h>

#define MAX 81

int main(void) {
    char line[MAX];
    FILE *fp;

    fopen_s(&fp, "infile.txt", "r");
    if (fp == NULL) {
        printf("File could not be opened for input.\n");
        exit(1);
    }
    while (!feof(fp)) {
        fgets(line, MAX, fp);
        printf("%s", line);
    }
    fclose(fp);
    return 0;
}
```

Example: Copy the contents of one file to another, line by line, and then output the new file.

```c
// file6.c

#include <stdio.h>
#include <stdlib.h>

#define MAX 81

int main(void) {
    char line[MAX];
    FILE *fpIn, *fpOut;

    fopen_s(&fpIn, "infile.txt", "r");
    if (fpIn == NULL) {
        printf("File could not be opened for input.\n");
        exit(1);
    }
    fopen_s(&fpOut, "outfile.txt", "w");
    if (fpOut == NULL) {
        printf("File could not be opened for output.\n");
        exit(1);
    }
    while (!feof(fpIn)) {
        fgets(line, MAX, fpIn);
        fputs(line, fpOut);
    }
    fclose(fpIn);
    fclose(fpOut);
    fopen_s(&fpIn, "outfile.txt", "r");
    if (fpIn == NULL) {
        printf("File could not be opened for input.\n");
        exit(1);
    }
    while(!feof(fpIn)) {
        fgets(line, MAX, fpIn);
        printf("%s", line);
    }
    return 0;
}
```

Example: Concatenate two files into a third file and output the third file.

```c
// file7.c

#include <stdio.h>
#include <stdlib.h>

#define MAX 81

int main(void) {
    char line[MAX];
    FILE *fpIn, *fpIn1, *fpIn2, *fpOut;

    fopen_s(&fpIn1, "infile1.txt", "r");
    if (fpIn1 == null)) {
        printf("File could not be opened for input.\n");
        exit(1);
    }
    fopen_s(&fpIn2, "infile2.txt", "r");
    if (fpIn2 == NULL) {
        printf("File could not be opened for input.\n");
        exit(1);
    }
    fopen_s(&fpOut, "outfile.txt", "w");
    if (fpOut == NULL) {
        printf("File could not be opened for output.\n");
        exit(1);
    }
    while (!feof(fpIn1)) {
        fgets(line, MAX, fpIn1);
        fputs(line, fpOut);
    }
    while (!feof(fpIn2)) {
        fgets(line, MAX, fpIn2);
        fputs(line, fpOut);
    }
    fclose(fpIn1);
    fclose(fpIn2);
    fclose(fpOut);
    fopen_s(&fpIn, "outfile.txt", "r");
    if (fpIn == NULL) {
        printf("File could not be opened for input.\n");
        exit(1);
    }
    while(!feof(fpIn)) {
        fgets(line, MAX, fpIn);
        printf("%s", line);
    }
    fclose(fpIn);
    return 0;
}
```

❖ Input-Output Homework

1. Write a section of code that attempts to open file `foo.txt` for input and, if the file does not exist, generates an error message and aborts the program.

2. What could happen if you attempt to open a file for input and you do not check to see whether or not the file exists.

3. Write a section of code that opens file `diary.txt` to add new data to the file without modifying the data that might already be in the file.

4. What could happen if you fail to close a file properly using the `fclose()` function.

5. Assume that a data file, `data.txt`, contains the data for a checking account. Each line in the data file contains a character for deposit or check cashed (`'D'` or `'C'`), and an amount that is represented as a `double`. Write a section of code that opens the `data.txt` input file, reads the data on each line in the file, and outputs the data to the terminal window.

6. Repeat the previous exercise but this time output each line of data to a new output file, `checking.txt`.

Chapter 10. Functions Revisited

Function Motivation
Functions Examples
Function Parameters
❖ Functions Revisited Homework
❖ Checking Account Lab
❖ Date Lab
❖ BlackJack Lab

Function Motivation

Suppose we wished to generate a table of powers with the following format:

```
--------------------------------------------------------------
          Number          Square             Cube
--------------------------------------------------------------
               1               1                1
               2               4                8
               3               9               27
               4              16               64
               5              25              125
               6              36              216
               7              49              343
               8              64              512
               9              81              729
              10             100             1000
--------------------------------------------------------------
```

Our code might look like this:

```c
// funct1.c
// Generate tables of powers

#include <stdio.h>

int main(void) {
    int i;

    for (i = 1; i <= 60; i++) {
        printf("%c", '-');
    }
    printf("\n");
    printf("%15s%15s%15s\n", "Number", "Square", "Cube");
    for (i = 1; i <= 60; i++) {
        printf("%c", '-');
    }
    printf("\n");
    for(i = 1; i <= 10; i++) {
        printf("%15d%15d%15d\n", i, i*i, i*i*i);
    }
    for (i = 1; i <= 60; i++) {
        printf("%c", '-');
    }
    printf("\n");
    return 0;
}
```

Note how we have duplicated our code to draw multiple dashed lines. We can rewrite our code to encapsulate the dashed line drawing within a function and then invoke the function at the appropriate time:

```c
// funct2.c
// Generate table of powers

#include <stdio.h>

void printLine(void);

int main(void) {
    int i;

    printLine();
    printf("%15s%15s%15s\n", "Number", "Square", "Cube");
    printLine();
    for(i = 1; i <= 10; i++) {
        printf("%15d%15d%15d\n", i, i*i, i*i*i);
    }
    printLine();
    return 0;
}

void printLine(void) {
    int i;

    for (i = 1; i <= 60; i++) {
        printf("%c", '-');
    }
    printf("\n");
}
```

We can even pass information to the function telling the function to draw the line with a certain width and with a certain character:

```c
// funct3.c

#include <stdio.h>

void printLine(int width, char ch);

int main(void) {
    int i;

    printLine(60, '*');
    printf("%15s%15s%15s\n", "Number", "Square", "Cube");
    printLine(50, '.');
    for(i = 1; i <= 10; i++) {
        printf("%15d%15d%15d\n", i, i*i, i*i*i);
    }
    printLine(55, '+');
    return 0;
}

void printLine(int width, char ch) {
    int i;

    for (i = 1; i <= width; i++) {
        printf("%c", ch);
    }
    printf("\n");
}
```

```
************************************************************
        Number         Square           Cube
..................................................
              1              1              1
              2              4              8
              3              9             27
              4             16             64
              5             25            125
              6             36            216
              7             49            343
              8             64            512
              9             81            729
             10            100           1000
+++++++++++++++++++++++++++++++++++++++++++++++++++++++++
```

Function Examples

Functions let you chop up a long program into named sections so that the sections can be reused throughout the program. A function is considered to be an independent set of statements for performing some computation. As we've seen, functions typically accept parameters and can also return a result.

Example 1: Leap Year Function
Here's an example of a function that returns false (0) or true (1) depending upon whether or not a year is a leap year. *We define a leap year as any year that is evenly divisible by 4 but not 100, except that years divisible by 400 are leap years:*

```
// leapYear1.c

int leapYear(int year) {
    int num;

    if ((year % 4 == 0 && year % 100 != 0) || year % 400 == 0) {
        num = 1;
    }
    else {
        num = 0;
    }
    return num;
}
```

This function contains one local variable, `num`, which is declared after the opening brace of the function. The local variable of a function vanishes as soon as the matching closing brace is reached in the function. While they exist, local variables live on the system stack. Actually, C allows you to declare variables after any opening brace, and they exist until the program reaches the matching closing brace and then they disappear.

Note that there is no semicolon after the parentheses in the function header. If you accidentally put one in, you would get a huge cascade of error messages from the compiler that make no sense.

The type of the value that is returned from the function, in this case `int`, is specified before the function name. The data value that is passed to the function, the *formal parameter*, appears in the parentheses after the function name. The data type of the parameter precedes the formal parameter (`int year`).

As we've discussed, function definitions may be placed in any order, but usually the `main()` function is placed first. The `return` expression indicates the function is to return the value of the expression back to the calling routine. The function is immediately exited and control of the program returns to the calling function. The return statement has the same effect as encountering the last brace in a function.

If there is no `return` statement in the function, control then passes back to the calling function when the closing brace of the body of the function is encountered.

Note that there can be more than one `return` statement in a function:

```
// leapYear2.c

int leapYear(int year) {
    if ((year % 4 == 0 && year % 100 != 0) || year % 400 == 0) {
        return 1;
    }
    else {
        return 0;
    }
}
```

The `return` statement may even include an expression:

```
// leapYear3.c

int leapYear(int year) {
    return (year % 4 == 0 && year % 100 != 0) || year % 400 == 0;
}
```

Remember from our discussion of control structures, the statement:

```
if (a == 0)
```

could be written as

```
if (!a)
```

Therefore our `leapYear()` function could finally be rewritten as:

```
// leapYear4.c

int leapYear(int year) {
    return (!(year % 4) && year % 100) || !(year % 400);
}
```

The `leapYear()` function might be called from another function, perhaps `main()`, in the following way:

```
// leapYearCall1.c

#include <stdio.h>

int main(void) {
    int num;

    num = leapYear(1996);
    if (num == 1) {
        printf("Leap year. ");
    }
    else {
        printf("No leap year. ");
    }
    return 0;
}
```

But here's a better way to make the call:

```
// leapYearCall2.c

#include <stdio.h>

int main(void) {
    if (leapYear(1996)) {
        printf("Leap year. ");
    }
    else {
        printf("No leap year. ");
    }
}
```

We could also make the call in the context of multiple calculations:

```c
// leapYearCall3.c

#include <stdio.h>

int main(void) {
    int i;

    for (i = 2000; i <= 2020; ++i) {
        if (leapYear(i)) {
            printf("Year = %d  Leap Year.\n", i);
        }
        else {
            printf("Year = %d  Not a leap year.\n", i);
        }
    }
}
```

Here's the output:

```
Year = 2000  Leap Year.
Year = 2001  Not a leap year.
Year = 2002  Not a leap year.
Year = 2003  Not a leap year.
Year = 2004  Leap Year.
Year = 2005  Not a leap year.
Year = 2006  Not a leap year.
Year = 2007  Not a leap year.
Year = 2008  Leap Year.
Year = 2009  Not a leap year.
Year = 2010  Not a leap year.
Year = 2011  Not a leap year.
Year = 2012  Leap Year.
Year = 2013  Not a leap year.
Year = 2014  Not a leap year.
Year = 2015  Not a leap year.
Year = 2016  Leap Year.
Year = 2017  Not a leap year.
Year = 2018  Not a leap year.
Year = 2019  Not a leap year.
Year = 2020  Leap Year.
```

Example 2: Power Function
Here's an example of a function that raises an `int` to the power of an `unsigned int` and returns the result as a `long`:

```
// power.c

long power(int base, unsigned expon) {
    int i;
    long num = 1;

    for (i = 0; i < expon; ++i) {
        num *= base;
    }
    return num;
}
```

The function follows a simple algorithm, multiplying `base` by itself `expon` times. A `for` loop is used to control the number of multiplications, and variable `num` stores the value to be returned.

The function header:

```
long power(int base, unsigned expon)
```

informs us the type of the return value, `long`, the name of the function, `power`, and a list of arguments used by the function, `int base, unsigned expon`. The arguments and their types are enclosed in parentheses, each pair separated by commas.

• The body of the function is bounded by a set of braces. Any variables declared here will be treated as local.

• Upon reaching a `return` statement, control of the program returns to the calling function. `num` is the value which is returned from the function. If the final closing brace is reached before any return value, then the function will return automatically, any return value will then be meaningless.

• The `return` value of a function is always converted to the type given by the type specifier of the function. In this case the solution to the function is being held in a `long` variable, `num`.

• This function can now be called by another function that looks like this:

```c
// power2.c

#include <stdio.h>

long power(int base, unsigned expon);

int main(void) {
    long result = power(3, 4);
    printf("%ld\n", result);
    return 0;
}

long power(int base, unsigned expon) {
    int i;
    long num = 1;

    for(i = 0; i < expon; ++i) {
        num *= base;
    }
    return num;
}
```

A statement in `main()` now calls the function `power()` assigning the return value to variable `result`, which is then output.

Example 3: Improved Power Function
We can further improve our `power()` function by allowing the `base` to be a `float`, by allowing `expon` to be a positive or negative `int` (or zero), and by allowing the function to return a `float`.

The program below:

```
// power3.c

#include <stdio.h>
#include <stdlib.h>

float power(float base, int expon);

int main(void) {
    float result = power(3.5, -6);
    printf("%f\n", result);
    return 0;
}

float power(float base, int expon) {
    int i;

    float num = 1.0;

    if (expon == 0) {
        return 1.0;
    }
    for (i = 0; i < abs(expon); ++i) {
        num *= base;
        if (expon >= 0) {
            return num;
        }
        else {
            return 1/num;
        }
    }
}
```

produces the following output:

```
0.000544
```

Note the use of the `abs()` function that returns the absolute value of `expon` is used in the `for` loop. The `abs()` function is a built-in C math function and its use requires the inclusion of the appropriate header file:

```
#include <stdlib.h>
```

Function Prototypes Revisited

In general, C does not care in what order you put your functions in the program, so long as a the function name is known to the compiler before it is called. This is ensured through the use of *function prototypes*. A function prototype declares the function name, its parameters, and its return type to the rest of the program *prior* to the function's actual declaration.

Function prototypes are placed at the beginning of a program before the first function declaration, which is usually `main()`, and consists of the function header with a semicolon after the closing brace. Here's an example:

```
// prototype.c

#include <stdio.h>

int main(void);
int add(int a, int b);
int mult(int a, int b);

int main(void) {
    int num1, num2;

    printf("Enter two integers: ");
    scanf_s("%d%d", &num1, &num2);
    printf("The sum of the two numbers is %d\n", add(num1, num2));
    printf("The product of the two numbers is %d\n", mult(num1, num2));
    return 0;
}

int add(int a, int b) {
    return a + b;
}

int mult(int a, int b) {
    return a * b;
}
```

Here's the output of the program:

```
Enter two integers: 4 5
The sum of the two numbers is 9
The product of the two numbers is 20
```

Note that we even provide a function prototype for `main()`.

Did you notice the `&` in front of `num1` and `num2` in the `scanf_s()` function? When reading in an `int`, `char`, or `float` with `scanf_s()`, we must provide to `scanf_s()` not the variable name but the *address* of the variable in memory. `&` is referred to as the *address of* operator in C, and when placed in front of a variable, returns the address in memory of the variable.

A Note on the Placement of `main()` and Function Prototypes...

Technically `main()` can be placed anywhere in a program. However, it is typically placed as the first function in a program. As you'll see, we generally do not place much detailed code in `main()`. When used correctly, it provides an abstraction to the rest of the program and its visibility as the first function in the program is useful.

But there's more to it than just style. Thinking that placing `main()` as the last function in a program will obviate the need for function prototypes is incorrect. Suppose your code was set up as follows:

```
void foo1() {
    ...
    ...
}

void foo2() {
    ...
    ...
}

int main() {
    ...
    ...
}
```

If `main()` calls `foo1()` or `foo2()` there's no problem. If `foo2()` calls `foo1()` there's no problem. But what happens if `foo1()` calls `foo2()`? The compiler will complain because it has not yet seen the declaration for `foo2()`. What kind of a function is it? How many parameters does it have? What are the data types of the parameters? Are there any return values? How can the compiler do error checking on the function call to `foo2()` if it cannot answer all these questions?

The use of function prototypes allows the compiler to see the function declarations before any code is looked at so error checking can be performed properly.

Of course you might want to switch the order of `foo1()` and `foo2()` in your program and all would be well. However, in a large program with dozens of functions, it might not be so easy to order the functions properly. With the use of function prototypes, we never have to worry about the order of our functions.

One last reason for the use of function prototypes deals with the building of larger programs and linking source codes together. This will be a topic for discussion at a later time.

Function Return Values

Note that even though a function returns a value, a program need not make use of it:

```
// return1.c

while (...) {
    :
    getchar();          // get a character and do nothing with it
    c = getchar();      // get another character and assign to c
    :
}
```

`void` Return Values and `void` Parameter List

If a function does not return any value, its return type should be specified as `void`. The `void` specifier informs the compiler that a function does not return a value. In a sense, the `void` data type is actually defining the absence of a data type and a function declared to be of type `void` has no return value and cannot be used in an expression as if it does.

```
// return2.c

void printHeader(void) {
    printf("Program Number 1\n");
    printf("by Richard Stegman\n");
    printf("Version 5.0, released 10/12/18\n");
}
```

As you can see, this function returns no value. You can call it with the following statement:

```
printHeader();
```

Note that you must include () in the call. If you do not, the function is not called, even though it will compile correctly on many systems.

If a function is not passed any parameters (i.e., there are no formal parameters declared), void should be specified in the parameter list within the parentheses after the function name. Here is a function that accepts no values and generates and returns a random number between 0 and 255:

```
// parameter1.c

int getRandomNumber(void)   {
    return (rand() % 255);
}
```

The function header:

```
int getRandomNumber(void)
```

declares the function:

```
getRandomNumber()
```

to the rest of the program and specifies that the function will accept no parameters and will return an int result.

Function Parameters

The value that is being passed to a function is called an *argument* or an *actual parameter*. The argument that appears in the function header is referred to as the *formal parameter*. We say that the actual parameter is passed to the formal parameter.

Function arguments are always passed *by value* in C. Each argument is evaluated and its value is used locally in place of the formal parameter in the function header. Therefore if an argument is passed to a function, the stored value of that argument will not be changed in the calling environment. For example:

```c
// parameter2.c

#include <stdio.h>

int main(void);
void foo(int num);

int main(void) {
    int num = 5;

    printf("%d\n", num);
    foo(num);
    printf("%d\n", num);
    return 0;
}

int foo(int num) {
    printf("%d\n", num);
    num = num + 1;
    printf("%d\n", num);
}
```

produces the following output:

```
5
5
6
5
```

If we want to pass an argument *by reference* (i.e., change the value of the argument in the function and have that new value be reflected back in the calling function), we must pass the *address* of the argument to the function, rather than the argument itself. Once the function has access to the memory location that is used to store the actual parameter, it can modify its contents, and thus modify the actual parameter.

For example:

```
// parameter3.c

#include <stdio.h>

int main(void);
void foo(int *num);

int main(void) {
    int num = 5;

    printf("%d\n", num);
    foo(&num);
    printf("%d\n", num);
    return 0;
}

void foo(int *num) {
    printf("%d\n", *num);
    *num = *num + 1;
    printf("%d\n", *num);
}
```

produces the following output:

```
5
5
6
6
```

Note that the value of the actual parameter has been changed by the call to `foo()`.

In order to pass by reference, we must first pass the address of the actual parameter to the function. This is accomplished by using the *address of operator* `(&)`. When `&` is placed in front of a variable, it returns the address of that variable.

So in the call from `main()`:

```
foo(&num);
```

we are passing the address of `num` to function `foo()`.

Now look at the declaration of the formal parameter for `foo()` in the function header. The `*` that appears in front of `num` is saying that the value being passed to `foo()` is actually a memory address rather than a data value. Now if we have a memory address and want to actually get to the data value stored in that memory location, we must use the *indirection operator* (`*`) to fetch it. The `*` is placed before the formal parameter name in every place we try and access the formal parameter in the function.

Here's a program that swaps the value of two integers passed by reference:

```c
// swap.c

#include <stdio.h>

void swap(int *x, int *y);

int main(void) {
    int a, b;

    a = 5;
    b = 9;
    printf("Before swap: a = %d   b = %d\n", a, b);
    swap(&a, &b);
    printf(" After swap: a = %d   b = %d\n", a, b);
    return 0;
}

void swap(int *x, int *y) {
    int temp;

    temp = *x;
    *x = *y;
    *y = temp;
}
```

Our program output looks like this:

```
Before swap: a = 5    b = 9
 After swap: a = 9    b = 5
```

Pass by Reference and scanf_s() Function

As previously indicated, scanf_s() needs to know the addresses of the items to be read. Therefore the names of variables are preceded by the address-of operator, &. However, if a parameter is passed by reference to a function and that variable is used in a scanf_s() statement, there is no need to place the address-of operator in front of the variable. This is because the variable already represents an address due to the fact that it was passed by reference.

```c
// scanf_s.c

#include <stdio.h>

void getValue(int *num);

int main(void) {
    int num;

    getValue(&num);
    printf("The value input = %d\n", num);
    return 0;
}

void getValue(int *num) {
    printf("Enter a number: ");
    scanf_s("%d", num);        // No address-of (&) operator required
}
```

Here's the output produced:

```
Enter a number: 35
The value input = 35
```

1. Write a function, `timeUpdate()`, that is passed three `int` parameters, `hour, min, sec,` representing the current time and returns the time updated by one second. The function should work with a 24-hour clock where 4:30 am is represented by 4:30 and 4:30 pm is represented by 16:30.

2. Explain the output of the following program. Does interchanging the arguments in the last `printf()` statement make any difference?

```c
#include<stdio.h>

int main(void) {
    char a = 127, b = 128;

    printf("%5d  %5d  %5d\n", a, a + 1, b);
    printf("%5d  %5d  %5d  %5d\n", a, a += 1, b, a);
    return 0;
}
```

Output:
```
127    128   -128
127   -128   -128    -128
```

❖ Checking Account Lab

Construct a C program, `check.c`, that reads the details of a monthly checking account and outputs a bank statement summarizing these transactions. An input file, `account.txt`, contains a list of transactions for the checking account for one month. Each line of the input file consists of a one-character transaction code along with a `double` containing the amount of the transaction. Valid transaction codes are as follows:

```
I    Initial balance brought forth from previous month
D    Deposit
C    Check
```

As each transaction is entered, you should output on a single line the type of transaction, the amount of the transaction (separate columns for deposits and checks), and the balance after the transaction has been processed:

```
Transaction        Deposit       Check       Balance
-----------        -------       -----       -------
Initial Balance                               478.83
Deposit            127.45                     606.28
Deposit            619.84                    1226.12
Check                            945.12       281.00
Check                              4.76       276.24
...
```

The bank's service charges (which should be deducted from the balance <u>at the end of the month</u>) are as follows:

```
$3.00 per month to maintain the account

$0.06 for each check cashed

$0.03 for each deposit made

$5.00 overdraft whenever a check cashed leaves the balance below $0.00
```

Note: Do not assess the overdraft service charge when the transaction is a deposit into an overdrawn account that does not bring the balance above zero.

The bank statement should also include the following summary information:

```
Total number deposits:
Total amount deposits:

  Total number checks:
  Total amount checks:

 Total service charge:

     Opening balance:
     Closing balance:
```

Shown below is the `main()` function that you should use for your program. Please do not modify the `main()` function.

```c
int main(void) {
    char code;
    double amount, service, balance;
    double amtCheck, amtDeposit, openBalance, closeBalance;
    int numCheck, numDeposit;

    fopen_s(&fpIn, "account.txt", "r");
    if (fpIn == NULL) {
        printf("account.txt could not be opened for input.");
        exit(1);
    }
    fopen_s(&fpOut, "csis.txt", "w");
    if (fpOut == NULL) {
        printf("csis.txt could not be opened for output.");
        exit (1);
    }

    amount        = 0.0;
    service       = 0.0;
    balance       = 0.0;
    amtCheck      = 0.0;
    amtDeposit    = 0.0;
    openBalance   = 0.0;
    closeBalance  = 0.0;
    numCheck      = 0;
    numDeposit    = 0;

    outputHeaders();
```

```
    while (!feof(fpIn)) {
        fscanf_s(fpIn, "%c %lf\n", &code, 1, &amount);
        if (code == 'I') {
            initialBalance(amount, &balance, &service, &openBalance);
        }
        else if (code == 'D') {
            deposit(amount, &balance, &service, &numDeposit,
                                                &amtDeposit);
        }
        else {
            check(amount, &balance, &service, &numCheck, &amtCheck);
        }
    }

    closeBalance = balance - service;
    outputSummary(numDeposit, amtDeposit, numCheck, amtCheck,
                            openBalance, service, closeBalance);
    fclose(fpIn);
    fclose(fpOut);
    return 0;
}
```

You will need to write five functions (and their prototypes) for your program:

```
outputHeaders()
initialBalance()
deposit()
check()
outputSummary()
```

These functions will use counters and summations to keep track of the different components of the checking account as well as output specific information relating to the bank statement. Note that some of the function parameters are passed as input parameters and some are passed as input-output parameters. Be sure to use the indirection operator (*) correctly in your functions.

Remember that the main() function should appear as the first function in the program. Be sure to use function prototypes for each of the functions that are used in your program.

The contents of `account.txt` are shown below:

```
I        478.83
D        127.45
D        619.84
C        945.12
C          4.76
D         32.81
C          1.06
D        184.32
C        495.18
C        141.81
C        255.10
D        250.00
D        123.88
D        245.05
D        873.25
C        981.12
D        317.84
C        812.73
D        606.12
```

You should not be using any global variables, other than declarations for file pointers, in your program other than file pointers. A global variable is a variable declared outside of `main()`.

Output from your program should be sent to the terminal window (your screen) as well as the requested `csis.txt` output file. Be sure to read the document on Capturing Program Output. Your full name must appear as a comment in the source file that contains `main()`. Be sure to include the `csis.txt` output file in your zip archive.

This assignment will focus on the use of functions and the passing of parameters. You are to construct a C program, `date.c`, which performs each of the following operations:

```
Converts a calendar date into a Julian date
Converts a Julian date into a calendar date.
Computes the number of days between any two calendar dates.
```

A calendar date is simply a date that contains a year, month, and day and a Julian date is an integer between 1 and 366, inclusive, which tells how many days have elapsed since the first of January in the current year (including the day for which the date is calculated). For example, calendar date 4/12/2008 is equivalent to Julian date 103, 2008.

Your program should contain a selection menu (*hint: think do-while loop*) that allows the user to choose one of the options. An illustration is given below:

```
DATE SELECTION MENU

1) Convert calendar date into Julian date
2) Convert Julian date into calendar date
3) Compute days between two calendar dates
4) Exit program

ENTER SELECTION (1 - 4):
```

Be sure your program contains separate functions for each of the required operations, passing parameters as necessary. Remember that no global variables are allowed in your program except for the file pointer. You should create at least the following functions for your program:

```
displayMenu          displays selection menu and prompts user for
                     selection
getCalendarDate      prompts and gets calendar date from user
getJulianDate        prompts and gets Julian date from user
toCalendar           converts Julian date into calendar date
toJulian             converts calendar date into Julian date
daysBetweenDates     calculates the number of days between two calendar
                     dates
```

Hint to compute the number of days between two calendar dates: For each date, figure out the number of days since January 1, 1900 and then subtract.

For this assignment we will define a leap year as any year that is evenly divisible by 4 but not 100, except that years divisible by 400 are leap years. Here's a function you can use to calculate leap years. Try and work through its details.

```
int isLeapYear(int year) {
    return ((!(year % 4) && year % 100) || !(year % 400));
}
```

Remember that the `main()` function should appear as the first function in the program. Be sure to use function prototypes for each of the functions that are used in your program.

Test data for the lab is given below.

```
Convert Calendar Date Into Julian Date
11    15    1922          (319,      1922)
2     29    1984          ( 60,      1984)
7     7     2000          (189,      2000)

Convert Julian Date Into Calendar Date
53    1947                ( 2/22/1947)
211   1995                ( 7/30/1995)
360   2006                (12/26/2006)

Compute Number of Days Between Two Calendar Dates
5     12    1949     8     16    1900        (17801)
12    15    1985     3     1     1986          (76)
1     1     1900     7     7     1993        (34155)
```

Be sure to turn in output for each of the test data provided above. The information appearing in the parentheses after each piece of the test data are the correct (hopefully) solutions. You may use these solutions to test your program on the supplied test data. Ultimately, however, your program should be able to run on any valid data.

Extra Credit

Given a calendar date and the number of days until some future event, determine the calendar date of the future event.

Given any calendar date, determine its corresponding day of the week. You may assume that January 1, 1900 was a Monday. (Hint: think mod 7).

Use the following extra credit test data:

```
Compute Future Date
  5   16   1947      2376       (11/16/1953)
  2   12   1912      6000       (7/17/1928)
 12   15   1933      2345       (5/17/1940)


Compute day of week
 12   31   1900              (Monday)
  4   18   1977              (Monday)
  8    1   1932              (Monday)
 11   30   1947              (Sunday)
 12   31   1986              (Wednesday)
 12   31   1988              (Saturday)
```

Output from your program should be sent to the terminal window (your screen) as well as the requested csis.txt output file. Be sure to read the document on Capturing Program Output. Your full name must appear as a comment in the source file that contains main(). Be sure to include the csis.txt output file in your zip archive.

This assignment will focus on the use of functions and the passing of parameters. You are to construct a C program that plays a simplified game of blackjack. The rules are as follows:

• A game consists of several hands, played until the cards run out. In each hand both the dealer and the player try to accumulate cards whose point value adds up as close to 21 as possible, but not more than 21.

• First the player gets a card, then the dealer gets a card, then the player gets a second card and the dealer gets a second card.

• The player then has the opportunity to call for more cards. Her strategy will be to refuse cards when she gets to 16 points or more (i.e., she "hits" 15 or under). If her point value goes over 21, the hand is over and the dealer wins.

• If the player's point value did not go over 21, the dealer calls for more cards. He must refuse cards when he gets to 17 or more (i.e., he "hits" 16 or under). If he goes over 21 the player wins the hand. Otherwise the hand with the point value closer to 21 wins the hand. In case of a tie, the dealer wins.

• If the player is dealt 21 on the first two cards, she has blackjack and immediately wins the hand. If the dealer has 21 on the first two cards, the hand is over and the dealer wins.

• Cards 2 through 10 count their face value; K, Q, J count 10 points; A counts 1 if the point value in the hand is greater than 10, otherwise A counts 11.

• A sample deck of cards can be found in: `cards.txt`.

The blackjack program should be organized as follows:

The program should contain a function called `playHand()` which contains two parameters: `dealerWin` and `ranOut` (both semi-boolean values). `playHand()` is to play a hand of blackjack and then set `dealerWin` to true (1) if the dealer wins and false (0) otherwise. The `main()` function should repeatedly call `playHand()` and keep track of the total number of wins in the game using two variables: `dealerTotal` and `playerTotal`. However, `playHand()` should set `ranOut` to true (1) if it ran out of cards. In this case the program should not count this hand, print the total number of wins for both the player and the dealer, and exit.

The program should also contain a function called getCard() which has one integer parameter, points. getCard() is used to get the next card from the input file and assign its value to points. It should read the next character (i.e., card) in the file and set points to the appropriate value from 1 to 11. Note that a 10 will be represented in the file as T).

Also note that before reading a card, getCard() should check whether EOF is true, and if it is, signal that there are no more cards in the file by assigning a value of zero to points. Each time playHand() calls getCard() it much check to see if points is 0, meaning the cards have run out.

You should also build a betting system into your program. Allow the player to make a bet at the start of each hand and print out the total wins and losses at the end of each hand. If the player has 21 on her first two cards, she has blackjack and wins double her bet.

All functions should output information explaining what is happening (e.g., getCard() should write out the card it reads and its score, playHand() should write out the running point values as each new card is obtained, etc.).

As usual, make sure the program is well structured and readable. Remember, careful thought put into its organization will pay off at debugging time.

Once again, you should not be using any global variables in your program. A global variable is a variable declared outside of main().

Output from your program should be sent to the terminal window (your screen) as well as the requested csis.txt output file. Be sure to read the document on Capturing Program Output. Your full name must appear as a comment in the source file that contains main(). Be sure to include the csis.txt output file in your zip archive.

Chapter 11. Arrays

Introduction to Arrays
Calculating Letter Frequency
Sieve of Eratosthenes
Arrays as Function Arguments
Parallel Arrays
Sorting an Array: Insertion Sort
Sorting an Array: qsort() Library Function
Searching an Array: Linear Search
Searching an Array: Binary Search
Two Dimensional Arrays
Symmetric Matrix Example
❖ Arrays Homework
❖ Statistics Lab
❖ Decode Lab
❖ Hamming Code Lab

Introduction to Arrays

We have so far been looking at scalar data types:

```
int
long
char
float
double
```

C also provides structured data types that are complex higher-level data types built from collections of simple scalar data types such as:

```
arrays
structures
files
pointers
```

Each one of these structured data types in C can also be defined in terms of other structured data types:

```
arrays of arrays
arrays of structures
structures containing arrays
files of structures
```

An array in C is a collection of memory locations that have the same name and the same data type. The array below is declared to hold 10 integers:

```
int num[10];
```

Our declared array of 10 elements looks like this:

The cells all contain some data, but we do not know what the values of the data in each cell are as each element of the array is uninitialized, i.e., has not yet been given a value. Here num is the name of the array and 10 is the size specifier. This specifier should be a positive integer constant such as 10, in this case.

```
#define MAX = 10
```

Accessing Array Elements

How do we access the individual elements of an array such as num, given that num now names 10 memory locations and not just one? Individual array elements are identified by an integer index or subscript, such as num[3] or num[i]. In C, the index begins at zero and is always written inside square brackets.

Because C uses zero-based indexing, elements of the array are stored in array locations num[0] through num[9]. Note that array location num[10] does not exist. However, the C compiler does no checking to determine if a subscript of an array is within the bounds of the array. Therefore, no error message is displayed if your program attempts to read or write to an element of the array that does not exist!

Initializing Array Elements

We can initialize individual array elements such as:

```
num[0] = 2;
num[1] = 18;
num[2] = -5;
num[3] = 6;
num[4] = 10;
num[5] = -2;
num[6] = 3;
num[7] = 3;
num[8] = -1;
num[9] = 2;
```

Our array now looks like this:

num

2	18	-5	6	10	-2	3	3	-1	2
[0]	[1]	[2]	[3]	[4]	[5]	[6]	[7]	[8]	[9]

We say the contents of `num[5]` is equal to -2 and the contents of `num[9]` is equal to 2.

- We can initialize array elements using a `for` loop:

```
for (i = 0; i < 10; ++i) {
    num[i] = 2*i;
}
```

Our array now looks like this:

num

0	2	4	6	8	10	12	14	16	18
[0]	[1]	[2]	[3]	[4]	[5]	[6]	[7]	[8]	[9]

- We can initialize an array at the time it's declared:

```
int num[5] = { 5, 10, 15, 20, 25 };
```

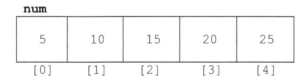

num

5	10	15	20	25
[0]	[1]	[2]	[3]	[4]

We can also initialize an array of characters at the time it's declared:

```
char letters[5] = { 'a', 'b', 'c', 'd', 'e' };
```

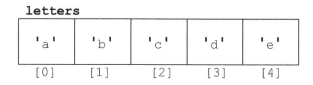

Note that it's not necessary to completely initialize an entire array. If less initial values are specified, then only as many elements will be initialized. The remaining elements in the array will be set to zero.

```
double sample[5] = { 10.5, 12.6, 31.2 };
```

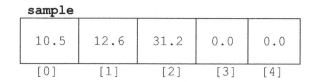

We can also define an array without specifying the number of elements in the array. The size of the array is automatically determined by the number of initialization elements:

```
int num[] = { 2, 3, 4, 7, 9 };
```

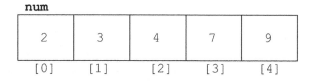

You will often see `#define` used with arrays. The syntax is:

```
#define some_name replacement_text
```

This statement would go right after the `#include` statement:

```
#include <stdio.h>

#define SIZE 100
```

For example, the following code will define the size of an array and initialize each array element to 0.

```
// array1.c

#include <stdio.h>

#define SIZE 100

int main(void) {
    int i, num[SIZE];

    for (i = 0; i < SIZE; i++) {
        num[i] = 0;
    }
    return 0;
}
```

Note that the text `SIZE` will be replaced with 100 before the program compiles.

Here's another way to initialize an array. The contents of the array are also output.

```c
// array2.c

#include <stdio.h>

#define SIZE 5

int main(void) {
    int i, num[SIZE] = { 100, 200, 300, 400, 500 };

    for (i = 0; i < SIZE; i++) {
        printf("%d\n", num[i]);
    }
    return 0;
}
```

Manipulating Array Elements

We can manipulate array elements in the same way that we can manipulate regular variables. For example:

```c
x = num[3] * 4;
```

assigns the product of the array element num[3] times 4 to x.

Here's another example:

```c
num[3] = num[5] + 2;
```

assigns the sum of array element num[5] plus 2 to array element num[3].

Example: Computing the Sum of the Elements in an Array
The code below provides an example of how we process the elements of an array, x, in sequence, from the start of the array (on the left), up to the number of elements in the array:

```c
// sumElements.c

#include <stdio.h>

#define MAX 10

int main (void) {
    int i, sum = 0;
    int x[MAX] = { 2, 4, 6, 8, 10, 12, 14, 16, 18, 20 };


    for (i = 0; i < MAX; i++) {
        sum = sum + x[i];
    }
    printf("The sum of the elements of the array = %d\n", sum);
    return 0;
}
```

What will be the value of sum after the for loop executes?

Example: Making a Copy of an Array

Quite often we have a need to make a duplicate copy of an array. Note that we cannot simply say:

```
dup = num
```

However, all that's necessary is to iterate through the original array and copy corresponding values to a second array.

```c
// copyArray.c
// Makes a copy of an array.

#include <stdio.h>

#define MAX 5

int main(void) {
    int i, num[MAX], dup[MAX];

    for (i = 0; i < MAX; ++i) {
        num[i] = i;
    }
    printf("Original array:\n");
    for (i = 0; i < MAX; ++i) {
        printf("%d  ", num[i]);
    }
    printf("\n\n");
    for (i = 0; i < MAX; ++i)
        dup[i] = num[i];
    printf("Duplicate array:\n");
    for (i = 0; i < MAX; ++i) {
        printf("%d  ", dup[i]);
    }
    printf("\n");
    return 0;
}
```

Here's the program output:

```
Original array:
0  1  2  3  4

Duplicate array:
0  1  2  3  4
```

Calculating Letter Frequency

Suppose that we wanted to calculate the number of times each letter (upper and lower case) appears in a text file. Looking at the ASCII (or Unicode) table we see that the numeric values for the capital letters range from 65 - 90 and the numeric values for the lower case letters range from 97 – 122.

A simple technique for counting the frequency occurrence of each letter would be to use an array, `letter`, to store a count of each of the characters read from the file. We could use each character's ASCII value as an index into the array where the count of that character would be kept.

For example, each time we saw the letter 'A' in a file, we could increment the counter in the `letter` array at index 65, as 65 is the numeric value for 'A':

```
letter[65] = letter[65] + 1;

or

++letter[65];

or

++letter['A'];
```

Here, the character 'A' would be cast into a numeric value (65), and that numeric value would be used as the index into the `letter` array.

We can generalize this for each letter in the file as:

```
++letter[c];
```

where `c` is a character read from the file.

Our code to calculate the frequency of letters in a text file looks like this:

```
// caclFreq.c
// Calculates the frequency of occurrence of each letter in a file.

#include <stdio.h>
#include <ctype.h>
#include <stdlib.h>

int main(void) {
    FILE *fp;
    int c, i;
    static int letter[256];

    fopen_s(fp, "getty.txt", "r");
    if (fp == NULL) {
        printf("File getty.txt could not be opened.\n");
        exit(1);
    }
    while ((c = getc(fp)) != EOF) {
        if (isupper(c) || islower(c)) {
            letter[c] += 1;
        }
    }
    for (i = 'A'; i < 'Z'; ++i) {
        if (letter[i] != 0) {
            printf("%d  %c  %d\n", i, i, letter[i]);
        }
    }
    puts("\n");

    for (i = 'a'; i < 'z'; ++i) {
        if (letter[i] != 0) {
            printf("%d  %c  %d\n", i, i, letter[i]);
        }
    }
    fclose(fp);
    return 0;
}
```

Note that although we are concerned with only upper or lower case characters, we declare an array of 256 locations to cover all possible characters, both printable and non-printable, that we might encounter in the file.

So each element of the array will be used as a counter for the letter with the numeric code of the index. But where do we initialize each element of the array, i.e., where do we initialize each counter to zero?

The answer is that the `letter` array was declared as `static` and an `int` array declared as `static` automatically initializes each element of the array to zero!

Here's a look at the output of the program:

```
66   B   1
70   F   1
73   I   3
78   N   1
84   T   2
87   W   2

97   a   100
98   b   13
99   c   31
100  d   54
101  e   165
102  f   24
103  g   26
104  h   79
105  i   66
107  k   3
108  l   41
109  m   13
110  n   75
111  o   91
112  p   16
113  q   1
114  r   81
115  s   45
116  t   122
117  u   20
118  v   23
119  w   25
121  y   10
```

Sieve of Eratosthenes

The Sieve of Eratosthenes algorithm for generating prime numbers was developed by a Greek scholar, Eratosthenes, who lived from about 275 B.C. to about 195 B.C. Around 240 B.C. Eratosthenes became the head of the library at Alexandria, Egypt, the most advanced center of learning that then existed in the world. He was widely known for his talents in poetry, drama, literature, geography, philosophy, and astronomy. Eratosthenes created accurate maps of the known world, calculated the circumference of the Earth and the tilt of its axis, and determined the size and distance from the Earth to the sun and the moon.

The sieve algorithm shown below generates and counts prime numbers from 1 to 1000 by setting up an array of all numbers up to 1000, and then filters out all numbers that are not prime. Knowing that 1, 2, and 3 are prime numbers, it filters out all multiples of 2 and 3. The next number in turn that is reached and not filtered out is considered prime and its multiples are then filtered out. The algorithm continues until nothing is left but prime numbers.

```c
// sieve.c

#include <stdio.h>

#define SIZE 1000

int main(void) {
    int i, mult, count;
    int flag[SIZE+1];

    count = 1;
    // Initialize flag array
    for (i = 1; i <= SIZE; ++i) {
        flag[i] = 1;
    }
    // Iterate through array
    for (i = 2; i <= SIZE; ++i) {
        if (flag[i] == 1) {      // Found a prime
            ++count;             // Count new prime
            mult = i;
            // loop deletes all multiples of new prime
            while (mult <= SIZE) {
                flag[mult] = 0;
                mult = mult + i;
            }
        }
    }
    printf("There are %d primes.\n", count);
    return 0;
}
```

Program output:

```
There are 169 primes.
```

Try the following:

See if you can modify the program to output all the prime numbers between 40,000 and 50,000, displayed 10 per line. Also display a count of how many primes there are.

Array Elements as Function Arguments

Elements of an array can be passed as function arguments in the same manner as any other variable. The example below passes two array elements by value. Note that the swap function attempts to swap the value of the two array elements but because the array elements are passed by value, the swapped values are not reflected back in `main()`.

```
// array3.c

#include <stdio.h>

#define SIZE 5

void swap(int x, int y);

int main(void) {
    int i, num[SIZE];

    for (i = 0; i < SIZE; ++i) {
        num[i] = i;
    }
    printf("Before swap: num[2] = %d   num[3] = %d\n", num[2], num[3]);
    swap(num[2], num[3]);
    printf(" After swap: num[2] = %d   num[3] = %d\n", num[2], num[3]);
    return 0;
}

void swap(int x, int y) {
    int temp;

    temp = x;
    x = y;
    y = temp;
}
```

Here's the output that's produced:

```
Before swap: num[2] = 2   num[3] = 3
 After swap: num[2] = 2   num[3] = 3
```

By placing the address-of operator `(&)` in front of each of the array element function parameters, we can pass the two array elements by reference. Of course, we also have to modify the `swap()` function to accept addresses rather than `int` values. Note that the swapped values are now reflected back in `main()`.

```c
// array4.c

#include <stdio.h>

#define SIZE 5

void swap(int *x, int *y);

int main(void) {
    int i, num[SIZE];

    for (i = 0; i < SIZE; ++i) {
        num[i] = i;
    }
    printf("Before swap: num[2] = %d   num[3] = %d\n", num[2], num[3]);
    swap(&num[2], &num[3]);
    printf(" After swap: num[2] = %d   num[3] = %d\n", num[2], num[3]);
    return 0;
}

void swap(int *x, int *y) {
    int temp;

    temp = *x;
    *x = *y;
    *y = temp;
}
```

Here's the output that's now produced:

```
Before swap: num[2] = 2   num[3] = 3
 After swap: num[2] = 3   num[3] = 2
```

Arrays as Function Arguments

When passing arrays as parameters, the entire contents of the array are not copied into the formal parameter array. Instead, a pointer (an address) to the first element of the array is passed to the formal parameter. Therefore, any changes made to the formal parameter array by the function are actually made to the original array passed to the function and not to a copy of the array. In other words, arrays are always passed by reference in C.

To pass an entire array to a function, it is only necessary to list the name of the array, without any subscripts, inside the call to the function. Although the receiving function need not know the size of the array, it's usually a good idea to pass the size of the array to the function.

Example: Passing an array by reference.
Our example will declare and initialize an array of ten elements. The array will be passed to a function where the elements of the array will be changed. The array is output both before and after the call to the function that changes the array elements.

```c
// array5.c

#include <stdio.h>

void updateArray(int num[], int size);

int main(void) {
    int i, x[10];

    for (i = 0; i < 10; i++) {
        x[i] = i * 10;
    }
    printf("Before: ");
    for (i = 0; i < 10; ++i) {
        printf("%5d", x[i]);
    }
    printf("\n\n");

    updateArray(x, 10);

    printf("After:  ");
    for (i = 0; i < 10; ++i) {
        printf("%5d", x[i]);
    }
    printf("\n");
    return 0;
}
```

```
// Function modifies elements of array that is passed by reference
void updateArray(int x[], int size) {
    int i;

    for (i = 0; i < size; ++i) {
        x[i] = i * -2;
    }
}
```

The program output looks like this:

```
Before:    0   10   20   30   40   50   60   70   80   90

After:     0   -2   -4   -6   -8  -10  -12  -14  -16  -18
```

Example: Function to sum array elements.
Our function to sum the elements of an array required that we iterate through the array visiting each array element. As we visit each array element, we place its contents into a summation variable. We must be sure to initialize the summation variable to zero before using it!

Once again we want our function to sum arrays of different sizes so we must pass the array size as an additional argument to the function.

```
// sumElements.c
// Function to sum array elements
int sumArray(int num[], int size) {
    int i, sum = 0;

    for (i = 0; i < size; ++i) {
        sum += num[i];
    }
    return(sum);
}
```

Example: Output array with format.
Suppose we wanted to write a function that prints max elements of an array num, 10 per line, with each column separated by one blank, and with each line (including the last) terminated by exactly one new line.

```
// outputArray1.c

#include <stdio.h>

#define MAX 100

void outputArrayWithFormat(int num[], int size);

int main (void) {
    int i, num[MAX];

    for (i = 0; i < MAX; i++) {
        num[i] = i;
    }
    outputArrayWithFormat(num, MAX);
    return 0;
}

void outputArrayWithFormat(int num[], int size) {
    int i;

    for (i = 0; i < size; ++i) {
        printf("%6d", num[i]);
        if (i % 10 == 9 || (i == size -1)) {
            printf("%c", '\n');
        }
        else {
            printf("%c", ' ');
        }
    }
}
```

Here's the output that's produced:

```
     0     1     2     3     4     5     6     7     8     9
    10    11    12    13    14    15    16    17    18    19
    20    21    22    23    24    25    26    27    28    29
    30    31    32    33    34    35    36    37    38    39
    40    41    42    43    44    45    46    47    48    49
    50    51    52    53    54    55    56    57    58    59
    60    61    62    63    64    65    66    67    68    69
    70    71    72    73    74    75    76    77    78    79
    80    81    82    83    84    85    86    87    88    89
    90    91    92    93    94    95    96    97    98    99
```

Here's the function from the example above with more compact code utilizing the conditional operator. Can you follow this?

```c
// outputArray2.c

void outputArrayWithFormat(int num[], int size) {
    int i;

    for (i = 0; i < size; ++i) {
        printf("%6d%c", num[i], (i % 10 == 9 || i == size-1) ?
                                                    '\n' : ' ');
    }
}
```

Example: Function to find the index of the smallest value in an array.
The function in this program declares a variable, `minIndex`, which will hold the index of the smallest array element seen so far. `minIndex` is first initialized to zero and the contents of each successive array element is inspected and compared against the element in location `minIndex`. If an array element is found to be smaller than the element at location `minIndex`, its array location is assigned to `minIndex`.

```c
// findIndex.c

#include <stdio.h>

int getMinIndex(int num[], int size);

int main(void) {
    int small;
    int num[10] = { 43, 66, 82, -16, 42, -8, 12, 33, -19, 11 };

    small = getMinIndex(num, 10);
    printf("The index of the smallest array element = %d.\n", small);
    printf("The value of the smallest array element = %d.\n",
                                                    num[small]);

    return 0;
}
```

```
// Function returns the index of the smallest value in an array
int getMinIndex(int num[], int size) {
    int i, minIndex = 0;

    for (i = 1; i < size; ++i) {
        if (num[i] < num[minIndex]) {
            minIndex = i;
        }
    }
    return minIndex;
}
```

Here's the output that's produced:

```
The index of the smallest array element = 8.
The value of the smallest array element = -19.
```

Suppose we now wanted to move the smallest element of the array, num, to the front of the array. The array as set up looks like this:

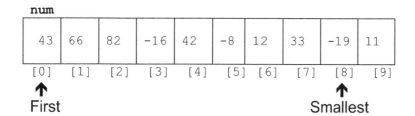

Once we have determined the index of the smallest element in the array num, (this index is 8 in the above example), we need to get this element to the front of the array. If we simply write the following statements in main():

```
small = getMinIndex(num, 10);
num[0] = num[small];
```

we will wipe out the value of num[0], which will be lost forever. So we can call our trusty swap() function to do this work:

```
// swap1.c

void swap(int *x, int *y) {
    int temp = *x;
    *x = *y;
    *y = temp;
}
```

The `swap()` function will swap any pair of `int` data items, even if those items are array elements.

Our relevant code in `main()` looks like this:

```
// swap2.c

small = getMinIndex(num, 10);
swap(&num[0], &num[small]);
```

Note that although arrays are automatically passed to functions by reference, individual array elements are passed by value unless preceded by the ampersand in the function call. Thus, `num[0]` and `num[small]` are just single elements of type `int` of array `num` and must be explicitly passed by reference.

Here's our code which first finds the index of the smallest item in the array and then swaps the integer at that location with the first integer in the array:

```
// swap3.c

#include <stdio.h>

int main(void);
int getMinIndex(int num[], int size);
void swap(int *x, int *y);

int main(void) {
    int i, small;
    int num[10] = { 43, 66, 12, -16, 42, -8, 12, 33, -19, 11 };

    small = getMinIndex(num, 10);
    swap(&num[0], &num[small]);
    for (i = 0; i < 10; ++i) {
        printf("%5d", num[i]);
    }
    return 0;
}

// Function returns the index of the smallest value in an array
int getMinIndex(int num[], int size) {
    int i, minIndex = 0;

    for (i = 1; i < size; ++i) {
        if (num[i] < num[minIndex]) {
            minIndex = i;
        }
    }
    return minIndex;
}

// Function swaps two integers
void swap(int *x, int *y) {
    int temp = *x;
    *x = *y;
    *y = temp;
}
```

Our array looks like this before the call to `swap()`:

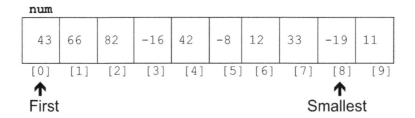

Our array looks like this after the call to `swap()`:

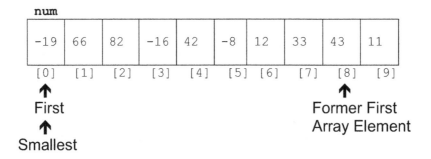

Example: Merge Arrays

Here's a program to merge two sorted (ordered) arrays into a single sorted array:

```c
// merge.c
// Merge two sorted arrays into a single array.

#include <stdio.h>

void mergeTwoArrays(int a[], int b[], int c[], int maxA, int maxB);

int main(void) {
    int k;

    int a[5] = {1, 5, 9, 11, 17};
    int b[5] = {2, 4, 6, 8, 20};
    int c[10];

    mergeTwoArrays(a, b, c, 5, 5);

    for (k = 0; k < 10; k++) {
        printf("%5d", c[k]);
    }
    return 0;
}


void mergeTwoArrays(int a[], int b[], int c[], int maxA, int maxB) {
    int i, j, k;
    i = j = k = 0;

    while (i < maxA && j < maxB) {
        if (a[i] <= b[j]) {
            c[k++] = a[i++];
        }
        else {
            c[k++] = b[j++];
        }
    }
    while (i < maxA) {
        c[k++] = a[i++];
    }
    while (j < maxB) {
        c[k++] = b[j++];
    }
}
```

Here's the output produced after the merge:

```
    1    2    4    5    6    8    9   11   17   20
```

Parallel Arrays

Arrays are very useful as they allow us to group together large amounts of data under a single name. However, one of the drawbacks of arrays is that the elements of the array are homogeneous, that is, each element of the array must be of the same data type, `int, char, float, double,` etc.

But what if we need to group together large amounts of information composed of different data types? For example, suppose we want to keep track of student names, grade point averages, and years of graduation. While we are unable to store all of this different information within a single array, we could declare three separate arrays with each array holding the information of the same data type, `char*` for name, `double` for grade point average, and `int` for year of graduation.)

To ensure that we can easily access the different data for a specific student, each student's data will be stored within the arrays at the same index location. For example, if we declare an array of `char*` called `name` to hold each student's name, and an array of `double` called `gpa` to store each student's grade point average, and an array of `int` called `year` to store each student's year of graduation, then array locations `name[2], gpa[2],` and `year[2]` will each hold data for the same student. These kinds of arrays are referred to as parallel arrays.

The code below create three parallel arrays with the same location within each array referring to the same student.

```c
// parallel.c

#include <stdio.h>

#define MAX 5

int main(void) {
    int i;

    char *name[MAX] = { "Bill", "Carol", "Sue", "Ted", "Jen" };
    double gpa[MAX] = { 3.75, 3.44, 3.95, 3.88, 2.95 };
    int year[MAX]   = { 2014, 2016, 2015, 2014, 2018 };

    printf("%-10s %-10s %-10s\n", "Name", "GPA", "Year");
    printf("%-10s %-10s %-10s\n", "----", "----", "----");
    for (i = 0; i < MAX; i++) {
        printf("%-10s %-10.2lf %-10d\n", name[i], gpa[i], year[i]);
    }
    return 0;
}
```

Our program output is shown below:

```
Name        GPA         Year
----        ----        ----
Bill        3.75        2014
Carol       3.44        2016
Sue         3.95        2015
Ted         3.88        2014
Jen         2.95        2018
```

Sorting an Array: Insertion Sort

Sorting is the process of rearranging items so that they are in order and is one of the most common tasks performed by computers today. Sorting is used to arrange names and numbers in meaningful ways. For example, it is relatively easy to look up the phone number of a friend because the names in the phone book have been sorted into alphabetical order. This example clearly illustrates one of the main reasons that sorting large quantities of information is desirable. That is, sorting greatly improves the efficiency of searching. If we were to open a phone book, and find that the names were not presented in any logical order, it would take an incredibly long time to look up someone's phone number!

Insertion sort works the way many people sort a poker or a rummy hand. We start with an empty left hand and the cards face down on the table. We then remove one card at a time from the table and insert it into the correct position in the left hand. To find the correct position for a card, we compare it with each of the cards already in the hand, from right to left. When we find the correct insertion point, we place the card in the hand at that location.

Insertion sort takes an item from an array and finds its correct position by comparing it with its predecessors. Given an array, num, of size max, we find the correct position for the ith element num[i] by comparing it with the elements num[1], num[2], ... num[i-1]. This ensures that at the ith stage of the algorithm, the first i elements in the array are sorted, such that by the nth stage, all n elements are in order.

Insertion Sort Example

To sort an array of data items, we move through the array from left to right and insert one data item at a time into its proper position among the data items to its left. Shown below is the insertion sort in action. The number in this shade is the number we're trying sort. The numbers in this shade are the sorted elements. The blank location in the array represent a possible insertion point. We begin with the assumption that the first element of the array is sorted:

5	3	8	2	9	4	6	7	

The next element of the array to be sorted is 3:

5	3	8	2	9	4	6	7	

We copy the data item to be sorted into a temporary location, thereby opening a possible insertion point in the sorted array for the data item:

5		8	2	9	4	6	7

3
temp

3 < 5 so we must open a new insertion point. We shift 5 to the right one position opening a new insertion point:

	5	8	2	9	4	6	7

3
temp

Reaching the start of the array tells us that the current insertion point is valid as the new data item is the smallest data item seen so far. So we insert the data item into the insertion point:

3	5	8	2	9	4	6	7

temp

At the end of the 1st pass, the first 2 data items are sorted.

We begin the 2nd pass. The next data item to sort is 8:

3	5	8	2	9	4	6	7

temp

The data item 8 is placed into the temporary memory location, thus opening a possible insertion point:

| 3 | 5 | | 2 | 9 | 4 | 6 | 7 |

| 8 |
temp

8 > 5 so the 8 gets placed into the insertion point:

| 3 | 5 | 8 | 2 | 9 | 4 | 6 | 7 |

| |
temp

At the end of the 2nd pass, the first 3 data items are sorted.

We begin the 3rd pass. The next data item to sort is 2:

| 3 | 5 | 8 | 2 | 9 | 4 | 6 | 7 |

| |
temp

The data item 2 is placed into the temporary memory location, thus opening a possible insertion point:

| 3 | 5 | 8 | | 9 | 4 | 6 | 7 |

| 2 |
temp

2 < 8 so we must open a new insertion point. We shift 8 to the right one position opening a new insertion point:

3	5		8	9	4	6	7	

2
temp

2 < 5 so we must open a new insertion point. We shift 5 to the right one position opening a new insertion point:

3		5	8	9	4	6	7	

2
temp

2 < 3 so we must open a new insertion point. We shift 3 to the right one position opening a new insertion point:

	3	5	8	9	4	6	7	

2
temp

Reaching the start of the array tells us that the current insertion point is valid as the new data item is the smallest data item seen so far. So we insert the data item into the insertion point:

2	3	5	8	9	4	6	7	

temp

At the end of the 3rd pass, the first 4 data items are sorted.

We begin the 4th pass. The next data item to sort is 9:

2	3	5	8	9	4	6	7

temp

The data item 9 is placed into the temporary memory location, thus opening a possible insertion point:

2	3	5	8		4	6	7

9

temp

9 > 8 so 9 gets placed into the insertion point:

2	3	5	8	9	4	6	7

temp

At the end of the 4th pass, the first 5 data items are sorted.

We begin the 5th pass. The next data item to sort is 4:

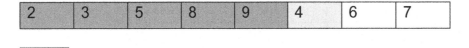

2	3	5	8	9	4	6	7

temp

The data item 4 is placed into the temporary memory location, thus opening a possible insertion point:

2	3	5	8	9		6	7

4
temp

4 < 9 so we must open a new insertion point. We shift 9 to the right one position opening a new insertion point:

2	3	5	8		9	6	7

4
temp

4 < 8 so we must open a new insertion point. We shift 8 to the right one position opening a new insertion point:

2	3	5		8	9	6	7

4
temp

4 < 5 so we must open a new insertion point. We shift 5 to the right one position opening a new insertion point:

2	3		5	8	9	6	7

4
temp

4 > 3 so 4 gets placed into the insertion point:

2	3	4	5	8	9	6	7

temp

At the end of the 5th pass, the first 6 data items are sorted.

We begin the 6th pass. The next data item to sort is 6:

2	3	4	5	8	9	6	7

temp

The data item 6 is placed into the temporary memory location, thus opening a possible insertion point:

2	3	4	5	8	9		7

6
temp

6 < 9 so we must open a new insertion point. We shift 9 to the right one position opening a new insertion point:

2	3	4	5	8		9	7

6
temp

6 < 8 so we must open a new insertion point. We shift 8 to the right one position opening a new insertion point:

2	3	4	5		8	9	7

6
temp

6 > 5 so 6 gets placed into the insertion point:

2	3	4	5	6	8	9	7

temp

At the end of the 6th pass, the first 7 data items are sorted.

We begin the 7th pass. The next data item to sort is 7:

2	3	4	5	6	8	9	7

temp

The data item 7 is placed into the temporary memory location, thus opening a possible insertion point:

2	3	4	5	6	8	9	

7
temp

7 < 9 so we must open a new insertion point. We shift 9 to the right one position opening a new insertion point:

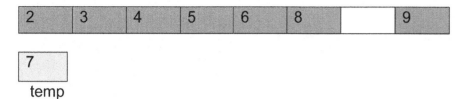

7 < 8 so we must open a new insertion point. We shift 8 to the right one position opening a new insertion point:

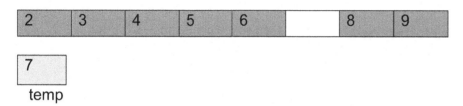

7 > 6 so 7 gets placed into the insertion point:

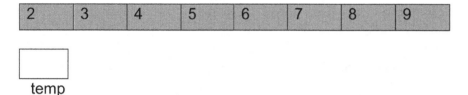

At the end of the 7th pass, the array is sorted. In general, an array of `max` data items requires `max-1` passes to be sorted.

```c
// insertionSort.c

void insertionSort(int list[], int max) {
    int i, j, temp;

    for (i = 1; i < max; i++) {
        temp = list[i];
        j = i - 1;
        while (j >= 0 && temp < list[j]) {
            list[j+1] = list[j];
            j = j - 1;
        }
        list[j+1] = temp;
    }
}
```

Sorting an Array: `qsort()` Library Function

The standard C libraries include an exceptionally powerful and generic sorting routine called `qsort()`. It is an implementation of a particular sorting algorithm called quicksort. The `qsort()` routine has four parameters:

• the base address of an array of data

• the number of items in the array

• the width (in bytes) of each item

• the address of a function that can compare two data items of the type contained in the array and return a signed value as follows:

```
< 0 if p < q
  0 if p = q
> 0 if p > q
```

If you're using one of C's primitive data types, you can usually construct an appropriate comparison function in a few lines of code. Here's an example:

```
// compare.c

int compare(const void *p, const void *q) {
    if (*(int *)p < *(int *)q) {
        return -1;
    }
    return *(int *)p > *(int *)q;
}
```

In the `compare()` function:

```
if p < q returns -1
if p = q returns  0
if p > q returns  1
```

The code below randomly populates a 100-element array with integers. The array contents are displayed, `qsort()` is called, and the array contents are displayed again showing the sorted data items.

```c
// qsort.c

#include <stdio.h>
#include <stdlib.h>
#include <time.h>

#define SIZE 100

int compare(const void *p, const void *q);
void output(int num[], int size);

int main() {
    int i, num[SIZE];

    srand((unsigned)time(NULL));
    for (i = 0 ; i < SIZE; i++) {
        num[i] = rand() % 50000;
    }
    printf("Before sort\n");
    output(num, SIZE);
    qsort(num, SIZE, sizeof(int), compare);
    printf("\nAfter sort\n");
    output(num, SIZE);
    return(0);
}

int compare(const void *p, const void *q) {
    if (*(int *)p < *(int *)q) {
        return -1;
    }
    return *(int *)p > *(int *)q;
}

void output(int num[], int size) {
    int i;

    for (i = 0; i < size; ++i) {
        printf("%6d", num[i]);
        if (i % 10 == 9 || (i == size -1)) {
            printf("%c", '\n');

        }
        else {
            printf("%c", ' ');
        }
    }
}
```

Here's the output that's produced:

```
Before sort
 30567  35439  21431   9013   3992  28690  24735   8148  14330  24847
 43747  10518  46366  40111  33228  46127  27945   8870  45536  21664
 35024  10674  27724  16905  30488  19128  32991   3856  21268  45855
 26816    803  39397   3986  44341  47219  33125  48655  36237   4323
 10188  33574  48866  45132  16189   3823   6746   9497  32622  16402
  8430  46630   1113   5271  47490  13727   7493  40531  46342  47608
 30989  49988  14230   3472  48785   9291    900  26877  24400  17550
 27638  19251  14013  41336  14304  39437  43991  30229  35682    654
 41083  27520  47042  26948  47726  41156  27658  33215  15557  44269
  2529  24729  16662  11997   9825  28596  25245  35327   7047  41915

After sort
   654    803    900   1113   2529   3472   3823   3856   3986   3992
  4323   5271   6746   7047   7493   8148   8430   8870   9013   9291
  9497   9825  10188  10518  10674  11997  13727  14013  14230  14304
 14330  15557  16189  16402  16662  16905  17550  19128  19251  21268
 21431  21664  24400  24729  24735  24847  25245  26816  26877  26948
 27520  27638  27658  27724  27945  28596  28690  30229  30488  30567
 30989  32622  32991  33125  33215  33228  33574  35024  35327  35439
 35682  36237  39397  39437  40111  40531  41083  41156  41336  41915
 43747  43991  44269  44341  45132  45536  45855  46127  46342  46366
 46630  47042  47219  47490  47608  47726  48655  48785  48866  49988
```

Note that the array is sorted in increasing order, as defined by the comparison function. To sort an array in decreasing order, reverse the sense of "greater than" and "less than" in the comparison function.

Even if you are not using a primitive C data type, qsort() will work just fine as long as you know enough about the data representation to tell whether one item is "smaller" than another.

In the case of strings, the standard library function strcmp() is perfectly suited for use with qsort() in the compare function.

```c
// compare2.c

int compare(const void *p, const void *q) {
    return strcmp((char *) p, (char *) q);
}
```

Here's a program that sorts strings with `qsort()`:

```c
// qsort2.c

#include <stdio.h>
#include <stdlib.h>
#include <string.h>

int compare(const void *p, const void *q);

int main() {
    char list[5][4] = { "cat", "car", "cab", "cap", "can" };
    qsort(list, 5, sizeof(list[0]), compare);
    for (i = 0; i < 5; ++i) {
        printf("%s  ", list[i]);
    }
    return(0);
}

int compare(const void *p, const void *q) {
    return strcmp((char *) p, (char *) q);
}
```

Searching an Array: Linear Search

The simplest search strategy is the linear or sequential search. The linear search is usually performed on unordered arrays. It starts at the beginning of the array, checks every element in order, until it either finds the data item it is looking for or until it reaches the end of the array, in which case the data item is not found in the array.

```c
// linearSearch.c

// returns the index in the array of data item found
// returns -1 if data item not in array

int linearSearch(int num[], int max, int key) {
    int i;

    for (i = 0; i < max; ++i) {
        if (num[i] == key) {
            return i;
        }
    }
    return -1;
}
```

Let's examine how long it will take to find a data item matching a key in the unsorted array. We can examine three different possibilities, average time, worst-case time, or best possible time. However, we will generally be most concerned with the worst-case time, as calculations based on worst-case times can lead to guaranteed performance predictions. Conveniently, the worst-case times are generally easier to calculate than average times.

To simplify analysis and comparison of algorithms, we look for a dominant operation and count the number of times that dominant operation has to be performed. In the case of searching, the dominant operation is the comparison.

If there are `max` items in our array, it is obvious that in the worst case when there is no item in the array with the desired `key`, then `max` comparisons of the `key` with the data items in the array will have to be made. In the best case we'll find our data item on the first comparison. In the average case we'll find our data item in `(1 + max) / 2` comparisons or approximately `max/2` comparisons.

Therefore, an array of 100 data items requires an average of 50 comparisons for a successful search. If we were to double the number of data items we had to search through, the number of comparisons would also double and therefore the run-time of our algorithm would double. We say that the number of comparisons is *proportional* to the number of data items n in the array. Accordingly, the search time of the algorithm is proportional to the number of data items `max` in the array. An array of 1000 data items takes 10 times longer to search than an array of 100 data items.

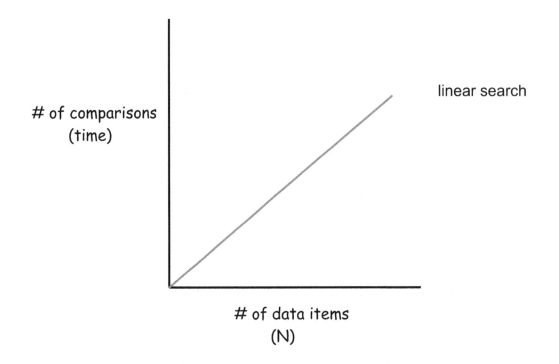

Searching an Array: Binary Search

As we saw earlier, the linear search algorithm is simple and convenient for small problems, but if the array is large and/or requires many repeated searches, it makes good sense to have a more efficient algorithm for searching an array.

The binary search algorithm works on a sorted array. It selects the median (middle) element in the array and compares its value to that of the target value, `key`. Because the array is known to be sorted, if the target value is less than the middle value then the target must be in the first half of the array. Likewise if the value of the target item is greater than that of the middle value in the array, it is known that the target lies in the second half of the array. In either case we can, in effect, "throw out" one half of the search space with only one comparison.

Now, knowing that the target must be in one half of the array or the other, the binary search examines the median value of the half in which the target must reside. The algorithm thus narrows the search area by half at each step until it has either found the target data or the search fails.

The algorithm is easy to remember if you think about a child's guessing game. Imagine I told you that I am thinking of a number between 1 and 1000 and asked you to guess the number. Each time you guessed I would tell you "higher" or "lower." Of course you would begin by guessing 500, then either 250 or 750 depending on my response. You would continue to refine your choice until you got the number correct.

Given a sorted array of items, say:

```
     ------------------------------
    | 12 | 29 | 30 | 32 | 35 | 49 |
     ------------------------------
      0    1    2    3    4    5

    low                  high
    index                index
```

Suppose we wish to search for the position of an element equal to `key`. We will search the array that begins at some low index and ends at some high index. In our case the low index of the effective array to be searched is 0 and the high index is 5. We can find the approximate midway index by integer division (`low + high`) `/ 2`, i.e. 2. We compare our value, key with the element at index 2. If they are equal, we have found what we were looking for; the index is 2. Otherwise, if key is greater than the item at this index, our new effective search array has a low index value of 3 and the high index remains unchanged at 5. If key is less than the element, the new effective search array has a high index of 1 and the low index remains at 0. The process repeats until the item is found, or there are no elements in the effective search array. The terminating condition is found when the low index exceeds the high index.

The binary search algorithm is implemented below:

```
// binarySearch.c

// Assumes array is in sorted order.
// Returns index of the location of the key in the array.
// Retuns -1 if not found.

int binarySearch(int num[], int n, int key) {
    int mid, i, j;

    i = 0;
    j = n-1;
    while (i <= j) {
        mid = (i + j) / 2;
        if (num[mid] > key) {
            j = mid - 1;
        }
        else if (num[mid] < key) {
            i = mid + 1;
        }
        else {
            return mid;
        }
    }
    return -1;
}
```

Analysis of Binary Search

Why use a binary search when a linear search is easier to code? The answer lies in the efficiency of the search. With a linear search, if you double the size of an array, you could potentially take twice as much time to find an item. With a binary search, doubling the size of the array merely adds one more item to look at. Each time you look with a binary search, you eliminate half of the remaining array items as possible matches.

For example, suppose we're given a search space of 1,000,000 data elements. Sequential search would take about 500,000 searches or comparisons on the average. If we were to double the search space to 2,000,000 data items, the number of comparisons would double to 1,000,000 and therefore our search time would effectively double. Binary search, on the other hand, would only require about 20 searches through a search space of 1,000,000 data items and doubling this data size to 2,000,000 would only increase the number of comparisons by 1. Binary search is indeed a powerful search algorithm!

So we say that binary search on an array takes approximately $\log_2 n$ comparisons because at each test you can "throw out" one-half of the search space. We can divide a set of n items in half at most $\log_2 n$ times. Thus the running time of a binary search is proportional to $\log_2 n$ and we say this is a `log n` algorithm.

It is noteworthy that for very small arrays a linear search can prove faster than a binary search. However as the size of the array to be searched increases, the binary search is the clear victor in terms of number of comparisons and therefore overall speed. Thus at large values of n, `log n` is much smaller than n, consequently a `log n` algorithm (binary search) is much faster than an algorithm whose time is proportional to n (linear search).

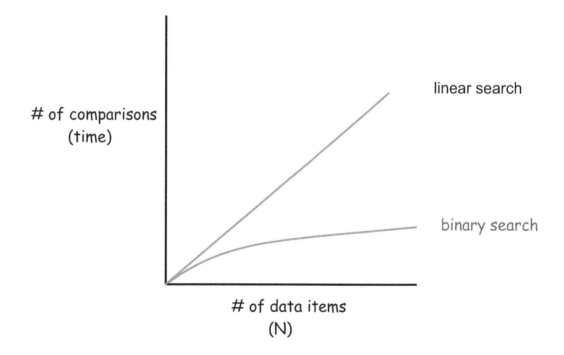

# of comparisons (time)

linear search

binary search

# of data items (N)

Still, the binary search has some drawbacks. First of all, it requires that the data to be searched be in sorted order. If there is even one element out of order in the data being searched it can throw off the entire process. When presented with a set of unsorted data the efficient programmer must decide whether to sort the data and apply a binary search or simply apply the less-efficient linear search. Even the best sorting algorithm is a complicated process. Is the cost of sorting the data is worth the increase in search speed gained with the binary search? If you are searching only once, it is probably better to do a linear search in most cases.

Once the data is sorted it can also prove very expensive to add or delete items. In a sorted array, for instance, such operations require a shift of array elements to open or close a "hole" in the array. This is an expensive operation as it requires, in worst case, $\log_2 n$ comparisons and n data movements.

Two-Dimensional Arrays

We can declare a two-dimensional array consisting of both rows and columns:

```
// 2dim1.c

int num [3][4];
```

This statement declares an array consisting of three rows and four columns:

	Col 0	Col 1	Col 2	Col 3
Row 0				
Row 1				
Row 2				

The elements of the two-dimensional array are identified as follows:

	Col 0	Col 1	Col 2	Col 3
Row 0	num[0][0]	num[0][1]	num[0][2]	num[0][3]
Row 1	num[1][0]	num[1][1]	num[1][2]	num[1][3]
Row 2	num[2][0]	num[2][1]	num[2][2]	num[2][3]

Note that the size in memory of the two-dimensional array is:

```
3 rows * 4 columns * sizeof(int) = 48 bytes
```

We can initialize a two-dimensional array at declaration time:

```
// 2dim2.c

int num[3][4] = {
                    { 2, 4, 6, 8 },
                    { 1, 3, 5, 7 },
                    { 3, 6, 9, 12 }
                };
```

Brace pairs are used to separate the list of initializers for one row from the next. Commas are required after each brace that closes off a row, except in the case of the last row.

Our two-dimensional array initialization looks like this:

	Col 0	Col 1	Col 2	Col 3
Row 0	2	4	6	8
Row 1	1	3	5	7
Row 2	3	6	9	12

Note that the inner pair of braces is also optional:

```
// 2dim3.c

int num[3][4] = { 2, 4, 6, 8, 1, 3, 5, 7, 3, 6, 9, 12 };
```

As with one-dimensional arrays, it is not necessary to initialize the entire array:

```
// 2dim4.c

int num[3][4] = {
                    { 2, 4 },
                    { 1, 3 },
                    { 3, 6 }
               };
```

This declaration initializes the first two elements of each row to the indicated values. The remaining values will be initialized to zero. Note that inner braces here are absolutely required to force the correct initialization!

Our two-dimensional array initialization looks like this:

	Col 0	Col 1	Col 2	Col 3
Row 0	2	4	0	0
Row 1	1	3	0	0
Row 2	3	6	0	0

We can output the contents of our two-dimensional array as follows:

```c
// 2dim5.c

#include <stdio.h>

int main(void) {
    int i, j, num[3][4] = {
                            { 2, 4, 6, 8 },
                            { 1, 3, 5, 7 },
                            { 3, 6, 9, 12 }
                  };
    for (i = 0; i < 3; ++i) {
        for (j = 0; j < 4; ++j) {
            printf("%4d", num[i][j]);
        }
        printf("\n");
    }
    return 0;
}
```

Our output looks like this:

```
   2    4    6    8
   1    3    5    7
   3    6    9   12
```

Two-Dimensional Array of Characters

The declaration for a two-dimensional array of characters must include the extra space for a null terminator if each row is to be treated as a character string:

```c
// 2dim6.c

char name[20][31];
```

This declares a two-dimensional array of 20 rows, each to contain 30 data characters plus the null terminator that the compiler appends to each string. The data is stored in row-major order, which means that each row forms an array or items in memory. Each row is itself a one-dimensional array and can be used in contexts where an array is allowed.

We can output each row of the two-dimensional array of character strings as follows:

```
// 2dim7.c

for (i = 0; i < 20; ++i) {
    printf("%s\n", name[i]);
}
```

Each individual element of the two-dimensional array can also still be accessed using subscripts:

```
name[i][j]
```

Passing Two-Dimensional Arrays as Function Arguments

Suppose you wanted to pass a two-dimensional array to a function:

```
// 2dim8.c

int main(void) {
    int num[3][4] = {
                        { 2, 4, 6, 8 },
                        { 1, 3, 5, 7 },
                        { 3, 6, 9, 12 }
                    };
    foo(num);
    return 0;
}
```

How should the two-dimensional array be received by the function `foo()`?

```
void foo(int num [][4]) {
    ...
    ...
}
```

This informs the compiler that it should break up the array into rows of 4 columns each.

Symmetric Matrix Example

An N x N matrix (two-dimensional array) is symmetric if the element `matrix[i][j]` equals the element `matrix[j][i]` for all `i` and `j` between 1 and N. We construct a program that initializes the elements of two `4` x `4` two-dimensional arrays, outputs the two-dimensional arrays in tabular format, and outputs a message as to whether or not the arrays are symmetric.

Case 1: `matrixYES` is symmetric.
Case 2: `matrixNO` is not symmetric.

```
// symmetric.c

#include <stdio.h>

void outputMatrix(int mat[][4]);
int isSymmetric(int mat[][4]);

int main(void) {
    int matrixYES[4][4] =   {
                                { 6, 2, 4, 6 },
                                { 2, 7, 1, 3 },
                                { 4, 1, 8, 5 },
                                { 6, 3, 5, 9 }
                            };
    int matrixNO[4][4] =    {
                                { 6, 2, 4, 6 },
                                { 2, 7, 1, 3 },
                                { 4, 1, 8, 5 },
                                { 6, 3, 1, 9 }
                            };
    puts("MatrixYES");
    outputMatrix(matrixYES);
    if (isSymmetric(matrixYES)) {
        printf("matrixYES is symmetric.\n\n");
    }
    else {
        printf("matrixYES is not symmetric.\n\n");
    }
    puts("MatrixNO");
    outputMatrix(matrixNO);
    if (isSymmetric(matrixNO)) {
        printf("matrixNo is symmetric.\n\n");
    }
    else {
        printf("matrixNo is not symmetric.\n\n");
    }
    return 0;
}
```

```
void outputMatrix(int mat[][4]) {
    int i, j;

    for (i = 0; i < 4; ++i) {
        for (j = 0; j < 4; ++j) {
            printf("%4d", mat[i][j]);
        }
        printf("\n");
    }
}

int isSymmetric(int mat[][4]) {
    int i, j;

    for (i = 0; i < 4; ++i) {
        for (j = 0; j < 4; ++j) {
            if (mat[i][j] != mat[j][i]) {
                return 0;
            }
        }
    }
    return 1;
}
```

Here's the output:

```
MatrixYES
   6    2    4    6
   2    7    1    3
   4    1    8    5
   6    3    5    9
matrixYES is symmetric.

MatrixNO
   6    2    4    6
   2    7    1    3
   4    1    8    5
   6    3    1    9
matrixNo is not symmetric.
```

1. Write some code to perform each of the following tasks:

  a) Define a constant MAX that holds a value of 50.

  b) Define an array of integers, num, containing MAX elements and initialize each of the elements of the array to 0.

c) What is the name of the fourth element of the array?

d) Output the value of the sixth element of the array.

e) Assign a value into the third element of array num.

f) Initialize each of the 50 elements of the array to 500.

g) Sum up the elements of array num into summation variable sum.

h) Copy the contents of array num into array foo, also of size MAX.

i) Increment each element of array foo by a value of 1.

2. The code below assigns a random number from 1 to 10,000 into each element of array num. Write a function that receives the array as a parameter and returns the smallest value of array.

```
srand((unsigned int) time(NULL));
for (i = 0; i < MAX; ++i) {
    num[i] = rand() % 10000 + 1;
}
```

3. As a practical joke, a friend gives you an int array for your birthday. As if that weren't bad enough, your friend tells you that the array contains almost all 0's except for a small string of consecutive 1's contained somewhere in the middle. Overwhelmed by the novelty of this you decide to write a function that will print out the location of the first 1 in the array, the location of the last 1 in the array, and the total number of 1's in the list of consecutive 1 values. Given below is the function prototype:

```
void joke (int  num[], int max);
```

where `num` is the array of `int` values and `max` contains the number of elements
in the array.

A set of data, (i.e. test scores), can be summarized by a frequency distribution chart. For example, if the list of test scores is:

```
90, 85, 100, 50, 50, 85, 60, 70, 55, 55, 80, 95, 70, 60, 95,

80, 100, 75, 70, 95, 90, 90, 70, 95, 50, 65, 85, 95, 100, 65
```

then the frequency distribution chart looks like the one below:

```
score        frequency
-----        ---------
100              3
 95              5
 90              3
 85              3
 80              2
 75              1
 70              4
 65              2
 60              2
 55              2
 50              3
```

a) Write a C program, `stats.c`, that initializes an array at compile time with the test scores shown above and outputs the test scores, five per line.

b) Sort the test scores into ascending order and output the scores, five per line.

c) Calculate and output the frequency distribution chart as shown above. Note that the scores are listed in decreasing value within the table.

d) Output the percentage of passing and failing test scores to one decimal place. Scores below 60 are failing.

e) Calculate and output the mean of the test scores to one decimal place.

f) Output the mode of the test scores.

g) The median of a list of numbers is that element such that when the numbers are arranged in ascending or descending order, half the elements lie above it and half below. This can happen only when there are an odd number of elements in the list. If the array contains an even number of items, the median is the average of the two numbers in the middle (to one decimal place). Your program should output the median of the test scores given to one decimal place. (Note: Your program should determine on its own whether there is an odd or even number of test scores).

Note that each section of the lab should be designed within its own function, passing parameters as necessary. Be sure to use the set of test data given above in your program and be sure you input the data in the order given.

Remember that the `main()` function should appear as the first function in the program. Be sure to use function prototypes for each of the functions that are used in your program.

Output from your program should be sent to the terminal window (your screen) as well as the requested `csis.txt` output file. Be sure to read the document on Capturing Program Output. Your full name must appear as a comment in the source file that contains `main()`. Be sure to include the `csis.txt` output file in your zip archive.

Your assignment is to write a C program, `decode.c`, which will decode a secret message. The message will be 26 characters in length, and will be given to you as a series of numbers. These numbers must be sorted and compared against a translation set of characters in order to decode it. This method is based upon the decoder rings that used to be available in packages of cereal.

Perhaps the easiest way to show how to decode a message is to first show how a message is encoded. First, the letters of the alphabet, the numbers, and any punctuation is scrambled into some sort of sequence.

For example, the string below can be found in `codefile.txt`:

```
CFL2AP(T9W,H!JEM86ND0BZ7UK1Y3VG4XR)ISOQ5.              ;-
```

Notice that the above string contains 52 characters (including the nine blanks near the end). Now, let's suppose that we want to encode the message:

```
HELP ME!
```

Looking up each of the letters in the above string we find that H is the 11th character (zero-based indexing), E is the 14th, L the 2nd, P the 5th, one of the blanks the 41st, M the 15th, E the 14th, and ! the 12th. Therefore, our initial coding is:

```
11      14      02      05      41      15      14      12
```

Next, each number is assigned a three-digit sequence number, in ascending order, to precede it. These numbers indicate relative position and need not be consecutive.

For example, we might assign the following numbers:

```
10111
12214
12802
12905
13541
13715
14214
15112
```

Finally, the order of the numbers is scrambled:

```
13541
12214
10111
15112
13715
12802
14214
12905
```

This is the list of numbers you would be given to decode. To decode a message, simply reverse the process: read the numbers into an array and sort them into ascending order. "Cut" each sorted number into two, using the last two digits (hint: think modulus operator) as the index to the correct character and print the character.

For this lab, the encoded message in numeric format is given below and can be found in: `msgfile.txt`:

```
19546
14501
17309
13027
16149
21512
18035
14014
15700
12515
16514
18207
13407
14837
16842
21037
15333
13244
21224
16321
14146
16014
20727
12804
18811
13711
```

You lab should include at least the following functions:

```
getCode()        - reads string from codefile.txt

getMessage()     - reads encoded message from msgfile.txt

sortMessage()    - sorts the encoded message array

decodeMessage()  - decodes and outputs the message
```

Note that the string used to hold the 52 characters read from `codefile.txt` should be declared to be of length 53 (to reserve a space for the terminating `NULL` character.

Be sure to do error checking when attempting to open a file for input or output. For extra credit, pass the file names to this lab as *command-line arguments*. Compiler specific information regarding command-line arguments can be found in Canvas at this location:

Files | Set Command-Line Arguments

Remember that the `main()` function should appear as the first function in the program. Be sure to use function prototypes for each of the functions that are used in your program.

Output from your program should be sent to the terminal window (your screen) as well as the requested `csis.txt` output file. Be sure to read the document on Capturing Program Output. Your full name must appear as a comment in the source file that contains `main()`. Be sure to include the `csis.txt` output file in your zip archive.

❖ Hamming Code Lab

Introduction

When data is transferred back and forth between two computers, the possibility exists that the bit pattern finally received may not be the one originally sent. To resolve this problem, a variety of techniques have been developed to detect and even correct transmission errors.

A popular and extremely simple method of detecting errors is based on the principle that if each of the bit patterns being manipulated has an even number of ones and a bit pattern is found with an odd number of ones, an error must have occurred. To use this principle, we need a system in which each pattern contains an even number of ones. This is easily obtained by first adding an additional bit, called the parity bit, to each pattern of a 7-bit ASCII code, producing an 8-bit code. In each case, we assign the value 1 or 0 to this new bit so that the resulting pattern will have an even number of ones.

For example, the 7-bit ASCII code for 'A' is `1000001` and for 'i' is `1001001`. Adding the parity bit as the most significant bit to the 7-bit ASCII code for 'A' produces `01000001` (parity bit 0), and for 'i' produces `11001001` (parity bit 1). Once our coding system has been modified in this way, a pattern with an odd number of 1's will indicate that an error has occurred and that the data being manipulated is incorrect.

The particular parity system just described is called *even parity*, because we designed our system so that each pattern would contain an even number of 1's. Another technique is to use *odd parity*. In such a system, each pattern is designed to have an odd number of 1's in it, and thus an error is signaled by the occurrence of a pattern with an even number of 1's.

Although the use of a parity bit is designed to allow the detection of an error, it does not provide the information to determine which bit is in error. Moreover, if errors had arisen in two different bit positions, the situation could not even be detected.

Hamming Code

A method not only for detecting transmission errors but for correcting them as well was devised by Richard Hamming (1950) and is known as a Hamming Code. In a Hamming Code, K parity bits are added to an N-bit character forming a new character of length N+K bits. The bits are numbered starting with bit 1 as the leftmost bit. All bits whose bit number is a power of two are parity bits, and all the remaining bits are used for data. Therefore, for a 7-bit ASCII character, four parity bits are added. Bits 1, 2, 4, and 8 are parity bits and bits 3, 5, 6, 7, 9, 10, and 11 are the seven data bits. A Hamming Code can be used on characters or messages of any length, although we will illustrate its use with 7-bit ASCII characters (and even parity).

For example, we can encode a 7-bit ASCII character 'E' (1000101) as an 11-bit codeword, using even parity:

```
P     P     1     P     0     0     0     P     1     0     1
-     -     -     -     -     -     -     -     -     -     -
1     2     3     4     5     6     7     8     9     10    11
```

Each of the bit positions containing a P represents a parity check bit. Each parity bit checks specific bit positions, and the parity bit is set so that the total number of 1's in the checked positions is odd or even. The bit positions checked by each of the parity bits are as follows:

```
parity bit 1:      checks bits 1, 3, 5, 7, 9, 11
parity bit 2:      checks bits 2, 3, 6, 7, 10, 11
parity bit 4:      checks bits 4, 5, 6, 7
parity bit 8:      checks bits 8, 9, 10, 11
```

In general, bit N is checked by those bits $b1$, $b2$, ..., bK such that $b1 + b2 + ... + bK = N$. For example, bit 5 is checked by bits 1 and 4 because 1 + 4 = 5. Bit 6 is checked by bits 2 and 4 because 2 + 4 = 6. Shown below is the construction of a Hamming Code for the character 'E' (1000101) using even parity.

```
1     0     1     0     0     0     0     0     1     0     1
|     |     |                       |
|     |     |                       |
|     |     |                       |
p     a     r     i     t     y     b     i     t     s
```

Consider what would happen if the leftmost bit were changed during transmission. The received codeword would be `00100000101` instead of `10100000101`. The four parity bits will be checked by the receiving computer with the result:

```
parity bit 1 incorrect:  bits 1, 3, 5, 7, 9, and 11 contain three 1's
parity bit 2 correct:    bits 2, 3, 6, 7, 10, and 11 contain two 1's
parity bit 4 correct:    bits 4, 5, 6, and 7 contain no 1's
parity bit 8 correct:    bits 8, 9, 10, 11 contain two 1's
```

The total number of 1's in bits 1, 3, 5, 7, 9, and 11 should be an even number because even parity is being used. The incorrect bit must be one of the bits checked by parity bit 1, namely, bits 1, 3, 5, 7, 9, or 11. Because parity bit 2 is correct, we know that bits 2, 3, 6, 7, 10, and 11 are correct. So the error was not in bits 3, 7, or 11. That leaves bits 1, 5, and 9. Parity bit 4 is correct, meaning that bits 4, 5, 6, and 7 contain no errors. That narrows the choice down to 1 or 9. Parity bit 8 is also correct, so bit 9 is correct. Consequently, the incorrect bit must be bit 1. Because it was received as a 1, it must have been transmitted as a 0. In this manner, errors can be both detected and corrected.

A simple method for determining whether there was a transmission error and, if so, for finding the incorrect bit, is to first re-compute all the parity bits in the received character. If all are correct, there was no error (or possibly more than one error, a burst error). If, on the other hand, one or more of the parity bits are incorrect, a transmission error did occur and we must locate and invert the incorrect bit. To accomplish this, we add up all the incorrect parity bits, counting 1 for bit 1, 2 for bit 2, 4 for bit 4, etc. The resulting sum is the position of the incorrect bit. For example, if parity bits 1 and 8 are correct, but 2 and 4 are incorrect, then bit 6 (2 + 4) has been accidentally changed. We can then simply invert it back to the intended value.

A Simple Algorithm Follows
When a codeword arrives, the receiver initializes a counter to zero. It then examines each check bit, `K` (K = 1, 2, 4, 8) to see if it has the correct parity. If not, it adds `K` to the counter. If the counter is zero after all the check bits have been examined (i.e., if they were all correct), the character is accepted as valid. If the counter is non-zero, it contains the number of the incorrect bit that should then be inverted. For example, if check bits 1, 2, and 8 are in error, the inverted bit is 11, because it is the only one checked by bits 1, 2, and 8.

Burst Errors

Hamming Codes can only correct single errors. However, there is a trick that can be used to permit Hamming Codes to correct burst errors. A sequence of R consecutive codewords are arranged as a matrix, one codeword per row. Below is the matrix format for the message "HELLO" before transmission with parity bits set for even parity.

H	1	1	1	1	0	0	1	1	0	0	0
E	1	0	1	0	0	0	0	0	1	0	1
L	1	0	1	1	0	0	1	1	1	0	0
L	1	0	1	1	0	0	1	1	1	0	0
O	0	0	1	1	0	0	1	1	1	1	1
	|	|	|			|			
	|	|	|			|			
	|	|	|			|			
	p	a	r	i	t	y	b	i	t	s

Normally the data would be transmitted one codeword at a time, from left to right. However, to correct burst errors, the data is transmitted one column at a time, starting with the leftmost column. When all R bits in the first column have been sent, the second column is sent, etc. When the message arrives at the receiver, the matrix is reconstructed, one column at a time. If burst errors of length R occurs, 1 bit in each of the R codewords will have been affected. Below is the reconstructed matrix containing a 5-bit burst error. A ' 'B represents the location of the burst errors.

1	1	1	1	0	0	1	**B**	0	0	0
1	0	1	0	0	0	0	**B**	1	0	1
1	0	1	1	0	0	**B**	1	1	0	0
1	0	1	1	0	0	**B**	1	1	0	0
0	0	1	1	0	0	**B**	1	1	1	1
|	|	|			|				
|	|	|			|				
|	|	|			|				
p	a	r	i	t	y	b	i	t	s

But, because the Hamming Code can correct one error per codeword, the entire matrix can be restored. The Hamming Code can thus locate and correct the single error that results in each of the corresponding rows. The entire R-bit burst error can therefore be detected and corrected. This method uses RK check bits to make blocks of RN data bits immune to a single burst error of length R or less.

Assignment

In this lab, you will implement a Hamming Code capable of detecting and correcting burst errors of up to 5 bits. The transmission of data to be received and evaluated will originate in a file called `transmit.txt`. This file contains the message already encoded into sequences of 0's and 1's. Note, however, that rather than dealing with the actual bit manipulation of data, each 0 and 1 will be represented and manipulated as a character of data.

You are to construct a C program, `hamming.c`, which receives the data transmission, detects and corrects any transmission errors that might have occurred, and stores the reconstructed message in a file called `csis.txt`. At the end of the data transmission, the complete received message should then be output to the terminal window.

Note that two additional files have been provided for testing your program:

```
testOK.txt      Contains a data transmission with no errors

testERR.txt     Contains a data transmission with errors
```

Remember that the `main()` function should appear as the first function in the program. Be sure to use function prototypes for each of the functions that are used in your program.

Output from your program should be sent to the terminal window (your screen) as well as the requested `csis.txt` output file. Be sure to read the document on Capturing Program Output. Your full name must appear as a comment in the source file that contains `main()`. Be sure to include the `csis.txt` output file in your zip archive.

Chapter 12. Pointers

Introduction to Pointers
Pointer Parameters in Functions
Pointers and Arrays
Pointer Arithmetic
Functions, Arrays and Pointers
❖ Pointers Homework

Introduction to Pointers

A simple variable in a program is stored in a certain number of bytes at a particular memory location or address in the machine. For example, if v is a variable, then `&v` is the address in memory of its stored value. In this context, the `&` is referred to as the *address-of* operator. When placed in front of any variable, it represents the address in memory of that variable. `&v` is therefore considered a constant.

A *pointer variable* is a variable holds the address of another variable. All pointer variables are typically the same size on any machine. Pointer variables can be declared in programs and then used to take addresses as values. For example:

```
int num;        num is an integer variable
int *ptr;       ptr is a pointer to integer variable
ptr = &num;     address of integer variable num is assigned to pointer
                variable ptr
```

The type specification identifies the type of the variable pointed to and the asterisk (`*`) identifies the variable itself as a pointer. Thus, the declaration:

```
int *ptr;

or

int* ptr;
```

says that `ptr` is a pointer variable and that the thing it points to, `*ptr`, is of type `int`.

As previously mentioned, the *address of operator*, `&`, when followed by a variable name, gives the address of that variable. `&num` is therefore the address in memory of the variable `num`.

The *indirection operator* (sometimes called the *dereference operator*), `*`, when followed by a pointer variable, gives the value stored at the pointed to address. It represents the thing being pointed to.

Let's analyze the following program:

```c
// pointer.c

#include <stdio.h>

(1)    int main(void) {
(2)        int x, y;
(3)        int *ptr;

(4)        x = 5;
(5)        ptr = &x;
(6)        y = *ptr;
(7)        printf("x = %d      y = %d\n", x, y);
(8)        return 0;
(9)    }
```

Line (3) declares `ptr` to be a pointer variable that will contain the address of some `int` variable. Line (5) uses the address of operator to assign the address of the `int` variable `x` to pointer variable `ptr`. Line (6) uses the indirection operator to take the thing that `ptr` points to (an `int` value) and assigns it to `y`. We say that the pointer variable `ptr` is dereferenced and gives us the thing pointed to, i.e., 5, to use in the assignment statement. The effect of statements (5) and (6) are the same as if we had made the assignment `y = x;`, i.e., to assign the value of 5 to `y`.

The output of the program is:

```
x = 5       y = 5
```

In order to print a memory address in a C program, you can use the `%p` format specifier and pass `printf()` the address value you'd like to print.

For example:

```
// address.c

#include <stdio.h>

int main(void) {
    int x = 5;

    printf("x = %d      &x = %p\n", x, &x);
}
```

prints both the value of variable x as well as its address in memory. The output will be similar to:

```
x = 5      &x = FFFFFFF4
```

Pointer Parameters in Functions

Except when passing arrays, C functions are always called by passing the value of each argument (actual parameters) to the function. Any change made to these arguments in the function (formal parameters) are not reflected back to the calling environment. Therefore the stored value of those arguments in the calling environment cannot be changed by the function. This is referred to as *pass by value*. For example:

```c
// value.c

#include <stdio.h>

int main(void);
void foo(int num);

int main(void) {
    int num = 5;

    printf("num = %d\n", num);
    foo(num);
    printf("num = %d\n", num);
    return 0;
}

void foo(int num) {
    printf("num = %d\n", num);
    num = num + 1;
    printf("num = %d\n", num);
}
```

The output of this program is:

```
num = 5
num = 5
num = 6
num = 5
```

This indicates that pass by value does not allow the actual parameter to be modified.

To simulate pass by reference, we can use pointers to pass the address of any data item to a function. When dealing with pointers sent to functions, the value of the pointer (i.e., the address of the actual parameter) is copied into the formal parameter when the function is called. By dereferencing the pointer within the function, we can access and modify the data (actual parameter) that it points to.

For example:

```c
// swap.c

#include <stdio.h>

void swap(int *u, int *v);

int main(void) {
    int x, y;

    x = 5;
    y = 7;
    printf("x = %d     y = %d\n", x, y);
    swap(&x, &y);
    printf("x = %d     y = %d\n", x, y);
    return 0;
}

void swap(int *u, int *v) {
    int temp;

    printf("u = %d     v = %d\n", *u, *v);
    temp = *u;
    *u = *v;
    *v = temp;
    printf("u = %d     v = %d\n", *u, *v);
}
```

The output to this program is:

```
x = 5     y = 7
u = 5     v = 7
u = 7     v = 5
x = 7     y = 5
```

Note that the call:

```
swap(&x, &y);
```

transmits the addresses of the actual parameters x and y rather than their values. This means that the formal parameters u and v will have addresses as their values. Therefore, they should be declared as pointers with the function prototype:

```
void swap(int *u, int *v);
```

Pointers and Arrays

Pointers and arrays are used in almost the exact same way to access memory. The difference is that *a pointer is a variable that takes addresses as values while an array name is an address, or pointer, that is fixed.*

When an array is declared, the compiler must allocate a base address and a sufficient amount of storage to contain all the elements of the array. The base address is the initial location in memory where the array is stored, i.e., the address of the first element (index 0) of the array. Therefore, *an array name is also a pointer to the first element of the array.* If we declare an integer array:

```
int num[100];
```

then the name of the array, num, is equivalent to the address of the first element of the array, &num[0]:

```
num == &num[0]
```

Both represent the memory address of that first element of the array and both are pointer constants because they remain fixed for the duration of the program. However, they can be assigned as values to a pointer variable and we can change the value of that pointer variable as we wish. For example:

```
int num[100];    // reserve sizeof(int)*100 bytes of memory
int *ptr;        // pointer variable
```

If ptr is assigned the address of the initial element of array num, we can then access the array storage using the pointer variable. So we can execute either

```
ptr = num;
```

or

```
ptr = &num[0];
```

The initial element of the array can now be accessed as *ptr, i.e., the thing pointed to by ptr.

Pointer Arithmetic

Pointer arithmetic is one of the most powerful features of C and provides an alternative to array indexing. The statements:

```
ptr = &num[1];

and

ptr = num + 1;
```

are equivalent and would assign the address of the second element of the array to `ptr`. What's interesting is that if the pointer variable `ptr` is a pointer to any particular type, then the expression `ptr + 1` yields the correct memory address for storing or accessing the next variable of that type. Each of the following statements are valid and would take us to the next variable of that type, i.e., the next element of the array:

```
ptr = ptr + 1;
ptr += 1;
++ptr;
ptr++;
```

Here is a program that sums the elements of an array of 100 integers using pointer arithmetic.

```c
// psum1.c

#include <stdio.h>

int main(void) {
    int i, num[100], sum, *ptr;

    for (i = 0; i < 100; i++) {
        num[i] = i;
    }
    for (sum = 0, ptr = num; ptr <= &num[99]; ptr++) {
        sum += *ptr;
    }
    printf("sum = %d\n", sum);
    return 0;
}
```

In this example, pointer variable `ptr` is first initialized to the base address of array `num`. The successive values of `ptr` are equivalent to `&num[0]`, `&num[1]`, …, `&num[99]`. In each iteration we then dereference the pointer `ptr` to access the contents of the array element that is added to the summation variable.

In general, given the following declarations:

```
int i, num[100];
int *ptr;
```

we can say that `ptr + i` is the ith offset from the address `ptr` and `num + i` is the ith offset from the base address of array `num`. Here is another way to sum the array:

```
// psum2.c

#include <stdio.h>

int main(void) {
    int i, num[100], sum;

    for (i = 0; i < 100; i++) {
        num[i] = i;
    }
    for (sum = 0, i = 0; i < 100; ++i) {
        sum += *(num + i);
    }
    printf("sum = %d\n", sum);
    return 0;
}
```

Note that because `num` is the name of an array, it is a `constant pointer` and the following expressions are illegal because we cannot change the value of `num`:

```
num = ptr;
++num;
num++;
num += 2;
```

In general, if `num` is an array of elements of type `x`, `px` is of type pointer to `x`, and `i` is an `int`, then:

```
px = num;
```

sets `px` to point to the first element of `num`,

```
*(px + i)
```

references the value contained in `num[i]`, and

```
px += i
```

sets `px` to point to `i` elements further in the array, no matter what type of element is contained within the array!

Comparing Pointer Variables

It is valid in C to compare two pointer variables. This is useful when comparing two pointers that point to the same array. For example, we could test `ptr` to see if it points past the end of an array containing 100 elements by comparing its value against a pointer to the last element in the array:

```
ptr > &num[99]

or

ptr > num + 99
```

We could also determine if a pointer has gone too far in the other direction:

```
ptr < &num[0]

or

ptr < num
```

Subtracting Pointers

When a pointer is subtracted from another pointer, the difference is divided by the size of the indirect value and the result (when dealing with arrays) is the number of elements contained between the two pointers. For example:

```
// diff.c

#include <stdio.h>

int main(void) {
    double num[100];
    double *pa, *pb;

    pa = num;
    pb = pa + 3;
    printf("difference = %d", pb - pa);
    return 0;
}
```

produces the output:

```
difference = 3
```

If `ptr` points to some element in array `num`, then:

```
i = ptr - num;
```

assigns to variable `i` the index number of the element inside `num` that `ptr` points to. Therefore if `ptr` had been set pointing to the 100th element in `num` by:

```
ptr = &num[99];
```

then the value of `i` after:

```
i = ptr - num;
```

would be: `99`

Summary

There is a very close connection between arrays and pointers. Keep in mind the following equalities:

```
num + 2 == &num[2]      // same address

and

*(num + 2) == num[2]    // same value
```

We can therefore use a pointer to identify an individual element of an array and get its value.

Be sure not to confuse:

```
*(num + 2)
```

which is the value of the third element of `num` with

```
*num + 2
```

which adds 2 to the value of the first element of num.

Also keep the following in mind:

```
*(++ptr)
```

first increments `ptr` and then fetches the data it points to, while

```
*ptr++
```

fetches the data pointed to by `ptr` before the pointer itself is incremented.

Functions, Arrays and Pointers

Given the following declarations:

```
int main(void) {
    int num[100];

    foo(num);
    return 0;
}

void foo(int list[]) {
    :
    :
}
```

Array `num` is an array containing 100 elements. How many elements are contained within array `list`? The answer is that there is no array list!! The formal parameter declaration:

```
int list[]
```

creates not an array, but a pointer. Why? Note our function call:

```
foo(num);
```

The argument is `num` and the name `num` is not only the name of the array, but is also a pointer to the first element of the 100 element array. So the function call passes a pointer, the address of the array, to the function `foo()`. This means that the argument of `foo()` is a pointer, and we could have written:

```
void foo(int *list) {
    :
    :
}
```

In other words, we have the following equality:

```
int list[] == int *list
```

Both declare `list` to be a pointer to an integer. The chief difference is that the first form reminds us that `list` points to an array.

We can now see why using an array name as a parameter is a call by reference and not a call by value. The function call initializes `list` to point to `num[0]`. If we come across the statement, `list[3]`, in the function, it's the same as saying `*(list + 3)`. But if list points to `num[0]`, then `list + 3` points to `num[3]`, i.e., `*(list + 3) == num[3]`. Therefore by modifying `list[3]` we are modifying `*(list + 3)` which is the same as modifying `num[3]`.

In general, when you use an array name as a function argument, you pass a pointer to the function. The function then uses this pointer to effect changes on the original array in the calling program.

The following two functions returns the sum of array `num`:

```
// sumaray1.c
int sumAray1(int num[], int max) {
    int i, sum;

    for (i = 0, sum = 0; i < max; i++) {
        sum += num[i];
    }
    return sum;
}


// sumaray2.c
int sumAray2(int *num, int max) {
    int i, sum;

    for (i = 0, sum = 0; i < max; i++) {
        sum += *(num + i);
    }
    return sum;
}
```

Note that we can also pass part of an array to a function by passing a pointer to the beginning of the subarray. For example, if `num` is an array, then:

```
foo(&num[2]);

and

foo(num + 2);
```

both pass to function `foo()` the address of element `num[2]`. Within `foo()`, the argument declaration can read:

```
void foo(int num[]) {
    :
    :
}

or

void foo(int *num) {
    :
    :
}
```

1. If x is a variable and p is a pointer to x, which of the following expressions are aliases for x?

a) *p   c) *&p   e) *x   g) *&x

b) &p   d) &*p   f) &x   h) &*x

2. If x is an `int` variable and p and q are pointers to `int`, which of the following assignments are legal?

a) p = x   d) p = &q   g) p = *q

b) *p = &x   e) p = *&q   h) *p = q

c) &p = q   f) p = q   i) *p = *q

3. Write a line of code for each of the examples below. Assume that `num1` and `num2` are `int` variables and `num1` is initialized to 5.

a) Define variable p to be a pointer to an `int`.

b) Assign the address of `num1` to pointer p.

c) Print the value of the variable pointed to by p.

d) Assign the value of the variable pointed to by p to variable `num2`.

e) Print the value of `num2`.

4. Suppose that the following declarations are in effect:

```
int a[] = { 5, 15, 34, 54, 14, 2, 52, 72 };
int *p = &a[1];
int *q = &a[5];
```

a) What is the value of * (p + 3)?

b) What is the value of * (q - 3)?

c) What is the value of q - p?

d) Is the condition $p < q$ true or false?

e) Is the condition $*p < *q$ true or false?

5. Suppose that num is a one-dimensional array and p is a pointer variable. Assuming that the assignment p = num has just been performed, which of the following expressions are illegal because of mismatched types? Of the remaining expressions, which are true (have a nonzero value)?

a) p == num[0]

c) *p == num[0]

b) p == &num[0]

d) p[0] == num[0];

Chapter 13. Strings

Introduction to Strings
Additional String Functions
Two String Examples
Strings and Pointers
Arrays of Character Strings
Command-Line Arguments
Set Command-Line Arguments in Visual Studio 12
Set Command-Line Arguments in Xcode 4
Variable Length Argument List
❖ Strings Homework
❖ Caesar Cipher Lab
❖ Text Format Lab
❖ Text Statistics Lab
❖ Grep Lab
❖ Text Encryption Lab
❖ String Manipulation Lab

Introduction to Strings

A string is defined as a character array that is terminated by the null character, `'\0'`. Strings can be initialized at the point of declaration as follows:

```
char name[] = { 'C', 'o', 'm', 'p', 'u', 't', 'e', 'r', '\0' };
```

Note that this array will contain 9 elements, one for each character plus one for the null character, `'\0'`. An alternate, and more widely used initialization, looks like this:

```
char name[] = "Computer";
```

Two widely used string I/O functions are:

- `gets(s1)`

Reads a string into string variable `s1` from `stdin`. Characters are placed into `s1` until a newline character is read, at which time the newline character is changed to a null character and is used to terminate `s1`. The value of `s1` (pointer to `char`) is returned. Note, unlike `scanf_s()`, this function allows input strings to contain white space characters.

Its function prototype is:
```
char *gets(char *s1);
```

- `puts(s1)`

The null terminated string `s1` is copied to `stdout`, except that the terminating null character itself is not copied. A newline character is appended.

Its function prototype is:
```
puts(char *s1);
```

The `string.h` library contains a variety of functions to manipulate strings. To use any of the functions, we must add the following declaration to our program:

```
#include <string.h>
```

We'll look closely at four string function that appear in the `string.h` library, `strlen()`, `strcpy()`, `strcat()`, `strcmp()`. We'll write our own code for each these string functions as well.

- `strlen(s1)`

Tells us the length of a string. It returns the number of characters in a string, not counting the null-terminating character.

Its function prototype is:
```
int strlen(char *s1);
```

For example:

```
strlen("Computer");
```

returns the value 8 and not 9.

We can actually write a simple function to calculate our own string lengths. Note that we use the location of the null character in the string to help us determine the end of the string:

```
// strlen1.c

int strlen(char s1[]) {
    int i = 0;

    while (s1[i] != '\0') {
        ++i;
    }
    return i;
}
```

The formal parameter `s1` is not really a character array, but a variable that holds the address of the initial element of the array. This is called a *character pointer*, and the function could have been declared as:

```
int strlen(char *s1)
```

When `strlen()` runs through its loop, it will look successively at `s1[0]`, `s1[1]`, etc. Since `s1` contains the initial address of the array, C understands that `s1[0]` means the character at that address.

- `strcpy(s1, s2) )`
Copies string `s2` to string `s1`, stopping after the terminating null character has been moved.

Its function prototype is:
```
void strcpy(char *s1, char *s2);
```

For example:

```
strcpy(s, "Computer");
```

copies the string `"Computer"` into string variable `s`.

Again, we can write our own `strcpy()` function and we can use the location of the null character in the string to help us determine the end of the string:

```c
// strcpy1.c

void strcpy(char s1[], chat s2[]) {
    int i = 0;

    while (s2[i] != '\0') {
        s1[i] = s2[i];
        ++i;
    }
    s1[i] = '\0';
}
```

We can write this more concisely:

```
// strcpy2.c

void strcpy(char s1[], chat s2[]) {
    int i = 0;

    while ((s1[i] = s2[i]) != '\0') {
        ++i;
    }
}
```

- `strcat(s1, s2) )`

Copies string `s2` to onto the end of string `s1`.

Its function prototype is:
`void strcat(char *s1, char *s2);`

For example:

```
char buf[32] = "Hello,";
strcat(buf, " world.");
printf("%s\n", buf);
```

outputs the string:

```
Hello, world.
```

Once again, we can write our own code to perform a string concatenation:

```c
// strcat1.c

void strcat(char s1[], char s2[]) {
    int i = 0, j = 0;

    while (s1[i] != '\0') {
        ++i;
    }
    while (s2[j] != '\0') {
        s1[i] = s2[j];
        ++i;
        ++j;
    }
    s1[i] = '\0';
}
```

We can simplify the code:

```c
// strcat2.c

void strcat(char s1[], char s2[]) {
    int i = 0, j = 0;

    while (s1[i]) {
        ++i;
    }
    while (s2[j]) {
        s1[i++] = s2[j++];
    }
    s1[i] = '\0';
}
```

We can simplify the code even further:

```
// strcat3.c

void strcat(char s1[], char s2[]) {
    int i = 0, j = 0;

    while (s1[i]) {
        ++i;
    }
    while (s1[i++] = s2[j++]) {
        ;
    }
}
```

- strcmp(s1, s2))

Performs a comparison of string s1 to string s2, starting with the first character in each string and continuing with subsequent characters until the corresponding characters differ or until the end of the strings is reached. The function returns a value that is:

```
< 0 if s1 is less than s2
== 0 if s1 is the same as s2
> 0 if s1 is greater than s2
```

Its function prototype is:
```
int strcmp(char *s1, char *s2);
```

We write our own code to perform a string comparison:

```
// strcmp1.c

int strcmp(char s1[], char s2[]) {
    int i = 0;

    while (s1[i] == s2[i] && s1[i] != '\0') {
        ++i;
    }
    return s1[i] - s2[i];
}
```

Here's an example of the use of the `strcmp()` function:

```c
// compareStrings.c

#include <stdio.h>
#include <string.h>

int main(void) {
    int num;

    char s1[] = "red";
    char s2[] = "blue";
    num = strcmp(s1, s2);
    if (num < 0) {
        printf("%s is smaller.\n", s1);
    }
    else if (num > 0) {
        printf("%s is smaller.\n", s2);
    }
    else {
        printf("The strings are the same.");
    }
    return 0;
}
```

The output produced looks like this:

```
blue is smaller.
```

Note that C does not allow us to directly compare two strings for equality using the equality operator:

```c
if (s1 == s2)
```

This is due to the fact that the equality operator can only be applied to simple variable types such as `int`, `float`, `char`, etc., but not to arrays, strings, or structures.

Additional String Functions

Here are additional string manipulation functions located in the string library:

- `strncpy(s1, s2, max)`

Copies up to `max` characters from string `s2` into string `s1`, truncating or null-padding `s1`. The target string `s1` might not be null-terminated if the length of `s2` is `max` or more.

Its function prototype is:
```
char *strncpy(char *s1, char *s2, int max);
```

- `strncmp(s1, s2, max)`

Makes the same comparison as `strcmp()`, but looks at no more than `max` characters. It starts with the first character in each string and continues with subsequent characters until the corresponding characters differ or until it has examined `max` characters. Returns an `int` value based on the result of comparing string `s1` (or part of it) to string `s2` (or part of it). The function returns a value that is:

```
< 0 if s1 is less than s2
== 0 if s1 is the same as s2
> 0 if s1 is greater than s2
```

Its function prototype is:
```
int strncmp(char *s1, char *s2, int max);
```

- `strchr(s1, c)`

Scans string `s1` for the first occurrence of character `c`. Returns a pointer to the first occurrence of the character `c` in `s1`. If `c` does not occur in `s`, `strchr()` returns null.

Its function prototype is:
```
char *strchr(char *s1, int c);
```

- `strrchr(s1, c)`

Scans a string for the last occurrence of a given character. `strrchr()` scans string `s1` in the reverse direction, looking for character `c`. Returns a pointer to the last occurrence of character `c`. If character `c` does not occur in string `s1`, `strrchr()` returns null.

Its function prototype is:
```
char *strrchr(char *s1, int c);
```

- `strstr(s1, s2)`

Scans string `s1` for the first occurrence of the substring `s2`. Returns a pointer to the element in `s1`, where `s2` begins (points to `s2` in `s1`). If `s2` does not occur in `s1`, `strstr()` returns null.

Its function prototype is:
```
char *strstr(char *s1, char *s2);
```

- `strset(s1, c)`

Sets all characters in string `s1` to character `c`. It quits when the terminating null character is found. Returns `s1`.

Its function prototype is:
```
char *strset(char *s1, int c);
```

- `strrev(s1)`

Reverses a string. `strrev()` changes all characters in a string to reverse order, except the terminating null character. Returns a pointer to the reversed string.

Its function prototype is:
```
char *strrev(char *s1);
```

- `strlwr(s1)`

Converts uppercase letters in string `s1` to lowercase. No other characters are changed. Returns `s1`.

Its function prototype is:
```
char *strlwr(char *s1);
```

- `strupr(s1)`

Converts lowercase letters in string `s1` to uppercase. No other characters are changed. Returns `s1`.

Its function prototype is:
```
char *strupr(char *s1);
```

Two String Examples

Below are two string functions. See if you can figure out how they work.

```c
// reverse.c
// Function to reverse a string in place

void reverse (char s[]) {
    int c, i, j;

    for (i = 0, j = (int)strlen(s)-1; i < j; ++i, --j) {
        c = s[i];
        s[i] = s[j];
        s[j] = c;
    }
}
```

```c
// convert.c
// Function converts a string of digits into its numeric equivalent

int atoi(char buf[]) {
    int i, num;

    num = 0;
    for (i = 0; buf[i] >= '0' && buf[i] <= '9'; ++i) {
        num = 10 * num + buf[i] - 48;
    }
    return num;
}
```

Strings and Pointers

Consider the following two declarations:

```
(1)  char word[]  =  "Computer";

(2)  char *word   =  "Computer";
```

In declaration (1) the compiler counts up the characters and sizes the array accordingly, for a total of 9 bytes (including the `'\0'` character). Here, the array name `word` is a *constant pointer* to the first element of the array:

```
word  ==  &word[0]
```

and we can show the following equalities:

```
*word  ==  'C'

*(word + 1)  ==  word[1]  ==  'o'
```

In declaration (2) pointer notation is used to set up a string. The compiler actually reserves 13 bytes of storage: 9 for the string and 4 for the pointer variable that will point to the string.

In each case `word` is a pointer to a string. In each case the string itself determines the amount of storage set aside for the string. But the forms are not identical. The array form sets up an array of 9 elements (including the `'\0'` character) in storage and the compiler recognizes the name `word` as a synonym for the address of the first array element, `&word[0]`. Note that `word` is a pointer constant that contains the base address of the array and that cannot change. You can reference `word + 1` to identify the next element in the array, but `++word` is not allowed.

The pointer form also causes 9 elements in storage to be set aside for the string. However, it also sets aside one more storage location for the pointer variable `word`. This variable initially points to the beginning of the string, but its value can change. Here, `++word` would point to the second character, etc.

Can you find the error in the following program?

```c
// error.c

#include <stdio.h>

int main(void) {
    char *name;

    printf("Please enter your name: ");
    gets(name);
    printf("Hello %s\n", name);
    return 0;
}
```

String Functions Revisited Using Pointers

The following two string functions return the number of characters in a string:

```c
// strlen2.c

int strlen(char *s) {
    int i = 0;

    while(*s++) {
        i++;
    }
    return i;
}


// strlen3.c

int strlen(char *s) {
    char *ptr = s;

    while(*ptr) {
        ptr++;
    }
    return(ptr - s);
}
```

The following four string functions copy string t into string s. Can you follow the pointers?

```
// strcpy3.c

void strcpy(char s[], char t[]) {
    int i;

    for (i = 0; t[i] != '\0'; i++) {
        s[i] = t[i];
    }
    s[i] = '\0';
}


// strcpy4.c

void strcpy(char *s, char *t) {
    for (; *t != '\0'; s++, t++) {
        *s = *t;
    }
    *s = '\0';
}


// strcpy5.c

void strcpy(char *s, char *t) {
    while (*t) {
        *s++ = *t++;
    }
    *s = '\0';
}


// strcpy6.c

void strcpy(char *s, char *t) {
    while (*s++ = *t++) {
        ;
    }
}
```

The following function concatenates string `t` onto the end of string `s` and returns a pointer to the concatenated string:

```
// strcat4.c

char *strcat(char *s, char *t) {
    while (*s) {
        s++;
    }
    while (*s++ = *t++) {
        ;
    }
    return s;
}
```

Note that in our final implementation of `strcat()`, we can actually return the concatenated string as the function return value.

Finally, the following function compares two strings:

```
// strcmp2.c

int strcmp(char *s, char *t) {
    while (*s== *t && *s) {
        s++;
        t++;
    }
    return *s - *t;
}
```

See if you can figure out the output to the following program:

```c
// doublep.c

#include <stdio.h>

int main(void);
void foo1(char *p);
void foo2(char **q);

int main(void) {
    char *p = "Hello";
    char *q = "Bye";

    printf("Function: main() --->    p = %s\n", p);
    foo1(p);
    printf("Function: main() --->    p = %s\n", p);
    printf("Function: main() --->    q = %s\n", q);
    foo2(&q);
    printf("Function: main() --->    q = %s\n", q);
    return 0;
}

void foo1(char *pp) {
    ++pp;
    printf("Function: foo1() --->  pp = %s\n", pp);
}

void foo2(char **qq) {
    ++*qq;
    printf("Function: foo2() ---> *qq = %s\n", *qq);
}
```

The output produced is as follows:

```
Function: main() --->    p = Hello
Function: foo1() --->   pp = ello
Function: main() --->    p = Hello
Function: main() --->    q = Bye
Function: foo2() --->  *qq = ye
Function: main() --->    q = ye
```

Arrays of Character Strings

Consider the following array declaration:

```
char name[5][10] = { "Haley", "Sammie", "Marc", "Lisa", "Zach" };
```

that sets up a rectangular two dimensional array of 5 rows each of length 10 columns. Note that it is necessary for us to declare a row's length large enough to at least hold the largest name:

```
name[0]  | H | a | l | e | y | \0 |   |   |   |   |
name[1]  | S | a | m | m | i | e | \0 |   |   |   |
name[2]  | M | a | r | c | \0 |   |   |   |   |   |
name[3]  | L | i | s | a | \0 |   |   |   |   |   |
name[4]  | Z | a | c | h | \0 |   |   |   |   |   |
```

As you can see, this is a great waste of storage. Fortunately, C gives us the ability to declare an array with each row's length determined by the string it's initialized to:

```
char *name[5] = { "Haley", "Sammie", "Marc", "Lisa", "Zach" };
```

Here, name is an array of 5 pointers to character strings. Each character string is an array of characters, so we have 5 pointers to arrays:

```
name[0]  | •===|===➜ | H | a | l | e | y | \0 |
name[1]  | •===|===➜ | S | a | m | m | i | e | \0 |
name[2]  | •===|===➜ | M | a | r | c | \0 |
name[3]  | •===|===➜ | L | i | s | a | \0 |
name[4]  | •===|===➜ | Z | a | c | h | \0 |
```

The first pointer is `name[0]` and it points to the first string, the second pointer is `name[1]` and it points to the second string, etc. Note that each pointer points to the first character in each string:

```
*name[0] == 'H'
*name[1] == 'S'
*name[2] == 'M'
*name[3] == 'L'
*name[4] == 'Z'
```

This array of pointers is sometimes known as a *ragged array*, because each row may be of a different size. The ragged array, therefore, doesn't waste any storage space!

Consider the following example that declares a ragged array which stores various error messages which might be needed by a program:

```c
// arrayString.c

char *errorMsg[5] = { "Memory allocation error",
                      "Stack overflow.",
                      "Cannot read sector.",
                      "File not found.",
                      "Division by zero."
                    };
```

To output an appropriate error message, it's simply a matter of accessing the appropriate array element:

```c
puts(errorMsg[3]);
```

If we wanted to output all error messages contained within the ragged array, it would simply be a matter of iterating through the array:

```c
for (i = 0; i < 5; i++) {
    puts(errorMsg[i]);
}
```

When a compiled program is executed, it's useful to supply initial values for some variables at runtime. These values are called *command-line arguments*. We have previously defined the `main()` function as:

```
int main(void);
```

but it is more generally defined as:

```
int main(int argc, char *argv[]);
```

The first argument, `argc`, stores the number of command-line arguments the program was invoked with (including the name of the program). The second argument, `argv`, is a pointer to ragged array of strings that stores the actual argument values passed to the program.

The declaration of `argv`:

```
char *argv[]
```

indicates that the pointer is to the initial element of the array and can also be written as:

```
char **argv
```

That is, `argv` is a pointer to a pointer to a `char`. If we look at the storage pointed to by `argv`, we will find an array of character pointers, each one pointing to a null-terminated string:

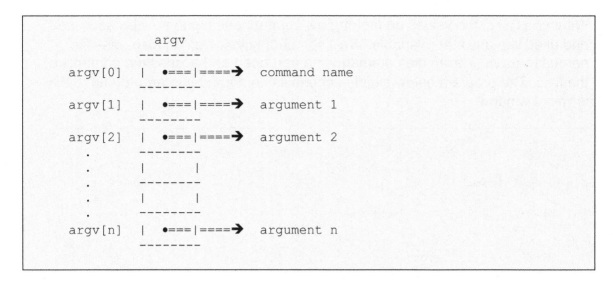

By convention:

`argc`   is at least one

`argv[0]`   is the name of the command itself (the name by which the program was invoked

`argv[1]`   points to the first argument string

`argv[2]`   points to the second argument string, etc

`argv[argc]` is always the last element of the array and always contains a null pointer

For example, if we were to execute a program, `foo`, with two arguments:

```
foo arg1 arg2
```

the program will receive a value for `argc` equal to 3 and `argv` will look like:

```
              argv
              --------
argv[0]      |  •===|====➔   foo
              --------
argv[1]      |  •===|====➔   arg1
              --------
argv[2]      |  •===|====➔   arg2
              --------
argv[argc]   | null |
              --------
```

Within `main()`, the values on the original command-line can now be accessed and used like any other variable. We'll see shortly that we can also pass file names to `main()` from the command-line and open and access the contents of the files. The program below simply echoes its command-line arguments to the terminal window:

```c
// echo1.c

#include <stdio.h>

int main(int argc, char *argv[]) {
    int i;

    for(i = 1; i < argc; i++) {
        printf("%s ", argv[i]);
    }
    printf("\n");
return 0;
}
```

Since `argv` is a pointer to an array of pointers, we can rewrite the above program without using array indexing:

```c
// echo2.c

#include <stdio.h>

int main(int argc, char *argv[]) {
    while(--argc > 0) {
        printf("%s ", *++argv);
    }
    printf("\n");
}
```

Since `argv` is a pointer to the beginning of the array of argument strings, incrementing it by 1, `++argv`, makes it point at `argv[1]` instead of `argv[0]`. Each successive iteration moves it along to the next argument. `*argv` is then the pointer to that argument. When `argc` becomes 0, there are no arguments left.

The program below passes a file name on the command-line to `main()` and capitalizes and displays all letters in the file:

```
// caps.c

#include <stdio.h>
#include <stdlib.h>
#include <ctype.h>

int main(int argc, char *argv[]) {
    int c;
    FILE *fp;

    fopen_s(&fp, argv[1], "r");
    if (fp == NULL) {
        puts("Could not open file. ");
        exit(1);
    }
    while((c = getc(fp)) != EOF) {
        if(islower(c)) {
            putchar(toupper(c));
        }
        else {
            putchar(c);
        }
    }
    fclose(fp);
    return 0;
}
```

Our final example shows how flags can be used to modify commands. The flags are usually preceded by a hyphen and occur as the second argument on the command-line. The program below outputs its command-line arguments and if the flag -c is present, the arguments will be output in capital letters; otherwise the arguments will be output as they appear on the command-line. Note that the argument that contains the flag will not be output.

```c
// flag.c

#include <stdio.h>
#include <string.h>

int main(int argc, char *argv[]) {
    int i = 1, flag = 0;

    if (!strcmp(argv[1], "-c")) {
        flag = 1;
        i = 2;
    }
    for ( ; i < argc; ++i) {
        if (flag) {
            strupr(argv[i]);
            printf("%s ", argv[i]);
        }
    }
    printf("\n");
    return 0;
}
```

Variable Length Argument List: Advanced

It is possible to create functions that receive an unspecified number of arguments! In fact, `printf()` takes a variable number of arguments. As a minimum, `printf()` must receive a string as its first argument, but can receive any number of additional arguments. The actual function prototype for `printf()` is:

```
int printf(char *fmt, ...);
```

The declaration `...` (ellipse) means that the number and types of these arguments may vary. The function may receive a variable number of arguments of any type. This declaration can only appear at the end of an argument list.

Declaring a function with a variable number of arguments can provide us great flexibility. Consider a function `average()` that can find the average of a variable number of arguments. It might be invoked as follows:

```
avg = average(a, b, c);

avg = average(a, b, c, d);
```

The secret to handling a variable number of arguments in C lies in the way arguments are passed to a function. Let's take a look at the contents of the stack at the moment a C function is entered. When a function is called, the arguments followed by the return address are placed on the stack:

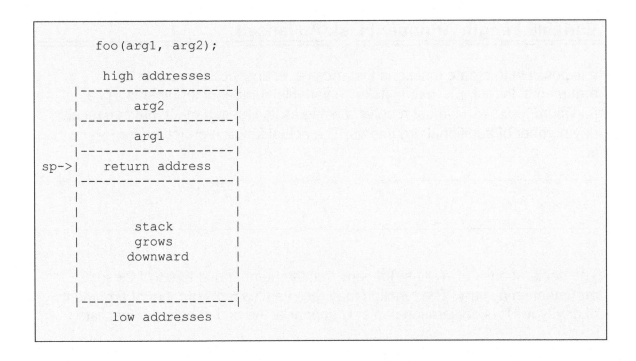

```
        foo(arg1, arg2);

        high addresses
      |----------------------|
      |         arg2         |
      |----------------------|
      |         arg1         |
      |----------------------|
sp->| return address         |
      |----------------------|
      |                      |
      |                      |
      |       stack          |
      |       grows          |
      |     downward         |
      |                      |
      |                      |
      |                      |
      |----------------------|
        low addresses
```

In C, the arguments of the functions are placed on the stack in the reverse order they appear in the function call. The result is that the first argument is always at a fixed offset from the stack pointer, sp. The offset is the number of bytes needed to store the return address. So no matter how many arguments are passed to a C function, the first argument is always easily reachable.

So upon entry to the C function, the first argument appears on the stack just above the return address, i.e., it has the next higher address. Additional arguments have successively higher addresses. Therefore, if you could get to the first argument on the stack and you know the size of all the other arguments, you could then retrieve the arguments one by one!

There is a standard C header file, stdarg.h, that contains a set of macros along with a newly defined data type that makes the task of handling a variable number of arguments straightforward. The implementation of this header file will vary from machine to machine, but the interface it presents is uniform. The first thing that stdarg.h contains is the definition of a new data type:

```
va_list
```

that is used to declare a variable that will refer to each argument in turn:

```
va_list ap;
```

We declare ap to be an argument pointer of type va_list. ap will be used by the other macros to process the variable-length argument list, i.e., ap will point to each argument in turn.

va_start is a macro which initializes the argument pointer, ap, to point to the first unnamed argument on the stack being passed to the function. va_start must be called once before ap is used to access any of the unnamed arguments.

The prototype for va_start is:

```
void va_start(va_list ap, lastarg);
```

The first argument, ap, is the argument pointer. The second argument, lastarg, is the name of the last fixed function parameter being passed to the called function. This is the rightmost argument in the argument list before the ellipse (...). Note that there must be at least one named argument to the function va_arg is a macro that advances the argument pointer, ap, to the next argument on the stack.

The first time va_arg is used, it returns the first argument in the list. Each successive time va_arg is used, it returns the next argument in the list. It does this by first dereferencing ap, and then incrementing ap to point to the following item.

The prototype for va_arg is:

```
type va_arg(va_list ap, type);
```

The first argument, ap, is the argument pointer. The second argument, type, represents the type of the value expected in the argument list such as int, double, etc. Note that we can't use char, unsigned char, or float. va_arg uses the type name to both perform the dereference to determine what type to return and to determine how big a step to take to locate the next argument on the stack. The macro returns the value of the argument type.

`va_end` is a macro which does whatever cleanup is necessary to help the called function perform a normal return. It must be called after `va_arg` has read all of the arguments and before the function returns. Failure to do so might cause strange, undefined behavior in your program. `va_end` is prototyped as follows:

```
void va_end(va_list ap);
```

The argument, `ap`, is the argument pointer.

The following program returns the average of a series of numbers. The first argument of the function `average()` is always the number of values to be averaged:

```
// arg1.c

#include <stdio.h>
#include <stdarg.h>

int main(void);
double average(int num, ...);

int main(void) {
    double a = 2.0, b = 4.0, c = 6.0, d = 8.0;

    printf("%5.1f\n", average(2, a, b));
    printf("%5.1f\n", average(3, a, b, c));
    printf("%5.1f\n", average(4, a, b, c, d));
    return 0;
}

double average(int num, ...) {
    int i;

    double total = 0.0;
    va_list ap;

    va_start(ap, num);
    for(i = 1; i <= num; i++) {
        total += va_arg(ap, double);
    }
    va_end(ap);
    return total / num;
}
```

The following program calculates the sum of a zero terminated list:

```
// arg2.c

#include <stdio.h>
#include <stdarg.h>

int main(void);
void sum(char *msg, ...);

int main(void) {
    sum("The total of 1+2+3+4 is %d\n", 1,2,3,4,0);
}

void sum(char *msg, ...) {
    int total = 0, arg;
    va_list ap;

    va_start(ap, msg);
    while ((arg = va_arg(ap,int)) != 0) {
        total += arg;
    }
    printf(msg, total);
    va_end(ap);
}
```

Finally, how does printf() and scanf_s() know what type to use in each va_arg macro? The answer is that they scan the format conversion specifiers in the format control string to determine the type of the next argument to be processed. Kernighan and Ritchie give an implementation of a minimal version of printf() to show how to write a function that processes a variable-length argument list. Its prototype is:

```
void myprintf(char *fmt, …);
```

Since the interest here is in argument passing, myprintf() processes the format string and arguments but calls the real printf() function to do the format conversions:

```
// arg3.c

#include <stdio.h>
#include <stdarg.h>

int main(void);
void myprintf(char *fmt, ...);

int main(void) {
    int x = 5, y = 10;
    float pi = 3.14;
    char *buf = "Hello";

    myprintf("%d %d\n", x, y);
    myprintf("%d %f %s %d\n", x, pi, buf, y);
}

void myprintf(char *fmt, ...) {
    char *p, *sval;
    int ival;
    double dval;
    va_list ap;

    va_start(ap, fmt);
    for(p = fmt; *p; p++) {
        if (*p != '%') {
            putchar(*p);
            continue;
        }
        switch(*++p) {
            case 'd': ival = va_arg(ap, int);
                      printf("%d", ival);
                      break;
            case 'f': dval = va_arg(ap, double);
                      printf("%f", dval);
                      break;
            case 's': for(sval = va_arg(ap, char *); *sval; sval++)
                          putchar(*sval);
                      break;
            default : putchar(*p);
                      break;
        }
    }
    va_end(ap);
}
```

Data Compression - Advanced

Data compression is the technique of reducing the number of bits needed to store or transmit data. Compression can be either *lossless* or *lossy*. Lossless and lossy compression are terms that describe whether or not all original data can be recovered when a file is uncompressed or a data transmission is received.

With lossless compression, every single bit of data that was originally in the file remains after the file is uncompressed. All of the information is completely restored. This is generally the technique of choice for text or spreadsheet files, where losing words or financial data could pose a problem. The Graphics Interchange File (GIF) is an image format used on the Web that provides lossless compression. Additional lossless compression algorithms are:

```
TIFF - Zip - RAR - FLAC - LZW - Huffman Code - PNG - Morse Code
```

On the other hand, lossy compression reduces a file by permanently eliminating certain information, especially redundant information. When the file is uncompressed, only a part of the original information is still there (although the user may not notice it). Lossy compression is generally used for video and audio, where a certain amount of information loss will not be detected by most users. The JPEG image file, commonly used for photographs and other complex still images on the web, is an image that has lossy compression. Using JPEG compression, the creator can decide how much loss to introduce and make a trade-off between file size and image quality. Additional lossy compression algorithms are:

```
MP3 - JPG - DivX
```

Dictionary Compression

By examining the relationships between successive data items in a dictionary, one can derive an efficient coding scheme to achieve a high level of data compression. The compression technique takes advantage of the fact that words in a dictionary, being in alphabetical order, tend to start with the same letters as their neighboring entries. The compression algorithm works as follows: each word in the compressed dictionary starts with a digit that indicates how many characters should be copied from the preceding word in the dictionary. The rest of the letters for the word follow the digit.

For example, if the original dictionary contained only five words:

```
can<LF>
canal<LF>
cancel<LF>
cancer<LF>
candid<LF>
```

it would be compressed as follows:

```
0can<LF>
3al<LF>
3cel<LF>
5r<LF>
3did<LF>
```

In the encoded version of the dictionary, only those letters appear which do not occur successively in the previous word. The number in front of the trailing end of each word represents the number of characters that are the same. Decoding demands sequential reading so that the preceding word is once again available. The count preceding the word to be decompressed provides the number of leading characters to be retained and the unencoded characters are then concatenated.

In the preceding example, the original dictionary contains 31 characters and the compressed version contains 22, for a space savings of 29%. Additional compression can be realized by reducing the number of newline characters, <LF>, at the end of each line. This can be achieved by outputting the words on one line until a predefined right margin is reached:

```
0can3al3cel5r3did<LF>
```

The compressed dictionary now contains 18 characters for a space savings of 42%. In practice, though, entries in an actual dictionary will be much closer to each other, lexicographically speaking, than those in this example, and the savings greater. With a larger dictionary, the compression ratio exceeds 50%.

A limitation of this dictionary compression scheme is that in order to decompress a word from the dictionary you have to know what the previous word is, whose decompression in turn depends on the next previous word, and so on. In practice, though, dictionary access is not limited to serial searches from the beginning, since the first word starting with a new letter copies no letters from its predecessor. Thus, with 26 pointers into the file, one to the start of the `a`'s through one to the start of the `z`'s, the dictionary can be searched quite rapidly. The pointer scheme may be extended with an index into the start of each two-letter pair (`aa`, `ab`, through `zy`, `zz`) so that even less of the dictionary must be read to look up a given word.

The function below, `compress()`, carries out this compression algorithm on alphabetically ordered ASCII text files with one word per line. The dictionary must be all lower case. The range of digits from 0 to 9 is extended in ASCII sequence with a colon (`:`) interpreted as 10, a semicolon (`;`) interpreted as 11, and so on.

The complementary function, `expand()`, performs the inverse function. It produces an ASCII text file with one word per line from a file that has been compressed by `compress()`.

```
// compress.c

/*
Reads an alphabetized file (one word per line) and writes a compressed
version of the file. Words in the output file are preceded by a count
of characters identical to the previous word plus an offset of 48
(ASCII '0'), and these identical characters are omitted. Multiple words
are output on each line until column MAX_COL is reached. At this point,
the current word is made the last on the line by printing '\n'.
*/

void compress(void) {
    char prev[MAX_CHAR], word[MAX_CHAR], buf[MAX_CHAR];
    char *s, *t;
    int chrcount, linelen = 0;
    FILE *fpIn, *fpOut;

    fopen_s(&fpIn, "dictionary.txt", "r");
    if (fpIn == NULL)) {
        printf("File could not be opened for input.\n");
        exit(1);
    }
    fopen_s(&fpOut, "compressedDictionary.txt", "w");
    if (fpOut == NULL) {
        printf("File could not be opened for output.\n");
        exit(1);
    }
    prev[0] = '\0';
    while (fgets(word, MAX_CHAR, fpIn)) {
        if (strchr(word, '\n')) {
            word[strlen(word)-2] = '\0';
        }
        s = word;
        t = prev;
        chrcount = 0;
        while ((*t != '\0') && (*s++ == *t++)) {
            ++chrcount;
        }
        buf[0] = chrcount + '0';
        buf[1] = '\0';
        strcat(buf, &word[chrcount]);
        fputs(buf, fpOut);
        linelen += 1 + strlen(&word[chrcount]);
        if (linelen >= MAX_COL) {
            linelen = 0;
            fputs("\n", fpOut);
        }
        strcpy(prev, word);
    }
    fclose(fpIn);
    fclose(fpOut);
}
```

```
// expand.c

/*
Reads a compressed file created by compress() and writes a standard
ASCII file, one word per line.
*/

void expand(void) {
    char prev[MAX_CHAR], word[MAX_CHAR];
    int samechr;
    FILE *fpIn, *fpOut;

    fopen_s(&fpIn, "compressedDictionary.txt", "r");
    if (fpIn == NULL) {
        printf("File could not be opened for input.\n");
        exit(1);
    }
    fopen_s(&fpOut, "newDictionary.txt", "w");
    if (fpOut == NULL) {
        printf("File could not be opened for output.\n");
        exit(1);
    }
    prev[0] = '\0';
    while ((samechr = getWord(word, fpIn)) >= 0) {
        strcpy(&prev[samechr], word);
        fputs(prev, fpOut);
        fputs("\n", fpOut);
    }
    fclose(fpIn);
    fclose(fpOut);
}

int getWord(char *t, FILE *fpIn) {
    int c, count;

    while ((c = fgetc(fpIn)) < 'a') {
        count = c - '0';
        if (c == EOF) {
            return (-1);
        }
    }
    ungetc(c, fpIn);
    while ((c = fgetc(fpIn)) >= 'a') {
        *t++ = c;
    }
    ungetc(c, fpIn);
    *t++ = '\0';
    return (count);
}
```

Implementation of `compress()` on a 50,000 word dictionary containing 482,884 bytes results in a file of 185,339 bytes, resulting in a compression of 61.62%.

1. The following function calls supposedly write a single new-line character, but some are incorrect. Identify which calls don't work and explain why.

        a)   `printf("%c", '\n');`

        b)   `printf("%c", "\n");`

        c)   `printf("%s", '\n');`

        d)   `printf("%s", "\n");`

        e)   `printf('\n');`

        f)   `printf("\n");`

        g)   `putchar('\n');`

        h)   `putchar("\n");`

        i)   `puts('\n');`

        j)   `puts("\n");`

        k)   `puts("");`

2. Suppose that `p` has been declared as follows:

    `char *p = "abc";`

Which of the following function calls are legal? Show the output produced by each legal call, and explain why the others are illegal.

        a)   `putchar(p);`

        b)   `putchar(*p);`

        c)   `puts(p);`

        d)   `puts(*p);`

3. Suppose that `str` is an array of characters. Which of the following statements is not equivalent to the other three?

    a)   `*str = 0;`

    b)   `str[0] = '\0';`

    c)   `strcpy(str, "");`

    d)   `strcat(str, "");`

4. What will be the value of the string `s1` after the following statements have been executed?

```
strcpy(s1, "computer");
strcpy(s2, "science");
if (strcmp(s1, s2) < 0)
    strcat(s1, s2);
else
    strcat(s2, s1);
s1[strlen(s1)-6] = '\0';
```

5. The following function supposedly creates an identical copy of a string. What's wrong with the function?

```
char *dup(char *p) {
    char *q;

    strcpy(q, p);
    return q;
}
```

6. What does the following program print?

```
#include <stdio.h>
int main(void) {
    char s[] = "Hello";
    char *p;

    for (p = s; *p; p++)
        --*p;
    puts(s);
    return 0;
}
```

❖ Cipher Lab

The purpose of this short assignment is to give you some practice using characters and Strings. You will create a program, `cipher.c`, which will encode a message by shifting each letter some number of places. Thus, if the shift is 2, then A becomes C, B becomes D, and so on. Like this:

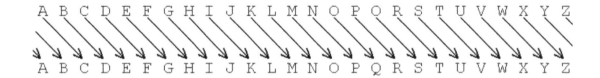

Surprisingly, you can do this by simply doing arithmetic with characters, but you should reassure C that the result is a character using a cast. If, for example, a letter contains the value `'A'`, then `'A' + 2` gives the integer result 67, which you can turn back into a character by saying `(char)(letter + 2)`, giving the value `'C'`.

Unfortunately, `(char)('Z' + 2)` does not give you the letter `'B'` (you can see why from the picture above). But if you realize you went past `'Z'`, you can subtract 26 (so the result is `'Z' + 2 - 26`, or `'Z' - 24`), and this will give you `'B'`.

This also means that if you encode a message with a shift of `n`, you can decode it with another shift of `26 - n`.

Your program should first call a function, `processFile()`, which reads a message from a file (`congress.txt`) into a very large character array. The function should convert all of the letters into uppercase characters. You may discard all the punctuation marks, digits, blanks, and anything else from the input string.

Your program should then accept the amount to shift as an input to a function, `cipher()`. The input parameter should be 13, although for your testing purposes, you can simplify things by using a shift of 1. Your function should encode each letter by shifting it the correct amount, and put the encoded letters into null-terminated array of characters.

Finally, you should create a function, `outputCode()`, which outputs the final encoded message in blocks of five letters, ten blocks per line. The last line may be shorter than five blocks, and the last block may be shorter than five letters.

For example, given a shift of 1, the program should turn this message:

```
Congress shall make no law respecting an establishment of religion, or
prohibiting the free exercise thereof; or abridging the freedom of
speech, or of the press; or the right of the people peaceably to
assemble, and to petition the government for a redress of grievances.
```

into this:

```
DPOHS FTTTI BMMNB LFOPM BXSFT QFDUJ OHBOF TUBCM JTINF OUPGS
FMJHJ POPSQ SPIJC JUJOH UIFGS FFFYF SDJTF UIFSF PGPSB CSJEH
JOHUI FGSFF EPNPG TQFFD IPSPG UIFQS FTTPS UIFSJ HIUPG UIFQF
PQMFQ FBDFB CMZUP BTTFN CMFBO EUPQF UJUJP OUIFH PWFSO NFOUG
PSBSF ESFTT PGHSJ FWBOD FT
```

Be sure that your final program submission shows the result of a shift of 13.

Remember that the `main()` function should appear as the first function in the program. Be sure to use function prototypes for each of the functions that are used in your program.

Output from your program should be sent to the terminal window (your screen) as well as the requested `csis.txt` output file. Be sure to read the document on Capturing Program Output. Your full name must appear as a comment in the source file that contains `main()`. Be sure to include the `csis.txt` output file in your zip archive.

Part I

The first part of this lab is to write a program, `word.c`, which reads words from a file, `getty.txt`, and displays each word on a line by itself. A word is defined as any sequence of characters separated by a blank, a tab, or a newline. Note that this definition for a word considers punctuation as part of the word.

You may use the following while loop which will read the next word from the file into a word buffer, `wbuf`, which is declared in `main()` as a character array:

```
while (!feof(fp)) {
    fscanf_s(fp,"%s",wbuf, sizeof(wbuf));
    ...
    ...
}
```

As each word is returned in the `wbuf` parameter, it is then sent to an output function, `output()`, which displays the contents of `wbuf` to standard output with a plus (+) sign both preceding and following the word:

```
+Four+
+score+
+and+
+seven+
+years+
+ago+
+our+
+fathers+
+brought+
+forth,+      ← Note that the comma is considered part of the word.
```

The plus signs should not be stored within `wbuf`, but should be output just before and just after the contents of `wbuf` are output.

Your output file for this part of the lab should be called `csis1.txt`.

Part II

The second part of this lab is to write a text aligner program, `align.c`. This is a program that attempts to fill the maximum number of words on a line, where a line is 62 characters, without breaking up individual words.

This program will use the `while` loop and character array, `wbuf`, defined in `word.c`, as well as a line buffer, `lbuf`, also declared as a character array in `main()`. This time, as each word is read from the file into `wbuf`, `wbuf` and `lbuf` are sent to `output()` where `wbuf` is placed into `lbuf`, until the line buffer is full, at which point the entire contents of `lbuf` is sent to standard output.

Here's a simple algorithm:

```
While there are more words to be read from the file
    Read the next word into wbuf
    Send wbuf and lbuf to the output() function
    If EOF has been reached and there are words in lbuf that have not
    yet been output
        Output lbuf. End of program.
    Otherwise
        Determine if the word in wbuf will fit into lbuf, being careful
        to allow room for the blank separating words.
        If there is room in lbuf,
            copy the contents of wbuf into lbuf
        Otherwise
            Output the contents of lbuf
            Print a newline to begin the next line
            Clear lbuf
            Copy the contents of wbuf into lbuf
```

Your output file for this part of the lab should be called `csis2.txt`.

Comments

Be sure to error check when opening your files for reading and writing. If the input file does not exist or if the output file cannot be created, your program should generate an error message and exit.

Note that I do not want you to read "lines" of input in your program. This is due to the fact that a line of input may be very long. No restrictions were put on the form of the input file. It would be valid in fact for the input to be all one (very long) line, which could easily overflow the size of `wbuf`. Although there are no long lines in the input files provided, a correct (and useful) program would have to handle them. Therefore, use my `while` loop to read one word at a time from the input file.

Extra Credit

For extra credit you will need to convert your text aligner program into a text formatter program, `format.c`. This is a program that outputs the words of the text on lines that are both left and right justified. Fortunately, we've modularized our program so well that this only involves adding a single new function, `fmt()`, which inserts additional spaces between words in `lbuf` to achieve full justification. This function should be called just prior to sending `lbuf` to standard output.

Each of your programs should run on the file: `getty.txt`.

```
Four score and seven years ago our fathers brought
forth,    upon    this   continent,    a   new   nation,
conceived   in   liberty,    and   dedicated   to    the
proposition that all men are created equal. Now we
are engaged in a great civil war,   testing whether
that nation,  or any nation,  so conceived, and so
dedicated,  can long endure.  We are met here on a
great   battlefield   of  that  war.   We  have  come   to
dedicate a portion of it as a final resting  place
for   those   who   here  gave their  lives  that  that
nation   might  live.   It is altogether fitting  and
proper   that we should do this.  But  in  a  larger
sense  we can not dedicate - we can not consecrate
- we  can not hallow this ground.  The brave  men,
living   and   dead,    who   struggled   here,    have
consecrated  it far above our poor power to add or
detract.  The  world will little  note,   nor  long
remember,   what we say here,   but can never forget
what   they   did  here.  It is for us,   the  living,
rather to be dedicated here to the unfinished work
which they have,  thus far,  so nobly carried on. It
is rather for us to be here dedicated to the great
task   remaining before us that from these  honored
dead we take increased devotion to that cause  for
which  they   here  gave the last full  measure  of
devotion - that we here highly resolve that  these
dead shall not have died in vain; that this nation
shall  have a new birth of freedom;  and that this
government of the people,  by the people,  for the
people,  shall not perish from the earth.
```

Remember that the `main()` function should appear as the first function in the program. Be sure to use function prototypes for each of the functions that are used in your program.

Output from your program should be sent to the terminal window (your screen) as well as the requested `csis1.txt` and `csis1.txt` output files. Be sure to read the document on Capturing Program Output. Your full name must appear as a comment in the source file that contains `main()`. Be sure to include the output files in your zip archive.

❖ Text Statistics Lab

The purpose of this assignment is to give you practice using text and data processing techniques in order to compute some statistics about a file of text. The assignment will also give you a chance to learn more about strings and files and about how to organize a moderate-sized program.

Construct a program, `stats.c`, to examine the characters and words in a data file, `getty.txt`. Your program should perform the following operations:

• Count the number of lines in the text.

• Count the number of words in the text.

• Calculate the average length of all the words in the text.

• Display a histogram of the length of words in the text, i.e., a bar graph such as:

```
1:  2  *  *

2:  6  *  *  *  *  *  *

3:  3  *  *  *

4:  8  *  *  *  *  *  *  *  *
```

to indicate that there are 2 one letter words in the text, 6 two letter words, 3 three letter words, 8 four letter words, etc.

• Count the number of characters in the text, excluding blanks and punctuation.

• Display a table showing the frequency of each letter in the text.

• Count the number of vowels in the text and output the frequency of each vowel as a percentage of the total number of vowels read.

Remember that the `main()` function should appear as the first function in the program. Be sure to use function prototypes for each of the functions that are used in your program.

Output from your program should be sent to the terminal window (your screen) as well as the requested `csis.txt` output file. Be sure to read the document on Capturing Program Output. Your full name must appear as a comment in the source file that contains `main()`. Be sure to include the `csis.txt` output file in your zip archive.

Be sure to do error checking when attempting to open a file for input or output. For extra credit, pass all file names to this lab as *command-line arguments*. Compiler specific information regarding command-line arguments can be found in Canvas at this location:

Files | Set Command-Line Arguments

The contents of `getty.txt` is given below:

```
Four score and seven years ago our fathers brought
forth,    upon    this continent,    a    new    nation,
conceived    in    liberty,    and    dedicated    to    the
proposition that all men are created equal. Now we
are engaged in a great civil war,    testing whether
that nation,    or any nation,    so conceived, and so
dedicated,    can long endure.    We are met here on a
great    battlefield    of that war.    We have come    to
dedicate a portion of it as a final resting    place
for    those    who    here gave their lives    that    that
nation    might live.    It is altogether fitting    and
proper    that we should do this.    But in    a    larger
sense    we can not dedicate - we can not consecrate
- we    can not hallow this ground.    The brave    men,
living    and    dead,    who    struggled    here,    have
consecrated    it far above our poor power to add or
detract.    The    world will little    note,    nor    long
remember,    what we say here,    but can never forget
what    they    did here.    It is for us,    the    living,
rather to be dedicated here to the unfinished work
which they have, thus far, so nobly carried on. It
is rather for us to be here dedicated to the great
task    remaining before us that from these    honored
dead we take increased devotion to that cause    for
which    they    here    gave the last full    measure    of
devotion - that we here highly resolve that    these
dead shall not have died in vain; that this nation
shall    have a new birth of freedom;    and that this
government of the people,    by the people,    for the
people, shall not perish from the earth.
```

For more practice with command-line arguments, write a program, `grep.c`, which searches a file, or a group of files, for a pattern and outputs each line of the file that contains an instance of the pattern. Your program should prefix the filename to each line that matches, so you can tell in which file the match takes place.

The syntax for the `grep` command is:

```
grep   [option]   pattern   file(s)
```

where `option` consists of one or more single characters preceded by a hyphen, `pattern` consists of the text to search for, and `file(s)` tells `grep` which file or files to search.

The following options should be recognized:

`-v`   **Non-match:** Only non-matching lines are printed. Only lines that do not contain the search string are considered to be non-matching lines.

`-i`   **Ignore case:** `grep` ignores upper/lowercase differences. `grep` treats all letters a-z as being identical to the corresponding letters A-Z in all situations.

`-n`   **Numbers:** Each matching line that `grep` prints is preceded by its relative line number in the file.

`-c`   **Count only:** Only a count of matching lines is printed. For each file that contains at least one matching line, `grep` prints the file name and a count of the number of matching lines. Matching lines are not printed.

`-l`   **List match files:** Only the name of each file containing a match is printed. After `grep` finds a match, it prints the filename and processing immediately moves on to the next file.

Note that matches will not cross line boundaries (i.e., a match must be contained on a single line). Be sure to include appropriate error checking routines in case the requested files do not exist.

Using the three files shown below, show the output generated for each of the following commands:

```
grep the genesis.txt
grep the getty.txt genesis.txt shakes.txt
grep hello getty.txt genesis.txt shakes.txt
grep the genesis.txt foo.txt shakes.txt
grep -v the getty.txt
grep -i and shakes.txt
grep -n the genesis.txt shakes.txt
grep -c the getty.txt shakes.txt genesis.txt
grep -l in getty.txt shakes.txt genesis.txt
```

Here are the contents of each of the files:

getty.txt
Four score and seven years ago our fathers brought forth, upon this
continent, a new nation, conceived in liberty, and dedicated to the
proposition that all men are created equal.

shakes.txt
All the world's a stage,
And all the men and women merely players.
They have their exits and their entrances;
And one man in his time plays many parts.

genesis.txt
In the beginning God created the heaven and the earth. Now the earth was
uniform and void, and darkness was upon the face of the earth and the spirit
of God hovered over the face of the waters. And God said: 'Let there be
light.' And there was light. And God saw the light, that it was good; and
God divided the light from the darkness. And God called the light day, and
the morning He called night. And there was evening and there was morning,
one day.

For extra credit, see if you can generalize your program so that it works with
more than one option at a time.

Remember that the `main()` function should appear as the first function in the
program. Be sure to use function prototypes for each of the functions that are
used in your program.

Output from your program should be sent to the terminal window (your screen) as well as the requested `csis.txt` output file. Be sure to read the document on Capturing Program Output. Your full name must appear as a comment in the source file that contains `main()`. Be sure to include the `csis.txt` output file in your zip archive.

Part 1

We have recently developed a NetNews reader for the campus wide bulletin board system. However, one part of the reader still needs to be completed. It is necessary to include an encryption scheme that uses simple substitution to allow private communications.

The encryption scheme is known as `ROT13` because it "rotates" each alphabetic character half-way around the alphabet (`'a'` becomes `'n'`, `'b'` becomes `'o'`, `'n'` becomes `'a'`, and so forth). Case is maintained. All white space, punctuation, numbers, etc., remain the same.

Write a program that takes an arbitrary amount of text from standard input, applies the `ROT13` transformation, and write it to standard output. No input or output line will exceed 80 characters.

```
Sample input:    This is 1 line to be rotated.
                 Guvf vf 1 yvar gb or ebgngrq.

Sample output:   Guvf vf 1 yvar gb or ebgngrq.
                 This is 1 line to be rotated.
```

Part 2

Write a program that asks the user to input a string password of arbitrary length. Then encode the password in the following way. Alternate placement of the vowels (`'a'`, `'e'`, `'i'`, `'o'`, `'u'`) so that the first vowel is moved to the front of the password, the second is moved to the rear, the third to the front, the fourth to the rear, etc. Encoding should stop when the last character of the input string has been examined. Print out the encoded password.

```
Sample input:    computer science
                 olympiad

Sample output:   eeocmptr scncuie
                 aolympdi
```

Remember that the `main()` function should appear as the first function in the program. Be sure to use function prototypes for each of the functions that are used in your program.

Output from your program should be sent to the terminal window (your screen) as well as the requested `csis.txt` output file. Be sure to read the document on Capturing Program Output. Your full name must appear as a comment in the source file that contains `main()`. Be sure to include the `csis.txt` output file in your zip archive.

❖ String Manipulation Lab

Write a program that contains the following:

A function that replaces the contents of a string with the string reversed.

A function that takes a string as an argument and removes the spaces from the string.

A function that outputs the command-line arguments in reverse order.

Remember that the main() function should appear as the first function in the program. Be sure to use function prototypes for each of the functions that are used in your program.

Output from your program should be sent to the terminal window (your screen) as well as the requested csis.txt output file. Be sure to read the document on Capturing Program Output. Your full name must appear as a comment in the source file that contains main(). Be sure to include the csis.txt output file in your zip archive.

Chapter 14. Storage Class

Storage Class
Storage Location
❖ Storage Class Homework

Storage Class

Every variable in C has two attributes, *storage type* and *storage class*. Storage type determines the meaning of values. Storage class determines storage location, lifetime and visibility or scope (region where a variable may be referenced.) There are four storage classes: *automatic (local), external, register and static.*

Automatic Variables

Automatic or local variables are the most common type of storage class. Variables declared within function bodies are, by default, automatic or local. These variables are known only within the function in which they are declared. As far as any other function is concerned, they don't exist.

Local variables are recreated each time the function is called and values from the previous calls will not be retained. Local variables may be given values in their declarations:

```
void foo(void) {
    int num = 5;
```

Note that automatic or local variables may be declared not only at the start of a function, but also at the start of a block:

```
// storage1.c

void foo(void) {
    char x;
    int num;
    ...
    ...
    if (num > 5) {
        int x;
        for (x = 0; x < num; x++) {
            ...
        }
    }
}
```

External Storage Class

When a variable is declared outside a function, storage is permanently assigned to it and its storage class is *external*. It is considered *global* and is visible to all functions declared after it. External variables can be a useful tool to transmit information across blocks and functions.

A declaration for an external variable looks just the same as a variable declaration inside a function or a block:

```
// storage2.c

#include <stdio.h>

int x = 1;
int y = 2;

int main(void) {
    z = foo();
    printf("%d %d %d\n", x, y, z);
}

int foo(void) {
    int y, z;

    x = y = z = 3;
    return x + y + z;
}
```

Output:

```
3   2   9
```

Note that external variables never disappear, but may be hidden if the identifier is redefined.

Information can be passed into a function in two ways: by use of external or global variables (which are not allowed in this class) or by use of parameters. The use of parameters is the preferred method to pass information into a function. It tends to improve the modularity of the code and the possibility of undesirable side effects is reduced.

For example:

```
// storage3.c

int num;

int main(void) {
    num = 0;
    while (num < 3) {
        foo();
        num++;
    }
}

void foo(void) {
    num = 0;
    while (num < 5) {
        puts("Hello.");
        num++;
    }
}
```

See if you can figure out the intent of the code and the output.

We should avoid using unnecessary external or global variables for three reasons:

1. They take up memory during the entire time your program is executing, not just when they are needed.

2. Using an external or global variable where a local variable will do makes your function less general because the function relies on something that must be defined outside of itself.

3. Using a large number of external or global variables can lead to program errors because of unknown and unwanted side effects.

Register Storage Class
Automatic (local) variables can be placed in the actual hardware registers of the computer by declaring them to have register storage class. This permits faster access during program execution. Register storage class is typically used for variables that are referenced often and this is an attempt to improve execution speed.

The syntax is as follows:

```
register type name;
```

Note that only certain data types can be placed in registers:

```
char
short
int
unsigned char
unsigned short
unsigned int
pointer variables as array parameters
```

Note that each machine is limited in the number of registers available for such variables. If a register is not available, this class defaults to automatic. So the implementation of register variables is machine dependent.

Also note that programs may not take the address (&) of a register variable, i.e., we cannot read into a register with `scanf_s()`.

Here's a program that counts to one million:

```
// storage4.c

int main(void) {
    register int units;
    register int thousands;

    thousands = 0;
    while (++thousands <= 1000) {
        units = 0;
        while (++units <= 1000) {
            ;
        }
    }
}
```

Register variables should be declared as close to its place of use as possible to allow maximum availability of the registers. Upon block exit the registers are freed.

Static Storage Class

Static storage class allows us to control whether the local variables retain their values between function calls. A static variable within a function is a local variable that retains its values from previous calls to that function. They are created the first time that a function is called and are not destroyed when the function is exited.

For example:

```c
void foo(void) {
    static int num = 0;
    ...
    ...
}
```

The value of `num` will be initialized to 0 only once when program execution begins. Here's a program to illustrate static and automatic variables:

```c
// storage5.c

int main(void) {
    int i;

    for (i = 0; i < 5; ++i) {
        foo();
    }
}

void foo(void) {
    int autoVar = 0;
    static int staticVar = 0;

    printf("Automatic = %d  Static = %d\n", autoVar, staticVar);
    ++autoVar;
    ++staticVar;
}
```

Output:

```
Automatic = 0     Static = 0
Automatic = 0     Static = 1
Automatic = 0     Static = 2
Automatic = 0     Static = 3
Automatic = 0     Static = 4
```

Note that the static variable, `staticVar`, is initialized once and keeps its value between function calls.

So a static variable is a variable that is only seen within the function in which it is defined (like a local variable) but whose lifetime is that of the entire program (like a global variable).

Initializing Arrays In Static Storage

C does not allow for the initialization of automatic (local) arrays. Only static or external arrays may be initialized with a list of values. Therefore, to initialize an array, it's best to declare the array as `static`.

If a static array is used within a function, then the initial values will be assigned to the array only once. Any changes made to the array elements will remain in effect throughout the execution of the program.

Here are some examples of initializing arrays in static storage:

```
// storage6.c

static short digits[10] = { 0,1,2,3,4,5,6,7,8,9 };

static char msg[6] = "Hello";
```

Note that a character string always includes a null terminator (`'\0'`) at the end.

If the array bound is greater than the number of initializers, the extra elements are initialized to 0, If no bound is given, the bound is taken to be the number of initializers.

Note that static and external variables that are not initialized will automatically be initialized to 0. Automatic and register variables that are not initialized will have unpredictable results!

A T T R I B U T E	AUTO	EXTERN	STATIC		REGISTER
			EXTERN	INTERN	
Retain value upon leaving block	NO	YES	YES	YES	NO
Available to multiple functions	NO	YES	YES	NO	NO
Available to other source files	NO	YES	NO	NO	NO
Zero default when not initialized	NO	YES	YES	YES	NO
Initialized once at compile time	NO	YES	YES	YES	NO
Initialize arrays and structures	NO	YES	YES	YES	NO
Variables in machine registers	NO	NO	NO	NO	YES

The table is headed **STORAGE CLASS**.

Storage Location

C divides memory into four separate locations: Stack, Heap, Data Area, Code Area.

High Memory

```
┌─────────────────────────────────────────────┐
│ Stack (changes size freely)                   │
│ • C maintains stack for us                    │
│ • automatic variables                         │
│ • pass parameters to functions                │
│ • store return addresses                      │
│ • set up at top of available memory and grows │
│ towards lower memory as it is filled          │
├─────────────────────────────────────────────┤
│                      │                        │
│                      ▼                        │
│                      ▲                        │
│                      │                        │
├─────────────────────────────────────────────┤
│ Heap (changes size freely)                    │
│ • allocating and using memory on heap         │
│ is our responsibility (malloc)                │
│ • starts in low memory and grows towards      │
│ higher memory                                 │
├─────────────────────────────────────────────┤
│ Data Area (fixed in size)                     │
│                                               │
│ • Uninitialized data                          │
│ • uninitialized static and external variables │
│ • all initialized to zero at once             │
│ - - - - - - - - - - - - - - - - - - - - - - - │
│ • Initialized data                            │
│ • initialized static and external variables   │
│ • initialized arrays and structures           │
├─────────────────────────────────────────────┤
│ Code Area (fixed in size)                     │
│ • program code                                │
│ • not changed when program runs               │
└─────────────────────────────────────────────┘
```

Low Memory

1. Answer each of the following questions with `auto`, `extern`, `register`, and//or `static`.

a) Which storage class is used primarily to indicate that a variable or function can be shared by several files?

b) Suppose that a variable x is to be shared by several functions in one file but hidden from functions in other files. Which storage class should x be declared to have?

c) Which storage classes can affect the storage duration of a variable?

2. Given function `foo()` below:

```
int foo(int i) {
    static int j = 0;
    return i * j++;
}
```

a) What will be the value of `foo(10)` if `foo()` has never been called before?

b) What will be the value of `foo(10)` if `foo()` has been called five times previously?

Chapter 15. Preprocessor

Preprocessor
* ❖ Preprocessor Homework
* ❖ Preprocessor Lab

Preprocessor

The C preprocessor is a simple tool that processes the source code of a C program before the compiler parses the source code. Sometimes the preprocessor is actually a separate program that reads the original source file and writes a new "preprocessed" source file that can then be used as input to the C compiler. The C preprocessor provides facilities for defining *macros, file inclusion, conditional compilation.*

#include

Lines that begin with a # in column 1 are called control lines which communicate with the preprocessor. The syntax for control lines is independent of the rest of the C language. A control line of the form:

```
#include "filename"
```

causes the preprocessor to replace the line with a copy of the contents of the named file. A search for the file is made first in the current directory and then in standard places. With the control line of the form:

```
#include <filename>
```

the preprocessor looks for the file only in the standard places and not in the current working directory.

An include file can contain other control lines, which will be expanded by the preprocessor:

#define

#define is used at the beginning of a program to define a symbolic name or symbolic constant to be a particular string of characters. The compiler will replace all unquoted occurrences of the name by the corresponding string. Use of #define makes program constants easier to read and allows a programmer to specify constants in a way to make it easier to change later.

Control lines with #define are called *macros* and can occur in two forms, macros without arguments and macros with arguments.

Macros Without Arguments: `#define identifier string`

The preprocessor replaces every occurrence of `identifier` with `string` in the remainder of the file, except in quoted strings.

```
#define MAXINT 2147483647
```

Note that there are no semicolons at the end of the macro. Macros are not recognized within character constants, string constants, or comments.

`#define` improves program readability and portability:

```
// macro1.c

#define PI       3.14159
#define FALSE    0
#define TRUE     1
#define BUFSIZE 512
#define FOREVER for(;;)
```

By convention, capital letters are used for identifiers in simple `#define` constants to allow the reader of a program to readily identify text that will be expanded by the preprocessor.

A collection of commonly used `#define` constants can be entered once into a file, `local.h`, and can be brought into a C source program using a `#include`:

```
#include "local.h"
```

Text inside a string or character constant does not get replaced by the preprocessor.

For example:

```
#define BLANK
```

The string:

```
"abcBLANKdef"
```

will be left unchanged. But:

```
"abc"BLANK"def"
```

is expanded to:

```
"abc""def"
```

Macros With Arguments: `#define identifier(arg1, arg2, …) string`
Note that there can be no space between the identifier and the left parenthesis of
the argument:

```
// macro2.c

#define SQ(x) ((x) * (x))
```

So:

```
SQ(7 + w)
```

expands to:

```
((7+w) * (7+w))
```

The use of parentheses is to protect against the macro expanding an expression that would then lead to an unanticipated order of evaluation. For example, if we defined the macro as:

```
// macro3.c

#define SQ(x) x * x
```

then:

```
SQ(a + b)
```

expands to:

```
a + b * a + b
```

which, because of operator precedence, is not the same as:

```
((a + b) * (a + b))
```

We would even run into errors if we defined the macro as:

```
// macro4.c

#define SQ(x) (x) * (x)
```

How would this macro expand the following expression:

```
4 / SQ(2)
```

This would expand to:

```
4 / (2) * (2)
```

which is not quite what we anticipated, which was this:

```
4 / ((2) * (2))
```

So if an operand appears in a macro definition, it's best to use parentheses.

Macros Within Macros

We can even define a macro by using other macros:

```
// macro5.c

#define SQ(x)      x * x
#define SQ(x)      (x) * (x)
#define SQ(x)      ((x) * (x))
#define CUBE(x)    (SQ(x) * (x))
#define FIFTH(x)   (CUBE(x) * SQ(x))
```

The preprocessor expands each #define identifier until no more appear in the text. Here's the macro expansion for FIFTH(2):

```
FIFTH(2)

(CUBE(2) * SQ(2))

((SQ(2) * (2)) * ((2) * (2)))

((((2) * (2)) * (2)) * ((2) * (2)))
```

Macros Can Replace Function Calls

Macros are frequently used to replace function calls by in-line code that is more efficient. For example, a macro `MIN()` could be used in a program instead of a function `min()`, where the macro definition is given by:

```
// macro6.c

#define MIN(x,y) (((x) < (y)) ? (x) : (y))
```

Therefore the call:

```
m = MIN(a, b);
```

gets correctly expanded by the preprocessor to:

```
m = (((a) < (b)) ? (a) : (b));
```

Here are some additional examples of how macros can replace function calls:

```
// macro7.c

#define MAX(x,y) (((x) > (y)) ? (x) : (y))

#define ABS(x) (((x) < 0) ? -(x) : (x))
```

Of course we must be careful that the macro arguments do not contain any side-effects. For example:

```
ABS(++n)
```

would expand to:

```
(((++n) < 0) ? -(++n) : (++n))
```

thus incrementing n twice!

Fun With Macros

You can also have some fun with macros. For example:

```
// macro8.c

#define print(x) printf("%d\n", x)
```

will expand:

```
print(5);
```

to the following:

```
printf("%d\n", 5)
```

Here are some additional macros to explore:

```
// macro9.c

#define print3(x,y,z) printf("x = %d\t y = %d\t z = %d\n", x, y, z);
```

How would this expand using the above macro definition?

```
print3(2, 4, 6);
```

Here's a macro that swaps it's two `int` arguments:

```
// macro10.c

#define SWAP(x,y) { int z; z = y; y = x; x = z; }
```

Here's another macro that swaps its two `int` arguments:

```
// macro11.c

#define SWAP(x,y) { x^=y, y^=x; x^=y; }
```

I'll give extra credit to the first student who can post a correct explanation of this code in the Open Discussion Forum!

Macros vs. Functions

So we see similarities between macros with arguments and functions. Which should we use? Well, there is a tradeoff between time and space. A macro produces "in-line" code, i.e., you get a statement in your program. If you use the macro 20 times, then you get 20 lines of code inserted into your program.

If you use a function 20 times, you have just one copy of the function statements in your program, so less space is used. But program control must shift to where the function is, then return back to the calling program, and this takes longer than executing in-line code. The general rule is to get your program working correctly first without defining any macro functions (i.e., macros with arguments). Then introduce them later, if you need the speed advantage.

1. Write a preprocessor directive to accomplish each of the following:

a) Define symbolic constant TRUE to have the value 1.

b) Define symbolic constant FALSE to have the value 0.

c) If symbolic constant YES is defined, undefine it and redefine it as 1.

d) Define a macro, AREA, that takes a single argument and computes the area of a square.

e) Define macro SUM that will sum two numbers.

f) Define macro MIN2 that will determine the smallest of two numeric values.

2. Write a macro that computes the remainder when n is divided by 4.

3. Let DOUBLE be the following macro:

```
#define DOUBLE(x)  2*x
```

    a) What is the value of DOUBLE(1+2)?

    b) What is the value of 4/DOUBLE(2)?

    c) Fix the definition of DOUBLE.

4. For each of the following macros, give an example that illustrates a problem with the macro and show how to fix it.

    a)   `#define AVG(x, y)    (x+y)/2`

    b)   `#define AREA(x, y)   (x) * (y)`

In this assignment we will construct a simple C preprocessor, `pre.c`, that will prepare a C program, `test.c`, for compilation. The preprocessor will parse the source code in `test.c` and create an output file, `out.c`, containing the preprocessed code. The contents of `out.c` should then be output, compiled and executed.

The preprocessor should perform the following operations:

• Remove all comments from the source code.

• Recognize the `#include` preprocessor command and insert the contents of the named file into `out.c`.

• Recognize the `#define` preprocessor command and substitute all symbolic names with their corresponding replacement strings.

To assist in the processing of the `#define` commands, we will use the following scheme:

Each defined symbol, along with its replacement string identified in `test.c`, should be placed in a file, `define.txt`. As each token is read from the source code, `test.c`, it must then be checked against the contents of `define.txt` in order to determine whether or not the token is a predefined symbol. If it is, the appropriate replacement string must be placed into `out.c`. Otherwise, the token itself is placed in `out.c`.

To prevent our having to compare each token against the contents of `define.txt`, we will utilize a simple hash table with each location initialized to 0. For each `#defined` symbol encountered, we will get its hash, set the contents of the appropriate location in the hash table to 1, and send the symbol and its replacement string to `define.txt`. For every other token in `test.c`, we must also get its hash and check its particular location in the hash table. If a 0 is found, the token is not a predefined symbol and should be placed into `out.c`. If, however, the token hashes to a location that contains a 1, it is possible that token is a predefined symbol. We must then search `define.txt` for that token. If a match is found, the replacement string should be placed in `out.c`, otherwise, the token itself should be placed in `out.c`.

Note that your program should not rely on file redirection but should utilize the I/O functions provided by the standard C library to set up and use external disk files.

Remember that the `main()` function should appear as the first function in the program. Be sure to use function prototypes for each of the functions that are used in your program.

Output from your program should be sent to the terminal window (your screen) as well as the requested `csis.txt` output file. Be sure to read the document on Capturing Program Output. Your full name must appear as a comment in the source file that contains `main()`. Be sure to include the `csis.txt` output file in your zip archive.

```c
test.c

#include <header.h>

#define TOTAL x + y
#define MESSAGE "ON A CLEAR DAY YOU CAN C FOREVER"
#define FORMAT1 "%s\n"
#define FORMAT2 "%d %d\n"

int main(void) {
    int x, y, z, i, sum;

    printf(FORMAT1, MESSAGE);
    printf(NEWLINE);

    sum = ZERO;
    for (i = MIN; i <= MAX; ++i) {
        sum += i;
    }
    x = MAX;
    y = MIN;
    z = TOTAL;
    printf(FORMAT2, sum, z);
    return 0;
}


header.h

#define MAX 30
#define MIN 20
#define ZERO 0
#define NEWLINE "\n"
```

Chapter 16. Enumerations & Typedef Statement

Enumerations
Typedef Statement
❖ Enumerations & Typedef Homework

Enumerations

When a data type will hold one of a limited list of values, you can choose to use an *enumerated data type*. A variable of an enumerated type may be assigned any "value" within its type.

```
// enum1.c

enum Day { Sat, Sun, Mon, Tues, Wed, Thurs, Fri };
enum Gender { male, female };

int main (void) {
    enum Day today = Wed;
    enum Day tomorrow = Thurs;
    enum Gender student = female;
    ...
}
```

Enumerated values are treated as constants by C compilers and each one is given an integer value, starting with 0. When we say `today = Wed;` the value of 4 is assigned to `today` and not the name `Wed`.

Variables with enumerated types can also be used in Boolean expressions:

```
if (student == female) {
    printf("female");
}
```

The other relational operators can also be used. Note that enumerating a data type automatically establishes order among the elements:

```c
// enum2.c

#include <stdio.h>

enum Day { Sat, Sun, Mon, Tues, Wed, Thurs, Fri };

int main (void) {
    enum Day today;

    for (today = Sat; today <= Fri; ++today) {
        if (today < Mon) {
            printf("Weekend\n");
        }
        else {
            printf("Weekday\n");
        }
    return 0;
}
```

Output:

```
Weekend
Weekend
Weekday
Weekday
Weekday
Weekday
Weekday
```

Suppose you wanted to output the different values of variable `today` while iterating through the `for` loop. You could try this.

```
// enum3.c

#include <stdio.h>

enum Day { Sat, Sun, Mon, Tues, Wed, Thurs, Fri };

int main (void) {
    enum Day today;

    for (today = Sat; today <= Fri; ++today) {
        printf("%d\n", today);
    }
    return 0;
}
```

But your output would look like this:

```
0
1
2
3
4
5
6
```

It turns out that values of an enumerated type cannot be written directly to output. A switch statement is normally used to achieve the desired result.

```
// enum4.c

#include <stdio.h>

enum Day { Sat, Sun, Mon, Tues, Wed, Thurs, Fri };

int main (void) {
    enum Day today;

    for (today = Sat; today <= Fri; ++today) {
        switch (today) {
            case Sat:   puts("Sat");    break;
            case Sun:   puts("Sun");    break;
            case Mon:   puts("Mon");    break;
            case Tues:  puts("Tues");   break;
            case Wed:   puts("Wed");    break;
            case Thurs: puts("Thurs");  break;
            case Fri:   puts("Fri");    break;
        }
    }
    return 0;
}
```

Output:

```
Sat
Sun
Mon
Tues
Wed
Thurs
Fri
```

There is no Boolean (true or false) data type in C. The integer values of 0 and 1 are used instead. However, it's easy to invent our own Boolean type:

```
// enum5.c

enum Boolean { false, true };
enum Boolean flag;
flag = true;

or as

enum Boolean { false, true } flag;
flag = false;
```

One annoying aspect of `enum` types is that they are not recognized by C input-output statements. For example:

```
// enum6.c

enum direction { north, south, east, west };

direction d1 = south;
printf("%d\n", south);
```

The value 1 gets output.

If it is desired to have a specific integer value associated with an enumerated value, then the integer can be assigned to the value when the data type is defined. Enumerated values that subsequently appear in the list will be assigned sequential values beginning with the specified integer value plus 1.

For example:

```
// enum7.c

enum direction { up, down, left = 10, right };
```

Each of the enumerated values will have the following numeric values:

```
up = 0
down = 1
left = 10
right = 11
```

The name of the data type can be omitted when defining an enumerated data type. Variables can also be declared to be of the particular enumerated data type when the data type is defined:

```
// enum8.c

enum { east, west, south, north } location;
```

Note that defining an enumerated data type within a function restricts the usage of that definition to variables defined within the function. Defining an enumerated data type at the beginning of the program, outside any function, makes the type definition global to the file.

Typedef Statement

The `typedef` statement enables a programmer to assign an alternate name to a data type. For example:

```
// typedef1.c

typedef int COUNTER;
```

defines the name COUNTER to be equivalent to the C data type `int`. Variables can now be declared to be of type COUNTER:

```
// typedef2.c

typedef int COUNTER;

COUNTER a, b, c;
```

This provides added readability to the program. Here's another example:

```
// typedef3.c

typedef char *STRING_PTR;
```

defines a name STRING_PTR to be a `char` pointer. We can now define variables to be of type STRING_PTR:

```
// typedef4.c

typedef char *STRING_PTR;

STRING_PTR buffer;
```

will be treated as a character pointer by the C compiler.

Another example:

```
// typedef5.c

typedef char STRING[81];
```

defines a type called STRING which is an array of 81 characters. We can now define variables to be of type STRING as in:

```
// typedef6.c

typedef char STRING[81];

STRING text;
```

This has the effect of defining the variable text to be a character array containing 81 characters and is equivalent to:

```
char text[81];
```

Procedure to Define a New Type Name
1. Write the statement as if a variable of the desired type were being defined.

2. Where the name of the defined variable would normally appear, substitute the new type name.

3. In front of everything, place the keyword typedef.

❖ Enumerations & Typedef Homework

1. a) Declare a tag for an enumeration whose values represent the seven days of the week.

b) Use `typedef` to define a name for the enumeration.

2. Which of the following statements about enumeration constants are true?

a) An enumeration constant may represent any integer specified by the programmer.

b) Enumeration constants have exactly the same properties as constants created using `#define`.

c) Enumeration constants have the values 0, 1, 2, … by default.

d) All constants in an enumeration must have different values.

e) Enumeration constants may be used as integers in expressions.

3. Suppose that `b` and `i` are declared as follows:

```
enum { FASLE, TRUE } b;
int i;
```

Which of the following statements are legal? Which ones are "safe" (always yield a meaningful result)?

a) `b = FALSE;`   d) `i = b;`

b) `b = i;`   e) `i = 2 * b + 1;`

c) `b++;`

4. Suppose that the direction variable is declared as follows:

```
enum { NORTH, SOUTH, EAST, WEST } direction;
```

Let x and y be int variables. Write a switch statement that tests the value of direction, incrementing x if direction is EAST, decrementing x if direction is WEST, incrementing y if direction is SOUTH, and decrementing y if direction is NORTH.

5. What are the integer values of the enumeration constants in each of the following declarations?

a) `enum { NORTH, EAST, SOUTH, WEST };`

b) `enum { DIAMONDS = 5, HEARTS, CLUBS, SPADES };`

c) `enum { MON = 8, TUES, WED, THURS = 14, FRI };`

d) `enum { RED = 5, BLUE, GREEN, YELLOW = 12, BROWN };`

Chapter 17. Structures

Introduction to Structures
Manipulating Entire Structures
Struct Example: Today's Date and Tomorrow's Date
Arrays of Structures
Nesting Structures
❖ Structures Homework
❖ Database Lab

Introduction to Structures

We have previously used arrays to store collections of data of the *same type* (and a specified size) using a single name:

```
int num[10];
```

We learned to reference individual elements of an array using subscripts such as `num[1]` or `num[i]`.

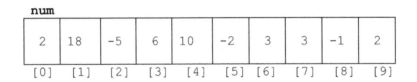

Often, we have a need to create collections of related data of *different types*. For example, if I wanted to collect information about students, I might be interested in the following information:

- The student's name (string of characters)

- The student's gpa (double)

- The student's expected graduation year (integer)

We can model such a collection in C using the data type called a `struct`. A `struct` is an example of a user-defined data type, i.e., we can define our own `struct` to model whatever data we want.

For example:

```
typedef struct {
    char name[30];
    double gpa;
    int year;
} Student;
```

This serves as a blueprint or template for the creation of a new data type called `Student`. This new user-defined data type, `Student`, can be used to declare variables just like any built-in data type:

```
// struct1.c

typedef struct {
    char name[30];
    double gpa;
    int year;
} Student;

int main(void) {
    Student s1, s2, s3;
    ...
    ...
    return 0;
}
```

Our declarations above create three variables of type `Student`: `s1`, `s2`, and `s3`. Each of these variables now has storage in memory for a character string, a `double`, and an `int`. Note that the name of our new data type begins with a capital letter. While it's not required, it's a good rule to follow.

Also note that the `struct` is declared outside of `main()` in the global scope. This allows the `struct` to be visible to all parts of the program. If the `struct` were only declared within `main()`, then it would be local to `main()` and only visible within `main()`.

The structure can be depicted as follows:

	name	gpa	year
s1	Larry	3.85	2016

Referencing elements of a `struct`.

We now have the same problem with structs as we had with arrays. How do we reference individual elements (called components or fields) of a `struct`? With arrays we used subscripts. With structs we use a period, also known as a *direct component selection operator* (or, more simply, the *selection operator*, for short).

For example, we can give values to each of the fields of the `struct` as follows:

```
// struct2.c

s1.gpa = 3.85;
s1.year = 2016;
strcpy(s1.name, "Larry");
```

Example: `Date` structure.

Suppose that we have a need to keep track of various dates. We can define a `Date` data type as follows:

```
// struct3.c

typedef struct {
    int month;
    int day;
    int year;
} Date;
```

Once we have defined a `Date` data type, we can create `Date` variables as follows:

```c
// struct4.c

typedef struct {
    int month;
    int day;
    int year;
} Date;

int main(void) {
    Date yesterday, today, tomorrow, appointment, birthday;
    ...
    ...
    return 0;
}
```

Structure Initialization

Structure initialization is similar to array initialization, except that the data types being initialized may be different for each member. For example:

```c
// struct5.c

Date birthday = { 8, 23, 96 };
```

Note that the elements listed inside the brackets are separated by commas. If there are fewer initializers than members, the remaining members are initialized to zero.

Manipulating Entire Structures

Entire structures can be manipulated, but only in limited ways.

- A `struct` of one type may be assigned to a `struct` of the same type.

- A `struct` may be passed by value or by reference to a function.

- A `struct` may be returned from a function (using the return statement).

Keep in mind, however, that you cannot do things like displaying an entire `struct` or read data into an entire `struct` without using a function to do the work.

Assigning Structures

Structures can be assigned in expressions as follows:

```c
// struct6.c

typedef struct {
    int month;
    int day;
    int year;
} Date;

int main(void) {
    Date today, appt;

    today.month = 5;
    today.day = 27;
    today.year = 2013;
    appt = today;
    ...
    ...
    return 0;
}
```

The statement:

```
appt = today;
```

is equivalent to the following three statements:

```
appt.month = today.month;
appt.day = today.day;
appt.year = today.year;
```

Passing a Structure to a Function by Value

Structures can also be passed as function arguments and returned as function values. When structures are arguments to functions, they are *passed by value*. A local value of the structure is made and all changes are to the local copy. (Note that this implies that arrays can be passed by value by making them a member of a structure.)

```
// struct7.c

#include <stdio.h>

typedef struct {
    int month;
    int day;
    int year;
} Date;

void foo(Date now);

int main(void) {
    Date today = { 5, 27, 2013 };
    foo(today);
    return 0;
}

void foo(Date now) {
    printf("month = %d  day = %d  year = %d\n", now.month,
                                    now.day, now.year);
}
```

Passing a Structure to a Function by Reference

Structures can also be passed to a function by reference. Therefore any changes made to the structure in the function that it was passed to will be reflected back to the calling function.

```
// struct8.c

#include <stdio.h>

typedef struct {
    int month;
    int day;
    int year;
} Date;

void foo(Date *now);

int main(void) {
    Date today = { 5, 27, 2013 };
    printf("month = %d  day = %d  year = %d\n", today.month,
                                        today.day, today.year);
    foo(&today);
    printf("month = %d  day = %d  year = %d\n", today.month,
                                        today.day, today.year);
    return 0;
}

void foo(Date *now) {
    (*now).month = 7;
    (*now).day = 29;
    (*now).year = 2014;
}
```

Here's a look at the output:

```
month = 5  day = 27  year = 2013
month = 7  day = 29  year = 2014
```

Note that if a `struct` is passed by reference, we must use the dereference operator, `*`, to access the value in each of the fields. Because the selection operator (period) has precedence over the dereference operator, we must use parentheses around the name of the structure and the dereference operator.

However, the use of the selection operator (the period) with enclosing parentheses becomes quite awkward and so a new, simpler operator has been added to C for just this purpose. It's referred to as the *arrow operator* and is made up of a hyphen and a greater than symbol: `->`

We can rewrite the function in the above example as follows:

```
// struct9.c

void foo(Date *now) {
    now->month = 7;
    now->day = 29;
    now->year = 2014;
}
```

So the selection operator `(.)` is used to access a member of a `struct`, while the arrow operator `(->)` is used to access a member of a `struct` that is referenced by a pointer.

Struct Example: Today's Date and Tomorrow's Date

Let's construct a program that accepts as input today's date and outputs tomorrow's date. We can develop a general algorithm for the flow of control of the program as follows:

```
Input todays date.
Calculate tomorrow's date.
Output today's date.
Output tomorrow's date.
```

As our program will be working with dates, it seems natural to model the concept of a date into our program by creating a new data type, `Date`, which will allow us to create multiple `Date` structures.

```c
// date1.c

typedef struct {
    int month;
    int day;
    int year;
} Date;
```

Our algorithm above now becomes the code for our `main()` function:

```c
// date2.c

#include <stdio.h>

int main(void) {
    Date today, tomorrow;

    getTodaysDate(&today);
    getTomorrowsDate(today, &tomorrow);
    printf("Today: ");
    outputDate(today);
    printf("Tomorrow: ");
    outputDate(tomorrow);
    return 0;
}
```

Let's first work on our I/O functions. Note that we've created a `Date` struct called `today` that will hold today's date. We must pass this `struct` by reference to the `getTodaysDate()` function that will prompt the user for the current month, day, and year.

```
// date3.c

void getTodaysDate(Date *today) {
    printf("Enter today's date mm/dd/yyyy: ");
    scanf_s("%d/%d/%d", &today->month, &today->day, &today->year);
}
```

Since `today` is defined as a pointer to a `Date` struct, we must use the arrow operator to dereference the `struct` and access each of the components of the `struct`. However, because each of the component variables `today->month`, `today->day`, and `today->year` are being used within a `scanf_s()` statement, we must use the address-of operator `(&)` with each of the variables as `scanf_s()` requires the address of variables.

Note the `scanf_s()` format string for reading in data:

```
"%d/%d/%d"
```

Specifying a non-format character such as `'/'` signals to the `scanf_s()` function that the `'/'` is expected as input. This is shown in the input prompt in the preceding `printf()` statement:

```
mm/dd/yyyy
```

Our output function is simpler as we can pass by value the `Date` struct we wish to output.

```
// date4.c

void outputDate(Date d) {
    printf("%d/%d/%d\n", d.month, d.day, d.year);
}
```

Next is our function to calculate tomorrow's date. We'll have to be careful when today's date falls at the end of a month or at the end of a year. We can easily determine if today's date falls at the end of a month by setting up an array of days in each month.

```
// date5.c

int daysPerMonth[] = {
    31, 28, 31, 30, 31, 30, 31, 31, 30, 31, 30, 31
};
```

A lookup inside the array for a particular month will then give the number of days in that month. For each month `i`, the value contained in `daysPerMonth[i-1]` corresponds to the number of days in that particular month.

If it is determined that today's date falls at the end of the month, then we can calculate tomorrow's date by adding 1 to the month number and setting the value of the day to 1.

```
Increment day.
If day is greater than the number of days in the month
        Set day to 1.
        Increment month.
```

We also must solve the problem of a date occurring at the end of the 12th month. If this is the case, not only must we set the value of the day to 1, we must also set the value of the month to 1 and increment the year by 1.

```
Increment day.
If day is greater than the number of days in the month
        Set day to 1.
        Increment month.
        If month is now greater than 12
                Set month to 1.
                Increment year.
```

We now implement our getTomorrowsDate() function as follows:

```c
// date6.c

void getTomorrowsDate(Date today, Date *tomorrow) {
    int daysPerMonth[] = {
        31, 28, 31, 30, 31, 30, 31, 31, 30, 31, 30, 31
    };

    *tomorrow = today;
    tomorrow->day++;
    if (tomorrow->day > daysPerMonth[tomorrow->month-1]) {
        tomorrow->day = 1;
        ++tomorrow->month;
        if (tomorrow->month > 12) {
            tomorrow->month = 1;
            ++tomorrow->year;
        }
    }
}
```

Note that we pass to the function today by value and we pass tomorrow by reference. Why? We do not wish to modify the contents of today but we do want to update the contents of tomorrow. Look how closely our code follows the algorithm we previously developed.

We have one final issue to deal with. What about leap years? We can use the leap year function we previously developed:

```
// date7.c

int isLeapYear(int year) {
    return ((!(year % 4) && year % 100) || !(year % 400));
}
```

Note how we work the test for leap year into the function:

```
// date8.c

int daysPerMonth[] = {31, 0, 31, 30, 31, 30, 31, 31, 30, 31, 30, 31};

if (isLeapYear(today.year)) {
    daysPerMonth[1] = 29;
}
else {
    daysPerMonth[1] = 28;
}
```

Our complete program looks like this:

```
// date9.c

#include <stdio.h>

typedef struct {
    int month;
    int day;
    int year;
} Date;

int main(void);
void getTodaysDate(Date *today);
void getTomorrowsDate(Date today, Date *tomorrow);
int isLeapYear(int year);
void outputDate(Date d);
```

```
int main(void) {
    Date today, tomorrow;

    getTodaysDate(&today);
    getTomorrowsDate(today, &tomorrow);
    printf("Today: ");
    outputDate(today);
    printf("Tomorrow: ");
    outputDate(tomorrow);
    return 0;
}

void getTodaysDate(Date *today) {
    printf("Enter today's date mm/dd/yyyy: ");
    scanf_s("%d/%d/%d", &today->month, &today->day, &today->year);
}

void getTomorrowsDate(Date today, Date *tomorrow) {
    int daysPerMonth[] = {
        31, 0, 31, 30, 31, 30, 31, 31, 30, 31, 30, 31
    };

    if (isLeapYear(today.year)) {
        daysPerMonth[1] = 29;
    }
    else {
        daysPerMonth[1] = 28;
    }
    *tomorrow = today;
    tomorrow->day++;
    if (tomorrow->day > daysPerMonth[tomorrow->month-1]) {
        tomorrow->day = 1;
        ++tomorrow->month;
        if (tomorrow->month > 12) {
            tomorrow->month = 1;
            ++tomorrow->year;
        }
    }
}

int isLeapYear(int year) {
    return ((!(year % 4) && year % 100) || !(year % 400));
}

void outputDate(Date d) {
    printf("%d/%d/%d\n", d.month, d.day, d.year);
}
```

Note that the definition of the `Date struct` appears in the global space, outside of any function. This allows all functions in the program to see and utilize the user-defined `Date` data type.

Shown below is the output for a few runs of the program:

```
Enter today's date mm/dd/yyyy: 02/28/1984
Today: 2/28/1984
Tomorrow: 2/29/1984


Enter today's date mm/dd/yyyy: 12/31/1999
Today: 12/31/1999
Tomorrow: 1/1/2000


Enter today's date mm/dd/yyyy: 5/31/2013
Today: 5/31/2013
Tomorrow: 6/1/2013
```

Just as we can declare arrays of integers, floats, doubles, etc., we can also declare arrays of structures. For example:

```
// arrayStruct1.c

#define SIZE 25

typedef struct {
    char name[30];
    float gpa;
    int year;
} Student;

int main(void) {
    Student myClass[SIZE];
    ...
    ...
    return 0;
}
```

This defines an array called `myClass` that consists of 1000 `Student` structs. Each element of the array is defined to be of type `Student`. The array might be illustrated as follows:

	name	gpa	year
[0]	Freda	3.75	2015
[1]	Karen	3.85	2016
[2]	Naomi	3.25	2017
...	...	...	...
[24]	Garrett	2.85	2019

The value of `myClass[2].gpa` is 3.25.

The value of `myClass[24].name` is Garrett.

The value of `myClass[0].year` is 2015.

We can now assign values to the different fields of each `myClass struct` as follows:

```
// arrayStruct2.c

myClass[21].year = 2018;
myclass[13].gpa = 3.50;
strcpy(myClass[4].name, "Griffin");
```

Once the array of structs is defined, we can iterate through the array and access each of the structs individually:

```
// arrayStruct3.c

for (i = 0; i < SIZE; ++i) {
    if (myClass[i].gpa > 3.75) {
        printf("Congratulations %s, you have made the honor roll.",
                                            myClass[i].name);
    }
}
```

We can initialize arrays containing structures:

```
// arrayStruct4.c

Student myClass[SIZE] = {
    { "Freda", 3.75, 2015 },
    { "Karen", 3.85, 2016 },
    { "Naomi", 3.25, 2017 },
    { "Garrett", 2.85, 2019 }
};
```

Note that the inner braces are optional.

We can also pass the array of structures to a function:

```c
// arrayStruct5.c

#include <stdio.h>

#define SIZE 4

typedef struct {
    char name[30];
    float gpa;
    int year;
} Student;

int main(void);
void foo(Student myClass[]);

int main(void) {
    Student myClass[SIZE] = {
        { "Freda", 3.75, 2015 },
        { "Karen", 3.85, 2016 },
        { "Naomi", 3.25, 2017 },
        { "Garrett", 2.85, 2019 }
    };
    foo(myClass);
    return 0;
}

void foo(Student myClass[]) {
    int i;

    for (i = 0; i < SIZE; ++i) {
        printf("%10s %5.2f %5d\n",
                myClass[i].name, myClass[i].gpa, myClass[i].year);
    }
}
```

The output to the above program is shown below:

```
    Freda  3.75  2015
    Karen  3.85  2016
    Naomi  3.25  2017
  Garrett  2.85  2019
```

Nesting Structures

C allows us to nest structures, i.e., to define structures within other structures. For example, suppose we want to keep track of the dimensions of various rooms in a house. We can first define a `Distance struct` as follows:

```
// nestingStructs1.c

typedef struct {
    int feet;
    float inches;
} Distance;
```

We can now define a `Room struct` that contains `Distance` variables as its components:

```
// nestingStructs2.c

typedef struct {
    Distance length, width;
} Room;
```

We now initialize each of the fields of the `struct` variables:

```
// nestingStructs3.c

int main(void) {

    Room bedroom, kitchen;

    bedroom.length.feet = 25;
    bedroom.length.inches = 6;
    bedroom.width.feet = 20;
    bedroom.width.inches = 8.5;

    kitchen.length.feet = 15;
    kitchen.length.inches = 3.25;
    kitchen.width.feet = 10;
    kitchen.width.inches = 6;
    return 0;
}
```

Here's another example. Suppose we need to set up a list of events that are to occur at a particular date and time. We want to associate both date and time together within a single entity.

First we define a `Date struct` and a `Time struct`:

```
// nestingStructs4.c

typedef struct {
    int month;
    int day;
    int year;
} Date;

typedef struct {
    int hour;
    int minute;
    int second;
} Time;
```

Now we can define a `DateTime struct` as follows:

```
// nestingStructs5.c

typedef struct {
    Date eventDate;
    Time eventTime;
} DateTime;
```

Let's now create a `DateTime` variable and initialize its components:

```
// nestingStructs6.c

int main(void) {
    DateTime appt;

    appt.eventDate.month = 8;
    appt.eventDate.day = 23;
    appt.eventDate.year = 2013;
    appt.eventTime.hour = 11;
    appt.eventTime.minute = 30;
    appt.eventTime.second = 45;
    return 0;
}
```

If we're implementing a calendar program, we might have a need for many `DateTime` variables. So let's create an array of `DateTime` structs:

```
// nestingStructs7.c

DateTime event[1000];
```

We can now initialize an element of the array as follows:

```
// nestingStructs8.c

event[35].eventDate.month = 7;
event[35].eventDate.day = 14;
event[35].eventDate.year = 2015;
event[35].eventTime.hour = 2;
event[35].eventTime.minute = 15;
event[35].eventTime.second = 00;
```

❖ Structures Homework

1. Write code to accomplish each of the following:

a) Using `typedef`, declare a structure, `Automobile`, with the following members:

       `model` - string of 25 characters maximum
       `year` – integer
       `range` – integer

b) Declare variable `car` to be of type `Automobile`.

c) Assign the information below to the appropriate fields of variable `car`:

       2017 Tesla has a range of 335 miles.

d) Declare an array, `vehicle`, of 500 `Automobile`s.

e) Assign variable `car` to the 5th element of the array.

f) Output the `Automobile` information located in the 5th array location. Show the output.

g) Declare variable `p` to be a pointer to an `Automobile` structure.

h) Assign to variable `p` the address of the 5th array location.

i) Using variable `p`, output the `Automobile` information located in the 5th array location. Show the output.

j) Declare variable `q` to be a pointer to an `Automobile` structure.

k) Assign to variable `q` the address of the first array location.

l) Using variable `q`, output the `Automobile` information located in the 5th array location. Show the output.

❖ Database Lab

This lab will focus on the use and manipulation of structures. Each section of the lab should be designed within its own function, passing parameters as necessary. You are to construct a C program, `database.c`, which will retrieve and manipulate a company's payroll database, `payfile.txt`. The data for each employee should be read into a `struct` containing the following field identifiers:

```
• first      7 characters maximum
• initial    1 character maximum
• last       9 characters maximum
• street     16 characters maximum
• city       11 characters maximum
• state      2 characters maximum
• zip        5 characters maximum
• age        integer
• sex        1 character maximum (M/F)
• tenure     integer representing years of employment
• salary     double representing weekly salary
```

Your program should perform each of the operations indicated below. Be sure to clearly label your output for each section. Remember, each section of the lab should be designed within its own function, passing parameters as necessary.

a) Read data for employees into an array of structures.

b) Output the contents of each structure into an easily read format, similar to the format of the input file.

c) Output the first and last name of all men on the payroll.

d) Output the first and last name of the highest paid woman on the payroll.

e) Output the first and last name of the lowest paid man on the payroll.

f) Output the average salary for all the employees.

g) Output the first and last name of all women earning less than the average salary.

h) Output to three decimal places the ratio of the number of men above the average salary to the number men below the average salary.

i) Output the first and last name of all employees who make more than $35,000 per year, have been with the company for at least 5 years, and who are over 30 years old.

j) Give a 10% raise to all employees who make less than $350.00 per week and output the first and last name and new salary for each of the employees who received the raise.

k) (Extra Credit) Sort the structures according to zip codes and output the first and last name and zip code for each of the employees.

Here is a C function, strsub(), that grabs a substring, sub, from a string, buf, given the start and end index within the string.

```
void strsub(char buf[], char sub[], int start, int end) {
    int i, j;

    for (j=0, i=start; i<=end; i++, j++) {
        sub[j] = buf[i];
    }
    sub[j] = '\0';
}
```

This function might be useful when you read a line of data from the file and need to grab the different information from the line of data to place into the fields of the struct. Remember that arrays use zero-based indexing.

```
while (!feof(fp)) {
    fgets(buf, MAX, fp);
    strsub(buf, workers[i].first, 0, 6);
    strsub(buf, workers[i].initial, 8, 8);
    strsub(buf, workers[i].last, 10, 18);
    ...
    ...
}
```

You can assume the following declaration:

```
#define MAX 100
```

The following three functions from the C library, `stdlib.h` and `string.h`, might be useful for the lab:

```
atoi() - converts a string to an integer

atof() - converts a string to a float

strcmp() - compares two strings
```

For the extra credit portion of the lab you will need to modify the sorting algorithm that we looked at to work with structs.

The contents of `payfile.txt` are given below:

```
ADA      A AGUSTA    33 BABBAGE ROAD  LOVELACE    GB 19569 28 F 2 350.50
ISSAC    A ASIMOV    99 FICTION WAY   AMHERST     MA 63948 58 M 6 423.88
HUMPHRY  R BOGART    71 SAM STREET    HOLLYWOOD   CA 48482 56 M 5 366.00
ALBERT   G EINSTEIN  94 ENERGY WAY    PRINCETON   NJ 47474 67 M 8 780.00
EMMYLOU  L HARRIS    66 COUNTRY ROAD  NASHVILLE   TN 72647 38 F 2 767.42
JAMES    T KIRK      11 SPACE STREET  VULCAN      CA 82828 46 M 1 235.70
TED      L KOPPEL    55 ABC PLACE     WASHINGTON  DC 37376 48 M 9 909.44
DAVID    T LETTERMAN 14 WNBC AVENUE   NEW YORK    NY 19338 47 M 5 445.65
STEVIE   R NICKS     31 MUSIC ROAD    CHICAGO     IL 23459 38 F 8 460.88
MONTY    P PYTHON    76 SILLY STREET  LONDON      GB 80939 44 M 2 320.50
ROGER    R RABBIT    15 LOONEY TOONS  HOLLYWOOD   CA 91343 24 M 4 259.53
SALLY    W RIDE      21 COLUMBIA WAY  HOUSTON     TX 91123 30 F 9 707.80
ROD      Q SERLING   11 TWLIGHT ZONE  SAN DIEGO   CA 93939 56 M 1 440.00
LUKE     R SKYWALKER 43 MILKY WAY     NEW YORK    NY 12343 35 M 5 660.00
```

Remember that the `main()` function should appear as the first function in the program. Be sure to use function prototypes for each of the functions that are used in your program.

Output from your program should be sent to the terminal window (your screen) as well as the requested `csis.txt` output file. Be sure to read the document on Capturing Program Output. Your full name must appear as a comment in the source file that contains `main()`. Be sure to include the `csis.txt` output file in your zip archive.

Chapter 18. Dynamic Allocation of Variables

Dynamic Allocation of Variables
Dynamic Arrays - Advanced

Dynamic Allocation of Variables

Dynamic variables are variables that can be created and disposed of as a program executes. When a variable is needed, storage is reserved for it. When it is no longer needed, the storage is released. Therefore, the storage for these dynamic variables that are no longer in use is available for other purposes. There is no predefined limit to the number of dynamic variables that can be created.

We reference a dynamic variable not by name but through a pointer. Remember a pointer is a variable that contains the address (location) in memory of the dynamic variable it references. Every new dynamic variable created has an associated pointer to reference it. So when we allocate storage for a dynamic variable, our method of accessing the variable is through a pointer.

In order to create a dynamic variable of type integer, it is first necessary to declare a pointer variable that can hold its address. The declaration:

```
int *p;
```

declares the variable p to be a pointer variable whose values will be pointers to (contain the address of) dynamic variables of type int.

But a pointer variable is of no use unless there is something for it to point to. In order to create a dynamic variable, we use the malloc() function as follows:

```
int *p;

p = (int *) malloc(sizeof(int));
```

malloc() dynamically allocates variable-sized blocks of memory from the heap and allows a program to allocate memory explicitly as it's needed. By definition, malloc() returns a void * and therefore must be cast to the appropriate type of the pointer that will receive the address on the heap of the new dynamic variable, in this case int *. It is our responsibility to tell malloc() exactly how much storage to allocate for the dynamic variable, in this case sizeof(int) bytes. malloc() is prototyped in both the alloc.h and stdlib.h header files.

If malloc() is successful, it returns a pointer to the newly allocated block of memory. Otherwise, if not enough space exists for the new block of storage, `malloc()` returns `NULL`, which is a special value that any pointer variable may have. The `NULL` pointer does not reference a storage location.

We say that `malloc()` creates a new dynamic variable of type `int` and gives the address of the new dynamic variable to pointer `p`. This dynamic variable is then referred to as "the thing pointed to by p" or `*p`.

```
*p = 5;
printf("%d\n", *p);
```

In fact, `*p` can be used anyplace that it is appropriate to use a variable of type `int`. When a dynamic variable is no longer needed, we can use the `free()` function to free the memory space allocated to the dynamic variable:

```
free(p);
```

`free()` deallocates a block of memory allocated by a previous call to `malloc()`. It destroys the dynamic variable referenced by pointer `p`. The storage allocated to this variable is returned (recycled) to be assigned to some other dynamic variable. Accordingly, any further reference to `*p` is illegal. `free()` is also prototyped in `alloc.h` and `stdlib.h`.

See if you can follow the pointers in the following program.

```c
// dynamic.c

#include <stdio.h>
#include <alloc.h>

int main(void) {
    int *p, *q;

    p = (int *) malloc(sizeof(int));
    *p = 3;
    q = (int *) malloc(sizeof(int));
    *q = 5;
    printf("*p = %d      *q = %d\n", *p, *q);
    free(p);
    p = q;
    printf("*p = %d      *q = %d\n", *p, *q);
    *q = 7;
    printf("*p = %d      *q = %d\n", *p, *q);
    q = (int *) malloc(sizeof(int));
    *q = 9;
    printf("*p = %d      *q = %d\n", *p, *q);
    *p = *q;
    printf("*p = %d      *q = %d\n", *p, *q);
    free(p);
    p = q;
    printf("*p = %d      *q = %d\n", *p, *q);
    free(p);
    printf("*p = %d      *q = %d\n", *p, *q);
    return 0;
}
```

The output to the above program is:

```
*p = 3      *q = 5
*p = 5      *q = 5
*p = 7      *q = 7
*p = 7      *q = 9
*p = 9      *q = 9
*p = 9      *q = 9
```

Note that the last statement in the program is illegal although the C compiler will not complain about it! In the preceding statement, free(p), the dynamic variable that pointer p points to is disposed of. It is therefore illegal to dereference the pointer p. If you do, your program will become unstable. Although the C compiler will not find the error, you can be sure that the error will be found after you have shipped the 100,000[th] copy of your program!

There is another reason that the last statement in the program is illegal. It is because pointer q is being dereferenced! You might be wondering why this would be illegal since we have not executed a `free(q)` statement. Well, at least not directly. At the time we execute the `free(p)` statement, both pointers p and q are pointing to the same memory location, to the same dynamic variable. Therefore, after executing `free(p)`, pointer q is no longer pointing to a dynamic variable. Its storage has already been reclaimed. It is therefore illegal to dereference both pointers p and q at this point in the program.

See if you can find the error in the following program:

```c
// oops.c

#include <stdio.h>
#include <string.h>

int main(void);
char* foo(void);

int main(void) {
    char *buf;

    buf = foo();
    puts(buf);
    return 0;
}

char* foo(void) {
    char buf[32];

    strcpy(buf, "Hello, world.");
    puts(buf);
    return buf;
}
```

The problem lies in the fact that the storage for buf is allocated on the stack and is local to function foo(). When foo() is exited, the storage on the stack is reclaimed and a pointer is returned that no longer points to any valid memory location. The solution to this problem is to return a pointer to a valid storage location that persists after foo() is exited.

```
// strdup.c

#include <stdio.h>
#include <string.h>
#include <alloc.h>

int main(void);
char* foo(void);

int main(void) {
    char *buf;

    buf = foo();
    puts(buf);
    free(buf);
    return 0;
}

char* foo(void) {
    char buf[32];

    strcpy(buf, "Hello, world.");
    puts(buf);
    return strdup(buf);
}
```

strdup() makes a duplicate of a string obtaining storage on the heap with a call to malloc(). The allocated space is strlen(s) + 1 bytes long. Because storage is allocated on the heap, it persists after function foo() has exited. Note that you are responsible for freeing the space allocated by strdup() with a call to free() when it is no longer needed. If strdup() is successful, it returns a pointer to the location containing the duplicated string on the heap. Otherwise, if space could not be allocated, it returns NULL.

Let's now take a look at a more interesting dynamic variable, one that is a user-defined struct, rather than a simple integer variable. Given the following struct declaration:

```
// dynamic1.c

typedef struct student {
    char name[30];
    int age;
    float gpa;
} STUDENT;
```

that declares a student `struct` with three fields, and given the following pointer definition:

```
STUDENT *ps;
```

which declares pointer `ps` to be a pointer to a `student` `struct`, we can dynamically create a `student` `struct` variable on the heap as follows:

```
ps = (STUDENT *) malloc(sizeof(struct student));
```

Note that we must cast the return value of `malloc()` to the appropriate type for pointer `ps`, which is `STUDENT *`, or a pointer to a `student` `struct`. We must also tell `malloc()` exactly how many bytes on the heap we want to allocate for this dynamic variable, in this case, `sizeof(struct student)` bytes.

We now have a pointer to a `struct`, `ps`. In order to access a field of the `struct`, we must first dereference the pointer (to get to the `struct` itself) and then use the direct component selector (`.`) operator to access the appropriate field of the `struct`.

For example:

```
*ps.age = 35;
```

Unfortunately, there's one problem here. The direct component selector (`.`) operator has precedence over the star (`*`) operator. Therefore, the above code will try to access a field of the `struct` *before* the pointer is dereferenced. Disaster always results from this!! The simple solution is to override precedence by using parenthesis:

```
(*ps).age = 35;
```

Now, the pointer to the `struct` is first dereferenced, giving us the `struct` itself, and *then* the appropriate field of the `struct` is accessed. Although this syntax is correct, C programmers almost never use it! The reason is that there is a shortcut syntax that requires less keystrokes and produces clearer code. The equivalent statement looks like this:

```
ps->age = 35;
```

This *indirect component selector operator*, `->`, is made up of a hyphen and the greater than symbol without a space between them. It automatically first dereferences the pointer and then selects the appropriate field of the `struct`. Note that this operator can only be used when you have a pointer to a `struct` and you want to access a field of the `struct`. The example below shows the use of this new operator:

```c
// student.c

#include <stdio.h>
#include <string.h>
#include <alloc.h>

typedef struct student {
    char name[30];
    int age;
    float gpa;
} STUDENT;

int main(void) {
    STUDENT *ps;

    ps = (STUDENT *) malloc(sizeof(struct student));
    strcpy(ps->name, "Lauren");
    ps->age = 35;
    ps->gpa = 3.75;
    printf("%s %d %4.2f\n", ps->name, ps->age, ps->gpa));
    free(ps);
    return 0;
}
```

Dynamic Arrays: Advanced

We know that we can declare arrays of common data types as well as arrays of user-defined data types. For example, we can declare an array of 5 integers:

```
int num[5];
```

or we can declare an array of 5 `student structs` shown in the program below:

```c
// array.c

#include <stdio.h>

typedef struct student {
    char name[30];
    int age;
    float gpa;
} STUDENT;

void initialize(STUDENT stud[]); // Function initializes student array.
                                 // Code not included.
int main(void) {
    int i;
    STUDENT stud[5];

    initialize(stud);
    for (i = 0; i < 5; i++) {
        printf("%s %d %4.2f\n", stud[i].name, stud[i].age,
                                                stud[i].gpa);
    }
}
```

In this program, storage for the entire array is allocated on the stack as shown below:

```
           stud
        ------------------
   0   | student struct |
        ------------------
   1   | student struct |
        ------------------
   2   | student struct |
        ------------------
   3   | student struct |
        ------------------
   4   | student struct |
        ------------------
```

Arrays of built-in or user-defined types may be stored on the heap and accessed with pointers. The following program declares an array of pointers to student structs. Storage for the array of pointers is allocated on the stack while storage for each of the actual student structs is allocated on the heap.

```c
// darray1.c

#include <stdio.h>
#include <alloc.h>

typedef struct student {
    char name[30];
    int age;
    float gpa;
} STUDENT;

void initialize(STUDENT *pstud[]);
```

```
int main(void) {
    int i;
    STUDENT *pstud[5];
    for(i = 0; i < 5; i++) {
        pstud[i] = (STUDENT *) malloc(sizeof(struct student));
        initialize(pstud);
    }
    for (i = 0; i < 5; i++) {
        printf("%s %d %4.2f\n", pstud[i]->name, pstud[i]->age,
                                                pstud[i]->gpa);
    }
    for (i = 0; i < 5; i++) {
        free(pstud[i]);
    }
    return 0;
}
```

Below is a representation of the dynamic array created in the preceding program:

```
    created on stack   created on heap

        pstud
        --------
    0  |  •===|====➔   [student struct]
        --------
    1  |  •===|====➔   [student struct]
        --------
    2  |  •===|====➔   [student struct]
        --------
    3  |  •===|====➔   [student struct]
        --------
    4  |  •===|====➔   [student struct]
        --------
```

An alternate approach to dynamically create an array of items on the heap is as follows:

```c
// darray2.c

#include <stdio.h>
#include <alloc.h>

typedef struct student {
    char name[30];
    int age;
    float gpa;
} STUDENT;

void initialize(STUDENT *pstud);

int main(void) {
    int i;
    STUDENT *pstud;

    pstud = (STUDENT *) malloc(5 * sizeof(struct student));
    initialize(pstud);
    for (i = 0; i < 5; i++) {
        printf("%s %d %4.2f\n", pstud[i].name, pstud[i].age,
                                                stud[i].gpa);
    }
    free(pstud);
    return 0;
}
```

As shown in the diagram below, the only storage that is allocated on the stack is the storage for the pointer to the `student struct` array. Storage for the array itself (i.e., storage for each `student struct`) is allocated on the heap.

```
   created on stack          created on heap

                          -------------------
    pstud=========➔     0 |  student struct  |
                          -------------------
                        1 |  student struct  |
                          -------------------
                        2 |  student struct  |
                          -------------------
                        3 |  student struct  |
                          -------------------
                        4 |  student struct  |
                          -------------------
```

In the above program, note that we use the direct component selector (.) operator rather than the indirect component selector (->) operator to access the fields of the `struct`. This is due to the fact that we do not have an array of pointers to structs this time, but rather the structs themselves are contained within the array.

Our final example also creates a dynamic array on the heap. This time, however, not only is an array of pointers created on the heap, but the `student structs` that the pointers point to are also created on the heap.

```c
// darray3.c

#include <stdio.h>
#include <alloc.h>

typedef struct student {
    char name[30];
    int age;
    float gpa;
} STUDENT;

void initialize(STUDENT **pstud);

int main(void)   {
    int i;
    STUDENT **pstud;

    pstud = (STUDENT **) malloc(5 * sizeof(STUDENT *));
    for (i = 0; i < 5; i++) {
        pstud[i] = (STUDENT *) malloc(sizeof(struct student));
        initialize(pstud);
        for (i = 0; i < 5; i++) {
            printf("%s %d %4.2f\n", pstud[i]->name, pstud[i]->age,
                                                    pstud[i]->gpa);

        }
    }
    for (i = 0; i < 5; i++) {
        free(pstud[i]);
    }
    free(pstud);
    return 0;
}
```

Below is a representation of the dynamic array created in the above program:

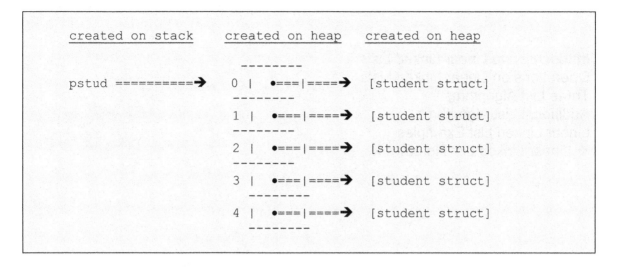

Chapter 19. Linear Linked Lists

Introduction to Linear Linked Lists
Operations on Linear Linked Lists
Three List Algorithms
Additional List Algorithms
Linear Linked List Examples
❖ Linear Linked List Homework

Introduction to Linear Linked Lists

Sequential Storage of Arrays

One of the big advantages of arrays is that you can allocate memory for a large number of variables without writing a lot of code. It's also simple to initialize or change their values "all at once" with a while or for loop. Additionally, we can have direct access to any array element with the use of the correct index into the array.

However, the big disadvantage of using an array is that the size of an array is fixed and you may not always know exactly how many items you will need to store. You may be reading in data from a file, and you won't necessarily know how big to make your array to hold the data.

Another problem with arrays is that rearranging elements in the array can be time consuming. Suppose you have 1,000 elements in an array and you decide that you want the 1,000[th] element to be the second element and the second to be the third and the third to be the fourth and so on. You'll have to shift all the elements down one place. This is not very efficient.

Linked Lists

In a sequential representation, the items of an array are implicitly ordered by the sequential order of storage. For example, if `num[i]` represents an element of an array, `num[i+1]` represents the next element of the array.

Now suppose that the items of a data structure were explicitly ordered. This would mean that every element of the data structure would have to contain within itself the address in memory of the next element of the data structure.

Note that in this new representation we can no longer use the fact that items are related by their location or address as in an array. Individual items in this data structure must have explicit pointers to the location of the other data items within the data structure. This gives rise to a new type of data structure called the *linear linked list*.

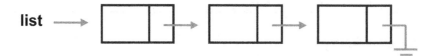

A linear linked list consists of a collection of nodes (items), each of which contains two fields:

- information field (info) – holds the actual data element on the list

- next address field (next) – contains the address in memory (pointer) to the next node in the list

---

Note that linear linked lists are typically drawn with boxes representing nodes, and pointers are drawn as arrows that connect one node to another. Thus, the arrows represent the links between the nodes, and each node contains data for one element.

The entire linked list is accessed via an external pointer, list, which points to (contains the address of) the first node in the list. Note that the external pointer is not included within a node but its value is accessed directly by referencing a pointer variable.

The next address field of the last node in the list contains a special pointer value, NULL, which is not a valid address but is used to signify the end of a list. The NULL pointer is represented by the symbol:

A list with no nodes is called the empty list or NULL list and is represented below. In this case the external pointer list has the NULL value:

list

list

Data elements of a linear linked list are contained in the `info` field of the list and must be of the same data type (`int`, `char`, `struct`, etc). As each node contains within itself (within its `next` field) a pointer to the next node in the list, we are able to traverse the list and access the nodes of the list in order (that is, from first to last).

The linked list is a dynamic structure and can change size as the program executes. Nodes can be inserted and deleted at any position of a list (beginning, between nodes, at the end). Only the first node, accessed by the list pointer, is known. From there links between nodes can be used to move from one node to another node. Theoretically, there is no upper limit on the length of a list, but practically a computer's memory size is the limit.

Here's an example of a new node being inserted into the middle of the list without causing the other elements to change their locations in memory. Notice that this can be done with just the manipulation of two pointers and requires no data movements:

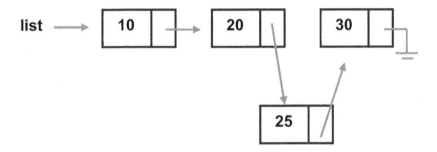

Working with linear linked lists can be fun because they are easy to draw, yet give a useful way to organize data. In certain places lists can be tricky, but a good drawing can go a long ways toward clarifying such a situation. Actually, I cannot emphasize this enough. It's very important to draw pictures when you're trying to build and understand linked list code. Generally, all you need to do is to draw a box for each node and an arrow going from each node to the next to represent the `next` pointer.

Linked Lists vs. Arrays

Notice that the above list gives numbers in numeric order. You might wonder how this compares with storing an ordered list of numbers in an array. The key difference is that an array gives random access in that you can directly access any data item by its index number. This allows one to use binary search instead of the slower sequential search, for example. A linked list gives only sequential access to the data, so that only sequential search is available. For example, to read the millionth element of a linked list, you must read the 999,999 elements that precede it!

However, there are other comparisons that could be made between the two. Although the array method allows the faster search to be used, if we want to insert a new item after the one found, we are in trouble! There is probably no room in the array to insert a new item at this point. Instead, all items to the right of this location have to be slid over to the next array location. This is a slow process but does make room to insert the new item. As we will see more clearly when we code linked lists, it is fairly easy to insert a new item into an ordered linked list. In fact, it is just a matter of changing a couple of pointers (as shown above).

Deletion of an item from an ordered list is also a simple matter of changing a pointer, whereas in an ordered array, all of the data to the right has to be shifted left to fill in the hole left upon deletion. Thus, once again, the linked list is faster and more flexible. In general, a linked list is probably the better method if you are going to dynamically insert and delete items a lot. (A linked list is one example of a *dynamic data structure*. This means that it can easily grow, contract, and change as needed. An array is a *static data structure*.)

Another comparison could be made based on the amount of space that the two methods use. With the array scheme, you would need to set the size of the array in advance, overestimating the amount of space needed. However, the linked list method also wastes space, in that it needs room in each node for a pointer. In general it is not possible to say which method wastes more space.

Writing linked list code is a bit more complicated than using arrays, but for many applications such as:

- Information retrieval
- Programming language development
- Simulation
- Storage management techniques

using a linked list instead of an array can be much more efficient.

If p is a pointer to a node:

- p = getNode()

Obtains an empty node and sets the contents of a pointer variable named p to the address of that node. This means that p is a pointer to this newly allocated node.

- freeNode(p)

Returns the node pointed to by p to the source of unused nodes and makes the node available for reuse.

p ⟶

- info(p)

Refers to the information portion of the node that is pointed to by p.

x = info(p) assigns the contents of the info field of the node pointed to by p to x.

p ⟶ | 10 | |

X = 10

`info(p)` = x assigns the contents of x to the `info` field of the node pointed to by p.

X = 10

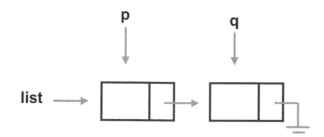

- `next(p)`

Refers to the `next` address portion of the node pointed to by p.

`q = next(p)` assigns the contents of the `next` field of the node pointed to by p to q.

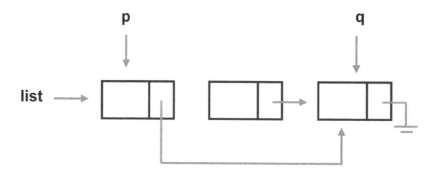

`next(p) = q` assigns the contents of pointer q to the `next` field of the node pointed to by p.

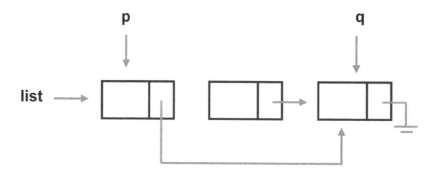

Algorithm 1: Given a linear linked list of integers, create an algorithm that will add a node with the data value of 10 to the front of the following list:

list ⟶ [20 | ⊣] ⟶ [30 | ⏚]

Step 1: `p = getnode()`

`p` is a pointer to a newly created node:

list ⟶ [20 | ⊣] ⟶ [30 | ⏚]

p ⟶ [|]

Step 2: `info(p) = x`

Inserts an integer `x` into the `info` portion of the node that `p` points to:

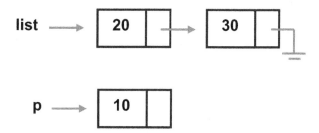

list ⟶ [20 | ⊣] ⟶ [30 | ⏚]

p ⟶ [10 |]

Step 3: next(p) = list

We now want the node pointed to by p to point to the node that list is pointing to (since list contains the address of the first node in the list). So we must set the next field of the node that p points to, to the node that list points to:

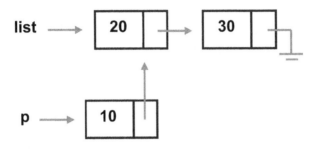

Step 4: list = p

Finally, since list is the external pointer to the linear linked list, its value must be modified to the address of the new first node of the list. This changes the value of list to the value of p:

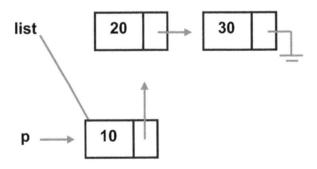

Note at this point the pointer p is not needed and can be simply disregarded:

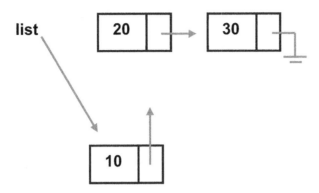

Put together, we have an algorithm for adding a node to the front of a linear linked list:

```
p = getNode()
info(p) = x
next(p) = list
list = p
```

Let's test this algorithm to see if it works for an initially empty list:

list ⏚

Step 1: `p = getNode()`

list ⏚

p ⟶ ☐☐

Step 2: `info(p) = x`

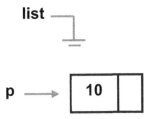

Step 3: `next(p) = list`

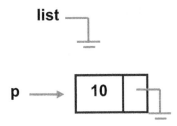

Step 4: `list = p`

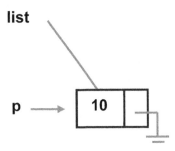

Again, pointer p is not needed and can be simply disregarded:

Algorithm 2: Remove the first node of a non-empty list and store the value of its `info` field into a variable `x`.

Step 1: `p = list`

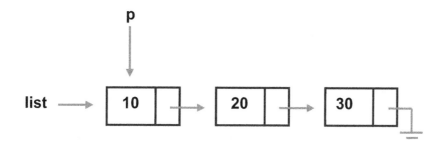

Step 2: `list = next(p)`

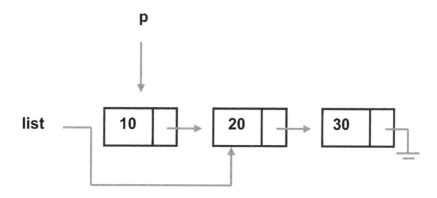

Step 3: `x = info(p)`

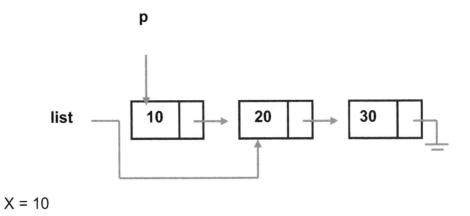

X = 10

Step 4: `freeNode(p)`

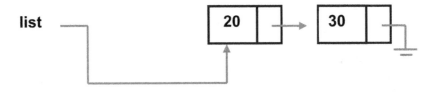

X = 10

Put together, we have an algorithm for deleting a node from the front of a linear linked list:

```
p = list
list = next(p)
x = info(p)
freeNode(p)
```

Finally, let's test this algorithm to see if it works for a list with a single node:

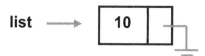

Step 1: p = list

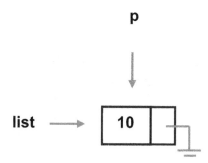

Step 2: list = next(p)

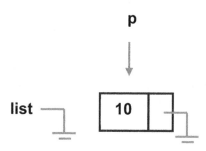

Step 3: x = info(p)

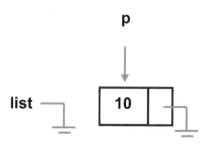

X = 10

Step 4: `freeNode(p)`

list ⌐
      ⏚

X = 10

Algorithm 3: Given a linear linked list of integers, create an algorithm that will traverse (visit) each node in the list and output the data in each of the `info` fields.

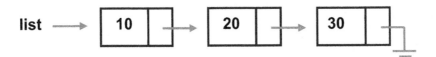

```
p = list
while (p != null)
    output(p.getInfo())
    p = p.getNext()
```

Can you see the importance of ensuring that there is a null value in the next field of the last node in the linear linked list?

Additional List Operations

It is easy to insert and delete elements from the middle of a list without any data movements. For example, the amount of work required to insert a node into the middle of a list is independent of the size of the list. All that is necessary is to:

- allocate a new node

- insert the information into the node

- adjust two pointers

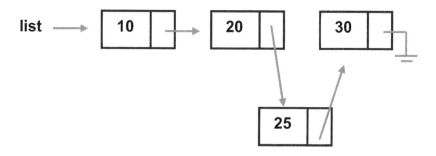

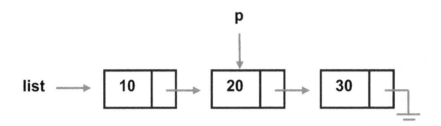

- q = getNode()

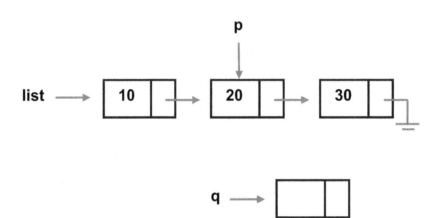

- info(q) = x

x = 25

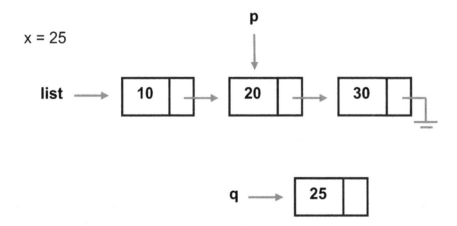

- `next(q) = next(p)`

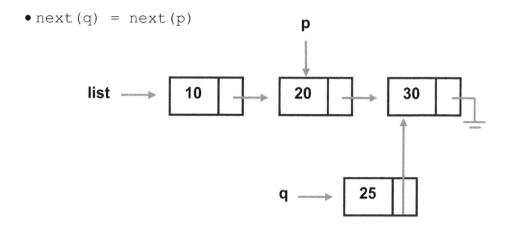

- `next(p) = q`

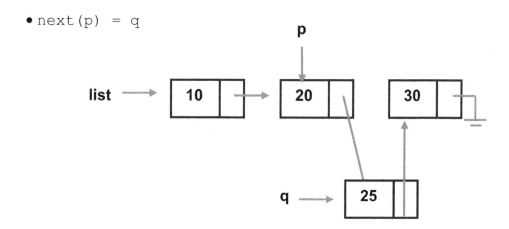

Note that an item can only be inserted after a given node, not before the node. This is because there is no way to proceed from a given node to its predecessor in a list without traversing the list from the beginning.

Here's the algorithm from above:

```
q = getNode()
info(q) = x
next(q) = next(p)
next(p) = q
```

Algorithm 5: Given a pointer `p` to a node in a linear linked list, write an algorithm, `deleteAfter`, that will delete a node after the node pointed to by `p`:

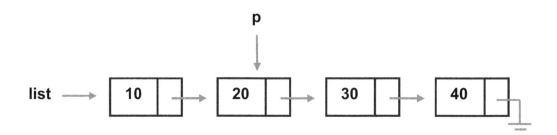

- `q = next(p)`

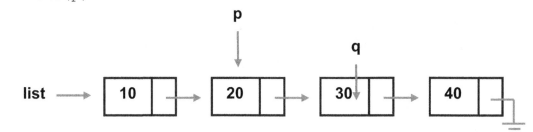

- `x = info(q)`

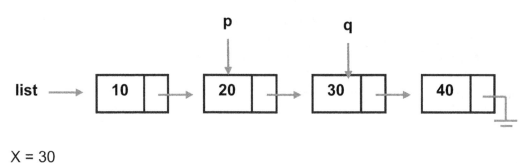

X = 30

- next(p) = next(q)

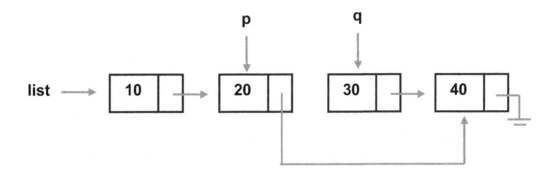

- freeNode(q)

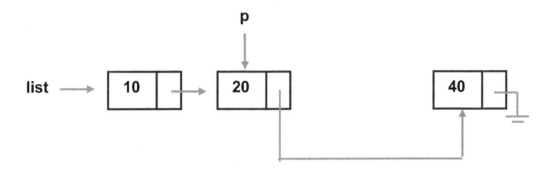

Again, we cannot just be given a pointer to the node we want to delete. This is because the next field of the node's predecessor must be changed to point to the node's successor and there is no direct way of reaching the predecessor of a given node.

Here's the algorithm from above:

```
q = next(p)
x = info(q)
next(p) = next(q)
freeNode(q)
```

Linear Linked List Examples

Example 1

Suppose we wanted to delete all occurrences of the number 4 from a linear linked list. We would have to traverse the list for nodes with 4 in the `info` field and delete that node. But to delete a node, its predecessor must be known. Therefore we must use two pointers, `p` and `q`, to traverse the list. `p` will be considered the *lead* pointer and `q` will be considered the *lag* pointer, i.e., `p` will traverse the list and `q` will always point to the predecessor of `p`. Note the practice of using two pointers, one following the other, is very common when working with lists.

Two functions will be used:

- `deleteFront()` will be used to delete the node from the front of the list.

- `deleteAfter()` will be used to delete a node from the middle of the list.

```
// deleteNumber.c

p = list
q = NULL
while p != NULL
    if info(p) == 4
        p = next(p)
        if q == NULL
            x = deleteFront(list)
        else
            x = deleteAfter(q)
    else
        q = p
        p = next(p)
```

It is left as an exercise to work through the algorithm. Be sure to draw pictures as you work through the algorithm line by line.

Example 2

Assume a linear linked list is ordered so that the smaller items precede the larger ones (i.e., the list is sorted). We want to insert an item x into this list in its proper place. Two functions are used:

- `insertFront()` will be used to insert a node at the front of the list.

- `insertAfter()` will be used to insert a node into the middle of the list.

```
insertItem.c

p = list
q = NULL
while p!= NULL and x > info(p)
    q = p
    p = next(p)
if q == NULL
    insertFront(list, x)
else
    insertAfter(q, x)
```

Again, it is left as an exercise to work through the algorithm. Be sure to draw pictures as you work through the algorithm line by line.

❖ Linear Linked List Homework

Write a pseudo code algorithm to perform each of the following operations:

1. Determine the number of nodes in a list.

2. Determine the sum of the integers in a list.

3. Append a node to the end of a list.

4. Concatenate two lists.

5. Free all the nodes in a list.

6. Delete the last element from a list.

7. Make a copy of a list.

Chapter 20. Implementation of Linear Linked Lists

Defining Nodes in C
Linear Linked List Operations
Separate Compilation
Linear Linked List Code
Addition of Polynomials
❖ Linear Linked List Lab
❖ Calculating Very Large Factorials Lab

Defining Nodes in C

We've seen that pointers allow us to build and manipulate linked lists of various types. By altering the values of pointers, nodes can be attached, detached, and reassembled in patterns that grow and shrink as execution of a program progresses.

We can create a chain of these nodes, and keep track of the first one in the list and then store within each node a pointer to the next node in the list. To accomplish this, each node will therefore be defined as a `struct` with one field containing the information and another field containing the address of the next node in the list. We make the declarations as follows:

```
// node1.c

struct node {
    int info;
    struct node *next;
};

typedef struct node *NODEPTR;
```

or, we can combine the two declarations above as follows:

```
// node2.c

typedef struct node {
    int info;
    struct node *next;
} *NODEPTR;
```

In either case, we declare NODEPTR to be a pointer to a node struct. Note that the next field in the node struct is a pointer that contains the address of the next node in the list.

We can now declare a NODEPTR p and dynamically create a new node:

```
// node3.c

NODEPTR p;
p = (NODEPTR) malloc(sizeof(struct node));
```

We access the `info` field of the node as:

```
p->info
```

and we can access the `next` field of the node as:

```
p->next
```

As before, we can use the `free()` function to dispose of the dynamically created node:

```
free(p);
```

Work through the following program to create a linked list containing five dynamically created nodes:

```c
// dynamic.c

#include <stdio.h>
#include <stdlib.h>

typedef struct node {
    int info;
    struct node *next;
} *NODEPTR;

int main(void) {
    int i;
    NODEPTR list, p, q;

    list = (NODEPTR) malloc(sizeof(struct node));
    p = list;
    p->info = 1;
    for (i = 2; i <= 5; i++) {
        q = (NODEPTR) malloc(sizeof(struct node));
        q->info = i;
        p->next = q;
        p = q;
    }
    p->next = NULL;
    return 0;
}
```

Linear Linked List Operations

Here are functions to manipulate a linear linked list of integers. It is very important for you to work through each of these functions to be sure that you understand how they work. Be sure to draw pictures of linked lists to assist you in visualizing the algorithms. It is extremely difficult to write code using linked lists without drawing pictures of the lists and how the list changes as your algorithm executes.

```c
// returns the address of a newly created node

NODEPTR getNode(void) {
    NODEPTR p;

    p = (NODEPTR) malloc(sizeof(struct node));
    if (p == NULL) {
        error("List overflow.");
    }
    return(p);
}


// frees the node pointed to by p

void freeNode(NODEPTR p) {
    free(p);
}


// adds a new node to the front of the list

void addFront(NODEPTR *list, int num) {
    NODEPTR p;

    p = getNode();
    p->info = num;
    p->next = *list;
    *list = p;
}
```

```
// deletes the node at the front of the list

int deleteFront(NODEPTR *list) {
    int temp;
    NODEPTR p;

    if (*list == NULL) {
        error("List underflow.");
    }
    p = *list;
    temp = p->info;
    *list = p->next;
    freeNode(p);
    return temp;
}


// adds an element to the end of a list

void addLast(NODEPTR *list, int num) {
    NODEPTR p, q;

    p = getNode();
    p->info = num;
    p->next = NULL;
    if (*list == NULL) {
        *list = p;
    }
    else {
        q = *list;
        while (q->next) {
            q = q->next;
        }
        q->next = p;
    }
}
```

```
// deletes the last element in a list

int deleteLast(NODEPTR *list) {
    NODEPTR p, q;
    int temp = -1;

    if (*list) {
        p = *list;
        q = NULL;
        while (p->next) {
            q = p;
            p = p->next;
        }
        if (!q) {
            *list = NULL;
        }
        else {
            q->next = NULL;
        }
        temp = p->info;
        freeNode(p);
    }
    return temp;
}


// inserts a new node after the node pointed to by p

void insertAfter(NODEPTR p, int num) {
    NODEPTR q;

    if (p == NULL) {
        error("Void insertion.");
    }
    q = getNode();
    q->info = num;
    q->next = p->next;
    p->next = q;
}
```

```c
// deletes the node after the node pointed to by p

int deleteAfter(NODEPTR p) {
    int temp;
    NODEPTR q;

    if (p == NULL || p->next == NULL) {
        error("Void deletion.");
    }
    q = p->next;
    temp = q->info;
    p->next = q->next;
    freeNode(q);
    return temp;
}


// insert a node into its correct location within a sorted list

void insert(NODEPTR *list, int num) {
    NODEPTR p, q;

    p = *list;
    q = NULL;
    while (p != NULL && p->info < num) {
        q = p;
        p = p->next;
    }
    if (q == NULL) {
        addFront(list, num);
    }
    else {
        insertAfter(q, num);
    }
}


// returns the number of nodes in the list

int numElements(NODEPTR list) {
    int count=0;

    while (list) {
        count++;
        list = list->next;
    }
    return count;
}
```

```
// returns sum of integers in the list

int sumElements(NODEPTR list) {
    int sum=0;

    while (list) {
        sum += list->info;
        list = list->next;
    }
    return sum;
}


// traverses a list and outputs contents of list

void outputList(NODEPTR list) {
    while (list) {
        printf("%8d", list->info);
        list = list->next;
    }
    printf("\n\n");
}


// Returns true if the item is found in the list

int contains(NODEPTR list, int num) {
    NODEPTR p;

    p = list;
    while (p != NULL && p->info != num) {
        p = p->next;
    }
    return p != NULL;
}


// determines whether or not a list is empty

int isEmpty(NODEPTR list) {
        return list == NULL;
}
```

```
// frees all the nodes in a list

void freeList(NODEPTR *list) {
    NODEPTR p;

    while (*list) {
        p = *list;
        *list = p->next;
        freeNode(p);
    }
}


// returns a pointer to the node with the requested value;
// otherwise returns NULL

NODEPTR select(NODEPTR list, int num) {
    while (list) {
        if (list->info == num) {
            return list;
        }
        else {
            list = list->next;
        }
    }
    return list;
}


// removes the first occurrence of an item in a list

int remove(NODEPTR *list, int num) {
    NODEPTR p, q;

    p = *list;
    q = NULL;
    while (p != NULL && p->info != num) {
        q = p;
        p = p->next;
    }
    if (p == NULL) {
        return -1;
    }
    else {
        return q == NULL ? deleteFront(list) : deleteAfter(q);
    }
}
```

```
// makes a copy of a list

NODEPTR copyList (NODEPTR list) {
    NODEPTR newlist, p, q;

    newlist = NULL;
    while (list) {
        p = getNode();
        p->info = list->info;
        p->next = NULL;
        if (newlist == NULL) {
            newlist = p;
        }
        else {
            q->next = p;
        }
        q = p;
        list = list->next;
    }
    return newlist;
}


// concatenates two lists

void concatList(NODEPTR *list1, NODEPTR list2) {
    NODEPTR p;

    if (*list1 == NULL) {
        *list1 = list2;
    }
    else if (list2) {
        p = *list1;
        while (p->next) {
            p = p->next;
        }
        p->next = list2;
    }
}
```

```
// returns a pointer to a new list containing the intersection of
// two lists

NODEPTR intersect(NODEPTR list1, NODEPTR list2) {
    NODEPTR p, q, r, s, newlist;
    int found;

    p = list1;
    newlist = NULL;
    r = NULL;
    while (p) {
        q = list2;
        found = 0;
        while (q && !found) {
            if (p->info == q->info) {
                found = 1;
            }
            else {
                q = q->next;
            }
        }
        if (found) {
            s = getNode();
            s->info = p->info;
            s->next = NULL;
            if (!r) {
                newlist = s;
            }
            else {
                r->next = s;
            }
            r = s;
        }
    p = p->next;
    }
    return newlist;
}


// display an error message and aborts the program

void error(char *msg) {
    puts(msg);
    exit(1);
}
```

C does not require that all of the statements for a particular program be contained within a single file. C programs can be constructed from functions written in separate files and linked into a single program. Up until this point, all of our C source code for each project has been placed within a single .c file. But now, as our programs become longer and longer, we will need to find a more efficient way to organize our code.

We can compile a source file to create *"object code"* and can link its functions with other functions in other source files. If a function from one file needs to call a function contained inside another file, then the function call can be made in the normal fashion and arguments can be passed and returned in the usual way. As we are revising and debugging a program, it's easier if each compilation processes only part of the large program. Once we have written and debugged a function, we do not need to keep recompiling it as we work on other functions in the program.

Consider the following two C source files:

```
File 1                          File 2
int main(void) {                void faa(void) {
    foo();                          puts("Green");
    faa();                      }
}

void foo(void) {
    puts("Red");
}
```

The C compiler finds the two function calls in File 1. The reference to foo() is resolved when the definition of foo() is found in the same file. The reference to faa() is resolved when the definition of faa() is found in File 2. All object files specified to the C compiler will be "pulled into" the C compiler and are automatically included in the final executable file.

In the case of our linked list declarations and functions, we create two files, list.h and list.c. The .h file is called a header file and typically contains declarations as well as function prototypes. Here is what the header file would look like for our linear linked list:

```
// list.h

#ifndef _LIST_H
#define _LIST_H

typedef struct node {
    int info;
    struct node *next;
} *NODEPTR;

NODEPTR getNode(void);
void    freeNode(NODEPTR p);
void    addFront(NODEPTR *list, int num);
int     deleteFront(NODEPTR *list);
void    addLast(NODEPTR *list, int num);
int     deleteLast(NODEPTR *list);
void    insertAfter(NODEPTR p, int num);
int     deleteAfter(NODEPTR p);
void    insert(NODEPTR *list, int num);
int     numElements(NODEPTR list);
int     sumElements(NODEPTR list);
void    outputList(NODEPTR list);
int     contains(NODEPTR list, int num);
int     isEmpty(NODEPTR list);
void    freeList(NODEPTR *list);
NODEPTR select(NODEPTR list, int num);
int     remove(NODEPTR *list, int num);
NODEPTR copyList (NODEPTR list);
void    concatList(NODEPTR *list1, NODEPTR list2);
NODEPTR intersect(NODEPTR list1, NODEPTR list2);
void    error(char *msg);

#endif
```

Note the placement of our NODEPTR struct definition and function prototypes in the header file. To prevent the compiler from looking at this header file more than one time we use a preprocessor conditional compilation command to tell the compiler to only bring this code into the project once:

```
#ifndef _LIST_H
#define _LIST_H

...
...

#endif
```

The includes in the linear linked list .c file would look like this:

```
// list.c

#include <stdio.h>
#include <stdlib.h>
#include "list.h"
```

Note the statement:

```
#include "list.h"
```

This instructs the compiler to read in the statements from the list.h header file. At this point, you should be able to compile the list.c file separately from the rest of your program. So when you are ready to use the linked list code in your program, you would create a new source code file within the project and include the header file for the linked list functions:

```
#include "list.h"
```

You will also need to bring in the list.c source code for linked lists by adding the source code file to the other source code files in the project.

```
// list.h

#ifndef _LIST_H
#define _LIST_H

typedef struct node {
    int info;
    struct node *next;
} *NODEPTR;

NODEPTR getNode(void);
void    freeNode(NODEPTR p);
void    addFront(NODEPTR *list, int num);
int     deleteFront(NODEPTR *list);
void    addLast(NODEPTR *list, int num);
int     deleteLast(NODEPTR *list);
void    insertAfter(NODEPTR p, int num);
int     deleteAfter(NODEPTR p);
void    insert(NODEPTR *list, int num);
int     numElements(NODEPTR list);
int     sumElements(NODEPTR list);
void    outputList(NODEPTR list);
int     contains(NODEPTR list, int num);
int     isEmpty(NODEPTR list);
void    freeList(NODEPTR *list);
NODEPTR select(NODEPTR list, int num);
int     remove(NODEPTR *list, int num);
NODEPTR copyList (NODEPTR list);
void    concatList(NODEPTR *list1, NODEPTR list2);
NODEPTR intersect(NODEPTR list1, NODEPTR list2);
void    error(char *msg);

#endif
```

```
// list.c

#include <stdio.h>
#include <stdlib.h>
#include "list.h"


// returns the address of a newly created node

NODEPTR getNode(void) {
    NODEPTR p;

    p = (NODEPTR) malloc(sizeof(struct node));
    if (p == NULL) {
        error("List overflow.");
    }
    return(p);
}


// frees the node pointed to by p

void freeNode(NODEPTR p) {
    free(p);
}


// adds a new node to the front of the list

void addFront(NODEPTR *list, int num) {
    NODEPTR p;

    p = getNode();
    p->info = num;
    p->next = *list;
    *list = p;
}
```

```
// deletes the node at the front of the list

int deleteFront(NODEPTR *list) {
    int temp;
    NODEPTR p;

    if (*list == NULL) {
        error("List underflow.");
    }
    p = *list;
    temp = p->info;
    *list = p->next;
    freeNode(p);
    return temp;
}


// adds an element to the end of a list

void addLast(NODEPTR *list, int num) {
    NODEPTR p, q;

    p = getNode();
    p->info = num;
    p->next = NULL;
    if (*list == NULL) {
        *list = p;
    }
    else {
        q = *list;
        while (q->next) {
            q = q->next;
        }
        q->next = p;
    }
}
```

```c
// deletes the last element in a list

int deleteLast(NODEPTR *list) {
    NODEPTR p, q;
    int temp = -1;

    if (*list) {
        p = *list;
        q = NULL;
        while (p->next) {
            q = p;
            p = p->next;
        }
        if (!q) {
            *list = NULL;
        }
        else {
            q->next = NULL;
        }
        temp = p->info;
        freeNode(p);
    }
    return temp;
}


// inserts a new node after the node pointed to by p

void insertAfter(NODEPTR p, int num) {
    NODEPTR q;

    if (p == NULL) {
        error("Void insertion.");
    }
    q = getNode();
    q->info = num;
    q->next = p->next;
    p->next = q;
}
```

```
// deletes the node after the node pointed to by p

int deleteAfter(NODEPTR p) {
    int temp;
    NODEPTR q;

    if (p == NULL || p->next == NULL) {
        error("Void deletion.");
    }
    q = p->next;
    temp = q->info;
    p->next = q->next;
    freeNode(q);
    return temp;
}


// insert a node into its correct location within a sorted list

void insert(NODEPTR *list, int num) {
    NODEPTR p, q;

    p = *list;
    q = NULL;
    while (p != NULL && p->info < num) {
        q = p;
        p = p->next;
    }
    if (q == NULL) {
        addFront(list, num);
    }
    else {
        insertAfter(q, num);
    }
}


// returns the number of nodes in the list

int numElements(NODEPTR list) {
    int count=0;

    while (list) {
        count++;
        list = list->next;
    }
    return count;
}
```

```
// returns sum of integers in the list

int sumElements(NODEPTR list) {
    int sum=0;

    while (list) {
        sum += list->info;
        list = list->next;
    }
    return sum;
}


// traverses a list and outputs contents of list

void outputList(NODEPTR list) {
    while (list) {
        printf("%8d", list->info);
        list = list->next;
    }
    printf("\n\n");
}


// Returns true if the item is found in the list

int contains(NODEPTR list, int num) {
    NODEPTR p;

    p = list;
    while (p != NULL && p->info != num) {
        p = p->next;
    }
    return p != NULL;
}


// determines whether or not a list is empty

int isEmpty(NODEPTR list) {
    return list == NULL;
}
```

```
// frees all the nodes in a list

void freeList(NODEPTR *list) {
    NODEPTR p;

    while (*list) {
        p = *list;
        *list = p->next;
        freeNode(p);
    }
}


// returns a pointer to the node with the requested value;
// otherwise returns NULL

NODEPTR select(NODEPTR list, int num) {
    while (list) {
        if (list->info == num) {
            return list;
        }
        else {
            list = list->next;
        }
    }
    return list;
}


// removes the first occurrence of an item in a list

int remove(NODEPTR *list, int num) {
    NODEPTR p, q;

    p = *list;
    q = NULL;
    while (p != NULL && p->info != num) {
        q = p;
        p = p->next;
    }
    if (p == NULL) {
        return -1;
    }
    else {
        return q == NULL ? deleteFront(list) : deleteAfter(q);
    }
}
```

```
// makes a copy of a list

NODEPTR copyList (NODEPTR list) {
    NODEPTR newlist, p, q;

    newlist = NULL;
    while (list) {
        p = getNode();
        p->info = list->info;
        p->next = NULL;
        if (newlist == NULL) {
            newlist = p;
        }
        else {
            q->next = p;
        }
        q = p;
        list = list->next;
    }
    return newlist;
}


// concatenates two lists

void concatList(NODEPTR *list1, NODEPTR list2) {
    NODEPTR p;

    if (*list1 == NULL) {
        *list1 = list2;
    }
    else if (list2) {
        p = *list1;
        while (p->next) {
            p = p->next;
        }
        p->next = list2;
    }
}
```

```
// returns a pointer to a new list containing the intersection of
// two lists

NODEPTR intersect(NODEPTR list1, NODEPTR list2) {
    NODEPTR p, q, r, s, newlist;
    int found;

    p = list1;
    newlist = NULL;
    r = NULL;
    while (p) {
        q = list2;
        found = 0;
        while (q && !found) {
            if (p->info == q->info) {
                found = 1;
            }
            else {
                q = q->next;
            }
        }
        if (found) {
            s = getNode();
            s->info = p->info;
            s->next = NULL;
            if (!r) {
                newlist = s;
            }
            else {
                r->next = s;
            }
            r = s;
        }
    p = p->next;
    }
    return newlist;
}


// display an error message and aborts the program

void error(char *msg) {
    puts(msg);
    exit(1);
}
```

Addition of Polynomials

In order to find a suitable representation for a polynomial (in one variable), we must distinguish between coefficients and exponents within each term of the polynomial. Shown below is one term of a polynomial represented as a node in a linear linked list.

coefficient	exponent	link to next term

So, for example:

$3X^2$ would be represented as:

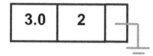

X^4 would be represented as:

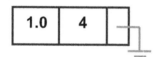

5 would be represented as:

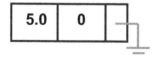

$3X^5 - 2X^3 + 4$ would be represented as:

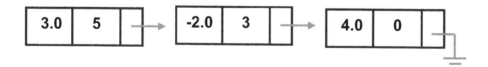

Polynomial Representation

Note the following three preconditions for representing a polynomial as a linear linked list:

- Terms must be stored in order of decreasing exponent within the linear linked list.

- No two terms may have the same exponent.

- No term may have a zero coefficient.

Each node of the linear linked list will represent one term of the polynomial and is a `struct` containing the following information:

- coefficient

- exponent

- pointer to the next term of the polynomial

```
typedef struct poly {
    float coeff;
    int expon;
    struct poly *next;
} *POLYPTR;
```

Adding Two Polynomials

To add two polynomials together, we only must scan through them once each:

- If we find terms with the same exponent in the two polynomials, then we add the coefficients and copy the new term to the end of the sum polynomial; otherwise we copy the term with the larger exponent into the sum polynomial and continue.

- When we reach the end of one of the polynomials, we copy the remaining part of the other to the sum polynomial.

• We must be careful not to include terms with 0 coefficient in the sum. For example:

$$6X^5 + 2X^4 + 3X^3 \qquad + 2X$$
$$+$$
$$\underline{3X^5 \quad - 2X^4 \qquad - 5X^2 - 8X + 7}$$
$$9X^5 \qquad\qquad + 3X^3 - 5X^2 - 6X + 7$$

```c
// poly.c

#include <stdlib.h>

typedef struct poly {
    float coeff;
    int expon;
    struct poly *next;
} *POLYPTR;

POLYPTR sum(POLYPTR p, POLYPTR q)  {
    float coeff;
    POLYPTR add = NULL;

    while (p != NULL && q != NULL) {
        if (p->expon == q->expon)  {
            coeff = p->coeff + q->coeff;
            if (coeff) {
                makeTerm(&add, coeff, p->expon);
                p = p->next;
                q = q->next;
            }
        }
        else if (p->expon > q->expon)  {
            makeTerm(&add, p->coeff, p->expon);
            p = p->next;
        }
        else {
            makeTerm(&add, q->coeff, q->expon);
            q = q->next;
        }
    }
    while (p) {
        makeTerm(&add, p->coeff, p->expon);
        p = p->next;
    }
    while (q) {
        makeTerm(&add, q->coeff, q->expon);
        q = q->next;
    }
    return add;
}
```

At several places in the algorithm we must create a new term with given coefficient and exponent and place it at the end of the sum polynomial, that is, after the term pointed to by `last`. Note that pointer `add` will always point to the first term created and pointer `last` will always point to the last term of the `sum` polynomial.

```c
void makeTerm(POLYPTR *add, float coeff, int expon) {
    POLYPTR t;
    POLYPTR last = NULL;

    t = (POLYPTR) malloc(sizeof(struct poly));
    t->coeff = coeff;
    t->expon = expon;
    t->next = NULL;
    if (last == NULL) {
        *add = t;
    }
    else {
        last->next = t;
    }
    last = t;
}
```

Other operations on polynomials can be programmed as functions of the same general nature as our function for addition. For extra credit, see if you can do the following:

• Write a method that will input a sequence of coefficients and exponents and form them into a linked polynomial as described earlier.

• Write a function that will subtract two polynomials.

• Write a function that will compute the first, second, and third derivative of a polynomial.

• Write a function that will multiply a polynomial by a scalar.

• Write a function that, given a polynomial and an integer, evaluates the polynomial at that integer.

• Write a function that will print a polynomial as a sequence of coefficients and exponents, arranged attractively.

This lab, similar in nature to the database lab, will focus on the manipulation of linear linked lists using dynamic storage allocation. Each section of the assignment should be structured within its own function, passing parameters as necessary.

You are to construct a C program, `dbase.c`, utilizing dynamic variables, which will retrieve and manipulate a company's payroll database, `payfile2.txt`. The data for each employee should be read into a `struct` containing the following fields:

```
•  firstName  -  10 characters maximum
•  lastName   -  15 characters maximum
•  gender     -  1 character maximum (M/F)
•  tenure     -  integer representing years of employment
•  rate       -  h/w
•  salary     -  float
```

Your program should perform each of the operations indicated below. Be sure to clearly label your output for each section.

a) Read the data from `payfile2.txt` into a `node struct` for each employee and insert the node onto the end of a linear linked list. Here's an `fscanf_s()` statement that will help you to read the data from the input file:

```
fscanf_s(fp, "%s %s %c %d %c %f\n", p->firstName, sizeof(firstName),
                                     p->lastName, sizeof(lastName),
                                     &(p->gender), 1,
                                     &(p->tenure),
                                     &(p->rate), 1,
                                     &(p->salary));
```

b) Output the contents of each of the nodes in the linked list into an easily read format, similar to the format of the input file.

c) Traverse the list and output the number of employees in the database.

d) Output the first and last name of all women on the payroll.

e) Output the first and last name and salary of all weekly employees who make more than $35,000 per year and who have been with the company for at least five years.

f) Give a raise of $.75 per hour to all employees who are paid on an hourly basis and make less than $10.00 per hour; and give a raise of $50.00 per week to all employees who are paid on a weekly basis and make less than $350.00 per week. Output the first and last name and new salary for each employee on the payroll who has received a raise.

g) Sort the nodes of the list into alphabetical order according to last name and output the first and last name and salary for each employee.

h) The file `hirefile2.txt` contains data for three employees to be hired by the company. Insert the record for each of the new employees into the correct location in the linear linked list and output the first and last name and salary for each employee in the database.

i) The file `firefile2.txt` contains data for two employees to be fired by the company. Delete the corresponding node for each of the employees to be fired and output the first and last name and salary for each employee in the database.

Note that previously we only looked at linear linked lists of nodes that contained `ints` and now we are looking at linear linked lists of nodes that contain `structs`. Accordingly, I have rewritten the linear linked list source code shown at the end of the lab write-up (`list.h` and `list.c`) to allow our lists to work with `employee structs` in the `info` field of each node and not just `ints`.

The `list.h` header file contains the declaration for the `employee struct` as well as the function prototypes. The `list.c` file contains list functions that I have rewritten for use with the `employee struct` for this lab.

Here is the `struct` declaration that appears in `list.h`:

```
typedef struct node {
    char    firstName[11];
    char    lastName[16];
    char    gender;
    int     tenure;
    char    rate;
    float   salary;
    struct node *next;
} *NODEPTR;
```

Here's a rather simple algorithm to sort a linked list. Assume `list` points to an unsorted list and `sortList` points to `NULL`.

```
while list != null
    remove first node from list
    insert node into correct location into sortList
list = sortList
```

Here is what the data files for the lab look like:

```
Payfile2.txt

Debbie     Starr          F 3 W 1000.00
Joan       Jacobus        F 9 W  925.00
David      Renn           M 3 H    4.75
Albert     Cahana         M 3 H   18.75
Douglas    Sheer          M 5 W  250.00
Shari      Buchman        F 9 W  325.00
Sara       Jones          F 1 H    7.50
Ricky      Mofsen         M 6 H   12.50
Jean       Brennan        F 6 H    5.40
Jamie      Michaels       F 8 W  150.00


Hirefile2.txt

Barry      Allen          M 0 H    6.75
Nina       Pinella        F 0 W  425.00
Lane       Wagger         M 0 W  725.00


Firefile2.txt

Jean       Brennan        F
Ricky      Mofsen         M
```

Presented below are the `list.h` and `list.c` files for implementation of linear linked list storing employee structs.

```
// list.h

#ifndef _LIST_H
#define _LIST_H

typedef struct node {
    char    firstName[11];
    char    lastName[16];
    char    gender;
    int     tenure;
    char    rate;
    float   salary;
    struct node *next;
} *NODEPTR;

NODEPTR getNode(void);
void    freeNode(NODEPTR p);
void    addNodeFront(NODEPTR *list, NODEPTR t);
NODEPTR removeNodeFront(NODEPTR *list);
void    addNodeLast(NODEPTR *list, NODEPTR t);
NODEPTR deleteNodeLast(NODEPTR *list);
void    insertNode(NODEPTR *list, NODEPTR t);
void    insertNodeAfter(NODEPTR p, NODEPTR t);
NODEPTR removeNode(NODEPTR *list, NODEPTR t);
NODEPTR deleteNodeAfter(NODEPTR *list, NODEPTR p);
int     numElements(NODEPTR list);
void    freeList(NODEPTR *list);
void    error(char *msg);

#endif
```

```c
// list.c

#include <stdio.h>
#include <stdlib.h>
#include <string.h>
#include "list.h"


// returns the address of a newly created node
NODEPTR getNode(void) {
    NODEPTR p;

    p = (NODEPTR) malloc(sizeof(struct node));
    if (p == NULL) {
        error("List overflow.");
    }
    return(p);
}


// frees the node pointed to by p
void freeNode(NODEPTR p) {
    free(p);
}


// adds a node to the front of the list
void addNodeFront(NODEPTR *list, NODEPTR t) {
    t->next = *list;
    *list = t;
}


// removes a node from the front of the list
NODEPTR removeNodeFront(NODEPTR *list) {
    NODEPTR p;

    if (*list == NULL) {
        error("List underflow.");
    }
    p = *list;
    *list = p->next;
    return p;
}
```

```
// adds a node to the end of a list
void addNodeLast(NODEPTR *list, NODEPTR t) {
    NODEPTR p;

    if (*list == NULL) {
        *list = t;
    }
    else {
        p = *list;
        while (p->next) {
            p = p->next;
        }
        p->next = t;
    }
}


// deletes the node at the end of a list
NODEPTR deleteNodeLast(NODEPTR *list) {
    NODEPTR p = NULL, q;

    if (*list) {
        p = *list;
        q = NULL;
        while (p->next) {
            q = p;
            p = p->next;
        }
        if (!q) {
            *list = NULL;
        }
        else {
            q->next = NULL;
        }
    }
    return p;
}
```

```c
// insert a node into its correct location within the sorted list
void insertNode(NODEPTR *list, NODEPTR t) {
    NODEPTR p, q;

    p = *list;
    q = NULL;
    while (p != NULL && strcmp(p->lastName, t->lastName) < 0) {
        q = p;
        p = p->next;
    }
    if (q == NULL) {
        addNodeFront(list, t);
    }
    else {
        insertNodeAfter(q, t);
    }
}



// inserts a node after the node pointed to by p
void insertNodeAfter(NODEPTR p, NODEPTR t) {
    if (p == NULL || t == NULL) {
        error("Void insertion.");
    }
    t->next = p->next;
    p->next = t;
}



// removes a node from a list
NODEPTR removeNode(NODEPTR *list, NODEPTR t) {
    NODEPTR p, q;

    p = *list;
    q = NULL;
    while (p != NULL && strcmp(p->firstName, t->firstName)
                        && strcmp(p->lastName, t->lastName)) {
        q = p;
        p = p->next;
    }
    return q == NULL ? removeNodeFront(list) : deleteNodeAfter(list, q);
}
```

```
// deletes the node after the node pointed to by p
NODEPTR deleteNodeAfter(NODEPTR *list, NODEPTR p) {
    NODEPTR q;

    if (p == NULL || p->next == NULL) {
        error("Void deletion.");
    }
    q = p->next;
    p->next = q->next;
    return q;
}



// returns the number of nodes in the list
int numElements(NODEPTR list) {
    int count=0;

    while (list) {
        count++;
        list = list->next;
    }
    return count;
}



// frees all the nodes in a list
void freeList(NODEPTR *list) {
    NODEPTR p;

    while (*list) {
        p = *list;
        *list = p->next;
        freeNode(p);
    }
}



// display an error message and aborts the program
void error(char *msg) {
    puts(msg);
    exit(1);
}
```

Output from your program should be sent to the terminal window (your screen) as well as the requested `csis.txt` output file. Be sure to read the document on Capturing Program Output. Your full name must appear as a comment in the source file that contains `main()`. Be sure to include the `csis.txt` output file in your zip archive.

❖ Calculating Very Large Factorials Lab

This assignment will focus on the manipulation of linear linked lists. You are to write a C program which queries the user for an integer, n, and returns the exact value of that integer's factorial, $n!$. The limit to the size of n can be quite large (up to 9,999), producing factorials containing hundreds and thousands of digits. Needless to say, our methodology will circumvent the inherent representation limitations of integers and longs in our programming languages.

The Storage of $n!$

Factorials will be stored in linear linked lists in which each node contains two fields. The first field, `info`, will hold an integer containing a value from 0 through 999. The second field, `next`, holds a reference to the next node in the linear linked list. To be certain that the nature of this storage plan is correctly conceptualized, depicted below are the representations of 10! and 15!:

```
10! = 3,628,800

 -------         -------         -------
|  3   |====> |  628 |====> |  800 |====X
 -------         -------         -------

15! = 1,307,674,368,000

 -------         -------         -------         -------         -------
|  1   |====> |  307 |====> |  674 |====> |  368 |====> |  000 |====X
 -------         -------         -------         -------         -------
```

Note that by storing only three digits per node, the placement of commas in the output is readily accomplished as just another action in stepping from one node to the next.

Multiplication

Suppose that the value of 15! is to be multiplied by 6. The value of 15!, stored in a linked list, is the multiplicand. The 6, stored as an ordinary scalar, is the multiplier. The multiplicand is always held in a linked list, and the multiplier is always a numeral between 0 and 9. The action consists of a sequence of individual multiplications where the number from a nodes `info` field is multiplied by the fixed multiplier. There are as many individual multiplications as there are nodes in the list holding the multiplicand.

The sequence of individual multiplications yields a sequence of individual products that have to be synthesized into the actual product of the full multiplicand times the multiplier. Realize that the actual product is to be stored in another linked list, identical in form to that of the multiplicand. This is accomplished by treating the thousands digit of each individual product as a "carry out" which is added to the units digit of the individual product from the node to the immediate left. This is perhaps more clearly seen through a concrete example. A diagram of the multiplication of 15! times 6 is shown below:

```
15! = 1,307,674,368,000

 _____      _____      _____      _____      _____
|  1  |====> | 307 |====> | 674 |====> | 368 |====> | 000 |====X
 _____      _____      _____      _____      _____



        1            307          674          368          000
      * 6            * 6          * 6          * 6          * 6
      ----          ----         ----         ----         ----
        6           1842         4044         2208         0|000


      + 1           + 4          + 2          + 0
      ----          ----         ----         ----
    0|007          1|846        4|046        2|208



15! * 6 = 7,846,046,208,000

 _____      _____      _____      _____      _____
|  7  |====> | 846 |====> | 046 |====> | 208 |====> | 000 |====X
 _____      _____      _____      _____      _____
```

A complication to be contended with when implementing this scheme for multiplication is that the individual multiplications have to start at the right-hand end of the multiplicand, which is stored at the rear of the list. In fact, it is necessary to proceed through the list taking the nodes in the reversed order. There are several ways to deal with this. One is to make the multiplicand's list doubly-linked, so that it is just as readily traversed from the rear to the front as from the front to the rear. Another approach is to store the 3-digit numbers in nodes, from front to rear, in the order in which they will need to be processed (instead of the order reflecting conventional representation):

```
15! = 1,307,674,368,000


 -------         -------         -------         -------         -------
| 000 |====> | 368 |====> | 674 |====> | 307 |====> | 001 |====X
 -------         -------         -------         -------         -------
```

A further complication entails extending the multiplication scheme so that it can deal with multiplications like 15! times 16, which is to say multiplications in which a factorial is multiplied by a number with two or more digits. The extension is directly analogous to the paper and pencil multiplication taught in grade school in which the digits in the multiplier are treated one-by-one. Just as each successive digit in the multiplier (i.e., the unit's digit, the ten's digit, the hundred's digit) requires another "round of multiplying" the multiplicand by a numeral (a number between 0 and 9) and another "intermediate product line", so it goes in the extension of the present multiplication scheme.

In implementing the multiplication of 15! times 16, first 15! would be multiplied times 6 and the result stored in a new linked list. Then, 15! would be multiplied times 1 (the numeral in the multiplier's tens place), and this result would be stored in a new linked list of its own. Next, the numerals in the linked list holding the product of 15! times 1 would be shifted one digit to the left, effecting a multiplication by ten to transform the 15! * 1 product to a 15! * 10 product. Lastly, the corresponding digits in the two "helping lists" would be added to give the final result. For example:

```
        15! * 16 =              1307674368000
                                         * 16
                                 -------------
                                 7846046208000
                                 1307674368000
                                 -------------
                                20922789888000

 -----     -----     -----     -----     -----
|001|===>|307|===>|674|===>|368|===>|000|===X       15!
 -----     -----     -----     -----     -----
                                         * 16         * 16
----------------------------------------------------------


 -----     -----     -----     -----     -----
|007|===>|846|===>|046|===>|208|===>|000|===X       15! * 6
 -----     -----     -----     -----     -----


 -----     -----     -----     -----     -----
|001|===>|307|===>|674|===>|368|===>|000|===X       15! * 1
 -----     -----     -----     -----     -----


 -----     -----     -----     -----     -----
|013|===>|076|===>|743|===>|680|===>|000|===X       15! * 10 (shifted)
 -----     -----     -----     -----     -----


 -----     -----     -----     -----     -----
|007|===>|846|===>|046|===>|208|===>|000|===X       15! * 6 (recopied)
 -----     -----     -----     -----     -----

+

 -----     -----     -----     -----     -----
|013|===>|076|===>|743|===>|680|===>|000|===X       15! * 10 (recopied)
 -----     -----     -----     -----     -----

 0020     0|922     0|789     0|888     0|000       (sum before carry
out)

 +  0    +   0    +   0    +   0

 -----     -----     -----     -----     -----
|020|===>|922|===>|789|===>|888|===>|000|===X       sum
 -----     -----     -----     -----     -----
```

Although the $15!$ times 16 example just happens not to show this, provision has to be made for a node-to-node carry when adding the intermediate products in the "helping lists" to get the final result.

Because the program will have to support the multiplication of factorial multiplicands (e.g., $567!$) times three-digit numbers (e.g., 568), or four-digit numbers, the idea embraced above will have to be enhanced to accommodate up to three or four intermediate products in three or four "helping lists".

General Computational Strategy

Supposed the user wished to calculate $15!$. $15!$ would be derived in the most straightforward of all possible ways, building it up from one factorial. One factorial, "hard wired" into the program as 1, would be used as the basis for computing $2!$. Two factorial would be the basis for computing $3!$. This would continue until $14!$ and this would be used as the basis for deriving $15!$.

Specification

The program will query the user for an integer, n, and return the exact value of that integer's factorial, $n!$. While there is no reason that there has to be a logical limit to the size of the **n** the program can handle, your program should be able to handle a number at least as high as $9,999!$.

Since $n!$ may be an integer hundreds or thousands of digits long, its display will spill across several lines. When this happens, print out $n!$ with the most significant digit at the left end of the top line and the units digit on the right-hand end of the number's lowest line. You should print a comma after every third digit (i.e., between the hundred's digit and the thousand's digit, between the hundred thousand's digit and the million's digit, etc.). Break lines at points where commas belong, and put the comma to the right of the number on the line being broken. This signifies that the number continues on the next line. Specifically, print no more than 45 digits per line. Your program should also output statistics on the following:

* Number of digits in each factorial

* Time, in milliseconds, taken by program to calculate $n!$.

Your program should be run and produce output on the following data:

```
10, 98, 234, 567, 999, 5432, 9999
```

Note that this lab has nothing to do with factorials and the multiplication of numbers. By this I mean that I am not looking for a cleaner or more efficient approach to calculating factorials. The goal of this lab is to manipulate linear linked lists using dynamic storage allocation! You are required to implement the algorithm specified.

Output from your program should be sent to the terminal window (your screen) as well as the requested `csis.txt` output file. Be sure to read the document on Capturing Program Output. Your full name must appear as a comment in the source file that contains `main()`. Be sure to include the `csis.txt` output file in your zip archive.

Chapter 21. Bitwise Operators

Introduction to Bitwise Operators
Bitwise And
Masks
WordStar
Bitwise Or
Bitwise Exclusive-Or
Bitwise Negate
Left Shift Operator
Right Shift Operator
Rotate Example
Extracting Bit Fields
❖ Bitwise Operator Homework
❖ Bitwise Operator Lab

Introduction to Bitwise Operators

C provides a host of operators specifically designed for performing operations on individual bits:

```
&       bit-and
|       bit-or
^       bit-exclusive or
~       bit-negate (one's complement)
<<      left shift
>>      right shift
```

All bitwise operators except the bit-negate are binary operators and therefore take two operands. Bit operations can be performed on any type of integer value in C, such as:

```
int         unsigned int
short       unsigned short
long        unsigned long
char        unsigned char
```

but not on:

```
float
double
long double
```

The bitwise operators are applied in parallel to the individual bit positions within each operand. This is unlike logical operators that treat each operand as one single zero (false) or non-zero (true) value.

Bitwise And

Similar to the logical AND operator (`&&`), the bitwise-and operator (`&`) produces a true value only if both operands are true (i.e., have non-zero values).

b1	b2	b1 & b2
0	0	0
0	1	0
1	0	0
1	1	1

We assume a 16-bit integer:

```
// and1.c

#include <stdio.h>

int main(void) {
    int x = 0x2719;        // 0010 0111 0001 1001
    int y = 0x35CD;        // 0011 0101 1100 1101
    int z;

    z = x & y;             // 0010 0101 0000 1001
    printf("z = 0x%x\n", z);
    return 0;
}
```

The output of this program is:

```
z = 0x2509
```

Note that each of the corresponding bits within each `int` variable are bit-anded together.

Here's another example:

```
// and2.c

#include <stdio.h>

int main(void) {
    int x = 0x1234;            // 0001 0010 0011 0100
    int y = 0x3468;            // 0011 0100 0110 1000
    int z = 0x5248;            // 0101 0010 0100 1000

    printf("0x%x\n", x & x);
    printf("0x%x\n", x & y);
    printf("0x%x\n", x & y & z);
    printf("0x%x\n", x & 1);
    return 0;
}
```

In the first `printf()` statement, any quantity bit-anded with itself returns itself as a value:

```
x = 0x1234 = 0001 0010 0011 0100
x = 0x1234 = 0001 0010 0011 0100
             -------------------
             0001 0010 0011 0100 = 0x1234
```

In the second `printf()` statement, variables x and y are bit-anded together producing:

```
x = 0x1234 = 0001 0010 0011 0100
y = 0x3468 = 0011 0100 0110 1000
             -------------------
             0001 0000 0010 0000 = 0x1020
```

In the third `printf()` statement, all three variables x, y, and z are bit-anded together producing:

```
x = 0x1234 = 0001 0010 0011 0100
y = 0x3468 = 0011 0100 0110 1000
z = 0x5248 = 0101 0010 0100 1000
             -------------------
             0001 0000 0000 0000 = 0x1000
```

The fourth `printf()` statement has the effect of extracting the rightmost bit of x, either a 0 or a 1.

```
x = 0x1234 = 0001 0010 0011 0100
    0x0001 = 0000 0000 0000 0001
             -------------------
             0000 0000 0000 0000 = 0x0
```

Note that this is a good test to see whether x is odd or even:

```
printf("%s", x & 1 ? "Odd" : "Even");
```

Keep in mind the distinction between the bitwise-and operator (&) and the logical-and operator (&&):

```
// and3.c

#include <stdio.h>

int main(void) {
    int x = 1;
    int y = 2;

    printf("bitwise = %d    logical = %d\n", x & y, x && y);
    return 0;
}
```

The output produced looks like this:

```
bitwise = 0    logical = 1
```

Masks

Bitwise ANDing is frequently used for masking operations. A *mask* is a constant or variable that is used to extract desired bits in a variable or expression. A mask can be used to set specific bits of a data item to 0. In the example below, we'll preserve the rightmost two bits from x and zero (mask) out all of the other bits:

```
// mask1.c

#include <stdio.h>

int main(void) {
    int x    = 0x0679;        // 0000 0110 0111 1001
    int mask = 0x0003;        // 0000 0000 0000 0011

    x = x & mask;             // 0000 0000 0000 0001
    printf("x = 0x%x\n", x);
    return 0;
}
```

The output produced is:

```
x = 0x1
```

Note that we could have written:

```
x &= mask;
```

Now suppose we want to set all but the rightmost four bits of a word to 0:

```
// mask2.c

#include <stdio.h>

int main(void) {
    int x    = 0x1234;        // 0001 0010 0011 0100
    int mask = 0x000F;        // 0000 0000 0000 1111

    x &= mask;                // 0000 0000 0000 0100
    printf("x = 0x%x\n", x);
    return 0;
}
```

The output produced is:

```
x = 0x4
```

We can also use a mask to determine the low-order bit of an `int` expression:

```
// mask3.c

#include <stdio.h>

int main(void) {
    int i;
    int mask = 0x0001;        // 0000 0000 0000 0001

    for (i = 0; i < 10; i++) {
        printf("%d ", i & mask);
    }
    return 0;
}
```

The above program prints an alternating sequence of 0's and 1's:

```
0 1 0 1 0 1 0 1 0 1
```

If we wished to find the value of a particular bit within an expression, we can use a mask that is 1 in that position and 0 elsewhere. For example, we can check the 5th bit from the right of an `int`:

```c
// mask4.c

#include <stdio.h>

int main(void) {
    int x    = 0x1234;        // 0001 0010 0011 0100
    int mask = 0x0010;        // 0000 0000 0001 0000

    if (x & mask) {
        printf("Bit is a 1.");
    }
    else {
        printf("Bit is a 0.");
    }
    return 0;
}
```

The output produced is:

```
Bit is a 1.
```

WordStar

WordStar was a word processor application that had a dominant market share during the early-to-mid 1980s. It used the high-order bit of an ASCII character for special formatting purposes.

WordStar would set the high order bit on the last character of a word to flag the location it can insert spaces to justify the right margin. It also set the high order bit on the spaces it inserts to know which spaces it can remove when it rejustifies the text. For example, it wouldn't want to remove the double space you put at the end of a sentence.

If you were to use a simple text editor to output the characters in a file created by WordStar, it might look something like this:

```
6Æ† WritÂ · functioÓ calle‰ find_strinÁ tÔ determinÂ iÊ onÂ† characteÚ ç
strinÁ† existÛ† insidÂ† anotheÚ† stringÆ† ThÂ firsÙ† argumenÙ† tÔ† thÂ ç
functioÓ shoul‰ bÂ thÂ characteÚ strinÁ thaÙ iÛ tÔ bÂ searche‰ an‰ thÂ ç
secon‰† argumenÙ† thÂ† strinÁ wÂ arÂ intereste‰† ióT findingÆ† IÊ† thÂ ç
functioÓ findÛ thÂ specifie‰ string"† theÓ havÂ iÙ returÓ thÂ locatioÓ ç
ió thÂ sourcÂ strinÁ wherÂ thÂ strinÁ waÛ foundÆ† IÊ thÂ functioÓ doeÛ ç
not find the string, then have it return -1.   (25)
```

In fact, this is a question from an exam that I created with WordStar in 1986. I recently came across the file and wanted to view its contents. The reason for all of the gobbledygook is due to the fact that WordStar has set the high order bit on many of the characters. Keep in mind that ASCII is actually a 7-bit code and never used the high-order bit to define a character. WordStar used this high order bit for its own purposes!

We can create a program that reads the file one character at a time. The program creates a mask to turn off the high-order bit before outputting the character:

```
putchar(c & 0x7f);
```

This statement `bit-ands` the character with the mask `01111111`, which effectively turns off the high-order bit.

Here's the code:

```
// strip.c

#include <stdio.h>
#include <stdlib.h>

int main(void) {
    int c;
    char fileName[32];
    FILE *fp;

    printf("Enter filename: ");
    gets(fileName);
    fopen_s(&fp, fileName, "r");
    if (fp == NULL) {
        printf("File could not be opened.\n");
        exit(1);
    }
    while((c = getc(fp)) != EOF) {
        putchar(c & 0x7f);
    }
    fclose(fp);
    return 0;
}
```

Here's the output:

```
6.  Write a function called find_string to determine if one  character
string  exists  inside  another  string.  The first  argument  to  the
function should be the character string that is to be searched and the
second  argument  the  string we are  interested  in  finding.  If  the
function finds the specified string,  then have it return the location
in the source string where the string was found.  If the function does
not find the string, then have it return -1.  (25)
```

Not a bad exam question!

Bitwise Or

Similar to the logical OR operator (| |), the bitwise-or operator (|) produces a true value if at least one operand is true (i.e., has a non-zero value).

b1	b2	b1	b2
0	0	0
0	1	1
1	0	1
1	1	1

```c
// or1.c

#include <stdio.h>

int main(void) {
    int x = 0x2719;      // 0010 0111 0001 1001
    int y = 0x85CD;      // 1000 0101 1100 1101
    int z;

    z = x | y;           // 1010 0111 1101 1101
    printf("z = 0x%x\n", z);
    return 0;
}
```

The output of this program is:

```
z = 0xA7DD
```

The bitwise-or operator is used to set specified bits of a word to 1 (i.e., to turn on bits). For example, suppose we want to set the rightmost 3 bits of an int to 1, regardless of the state of these bits before the operation was performed:

```
// or2.c

#include <stdio.h>

int main(void) {
    int x    = 0x1234;        // 0001 0010 0011 0100
    int mask = 0x0007;        // 0000 0000 0000 0111
    int z;

    z = x | mask;             // 0001 0010 0011 0111
    printf("z = 0x%x\n", z);
    return 0;
}
```

The output of this program is:

```
z = 0x1237
```

Now suppose we wanted to write a program to *flip* (if on, turn off; if off, turn on) the 5th bit of an `int`. One approach would be:

```
// flip1.c

#include <stdio.h>

int main(void) {
    int x    = 0x1234;              // 0001 0010 0011 0100
    int mask = 0x0010;              // 0000 0000 0001 0000

    if (x & mask) {                 // bit is on, turn it off
        x &= 0xFFEF;
    }
    else {                          // bit is off, turn it on
        x |= 0x0010;
    }
    printf("x = 0x%x\n", x);   // 0001 0010 0010 0100
    return 0;
}
```

The output produced is:

```
x = 0x1224
```

This code works fine but can be simplified with the use of the bitwise exclusive-or operator.

Bitwise Exclusive-Or

The bitwise exclusive-or operator produces a 1 when the two operands are of a different value and produced a 0 when the two operands are the same.

b1	b2	b1 ^ b2
0	0	0
0	1	1
1	0	1
1	1	0

For example:

```
// xor1.c

#include <stdio.h>

int main(void) {
    int x = 0x1234;              // 0001 0010 0011 0100
    int y = 0x85CD;              // 1000 0101 1100 1101
    int z;

    z = x ^ y;                   // 1001 0111 1111 1001
    printf("z = 0x%x\n", z);
    return 0;
}
```

The output of this program is:

```
z = 0x97F9
```

Note that any value exclusive-ored with itself produces 0:

```
// xor2.c

#include <stdio.h>

int main(void) {
    int x = 0x1234;                      // 0001 0010 0011 0100
    printf("x = 0x%x\n", x ^ x);         // 0000 0000 0000 0000
    return 0;
}
```

The output of this program is:

```
x = 0x0
```

This concept is frequently used in assembler language to clear a register:

```
XOR    AL, AL
```

We can now use the bitwise exclusive-or operator to rewrite the previous program which flips the 5th bit from the right of an `int`:

```
// flip2.c

#include <stdio.h>

int main(void) {
    int x    = 0x1234;        // 0001 0010 0011 0100
    int mask = 0x0010;        // 0000 0000 0001 0000

    x ^= mask;                // 0001 0010 0010 0100
    printf("x = 0x%x\n", x);
    return 0;
}
```

The output produced is:

```
x = 0x1224
```

The bitwise exclusive-or operator can also be used to exchange two values without the need for a temporary third variable:

```
// xor3.c

#include <stdio.h>

int main(void) {
    int x = 0x1234;            // 0001 0010 0011 0100
    int y = 0xABCD;            // 1010 1011 1100 1101

    x ^= y;
    y ^= x;
    x ^= y;
    printf("x = 0x%x\n", x);
    printf("y = 0x%x\n", y);
    return 0;
}
```

The output produced is:

```
x = 0xABCD
y = 0x1234
```

Bitwise Negate

The bitwise-negate operator is a unary operator. That means the operator requires only one operand. Its effect is to flip the bit of the operand.

```
b          ~b
0          1
1          0
```

For example:

```c
// negate1.c

#include <stdio.h>

int main(void) {
    int x = 0x1234;              // 0001 0010 0011 0100
    int y;

    y = ~x;                      // 1110 1101 1100 1011
    printf("y = 0x%x\n", y);
    return 0;
}
```

The output of this program is:

```
y = 0xEDCB
```

Remember not to confuse the bit-negate (~) operator with the arithmetic minus (-) operator or with the logical negation (!) operator. For example, if x is equal to 0:

```
-x = 0

!x = 1   (true)

~x = -1 (when treated as a signed value)
```

Note that the result of bitwise-and, bitwise-or, and bitwise-exclusive-or does not depend on the word size of the computer, but the result of bit-negate does. We can use this to our advantage.

Suppose we want to write a binary value which consists of all 1-bits except for the low-order 3-bits. We should write the value not as:

```
0xFFF8 (16-bit value)
```

nor as:

```
0xfffffff8 (32-bit value)
```

but as:

```
~7
```

which is appropriate for any word size!!!

When a bitwise operation is performed between two values that are of different sizes (`long` and `short`), the system aligns the operands on the right. If the shorter of the two items is a signed quantity, and the value is negative, the sign is extended to the left to match the number of bits contained in the larger sized value.

Finally, the precedence of the bitwise operators (`&`, `|`, `^`) falls below that of `==` and `!=`. This implies that bit-testing expressions like:

```
if ((x & mask) == 0)
```

must be fully parenthesized to give proper results.

Left Shift Operator

When a left shift ($<<$) operation is performed on a value, the bits contained within the value are literally shifted to the left. Bits that are shifted out through the high-order bit are lost and 0's are always shifted into the low-order bit.

For example:

```
// lshift.c

#include <stdio.h>

int main(void) {
    int num = 3;                // 0000 0000 0000 0110

    num = num << 1;             // 0000 0000 0000 1100
    printf("num = %d\n", num);
    return 0;
}
```

In the program above, all bits of `num` are shifted by one position to the left. The output produced is:

```
num = 6
```

Notice that left shifting a value by one results in multiplying the value that is shifted by 2. The left shift operation could also have been written as:

```
num <<= 1;
```

Below is a function that outputs the bit representation of a 16-bit `int` value:

```
// bitprnt1.c

int bitprnt1(int num) {
    int i, mask;

    mask = 1;
    mask <<= 15;
    for (i = 1; i <= 16; i++) {
        printf(num & mask ? "1" : "0");
        num <<= 1;
    }
    return 0;
}
```

Unfortunately this function is not portable due to the fact that the `sizeof(int)` will vary on different computers. We thus modify the program to make it portable to different computers as follows:

```
// bitprnt2.c

int bitprnt2(int num) {
    int i, mask;

    mask = 1;
    mask <<= (sizeof(int)*8)-1;
    for (i = 1; i <= sizeof(int)*8; i++) {
        printf(num & mask ? "1" : "0");
        num <<= 1;
    }
    return 0;
}
```

Right Shift Operator

The right shift (`>>`) operator shifts the bits of a value to the right. Bits that are shifted out of the low-order bit are lost. Right shifting an unsigned value will always result in 0's being shifted in on the left.

For example:

```
// rshift.c

#include <stdio.h>

int main(void) {
    int num = 12;                    // 0000 0000 0000 1100

    num = num >> 1;                  // 0000 0000 0000 0110
    printf("num = %d\n", num);
    return 0;
}
```

In the program above, all bits of `num` are left shifted by one position to the right. The output produced is:

```
num = 6
```

Notice that right shifting a value by one results in dividing the value that is shifted by 2. The right shift operation could also have been written as:

```
num >>= 1;
```

What is shifted in on the left for signed values depends on the sign of the value that is being shifted and also how this operation is implemented on your system. If the sign bit is 0 (positive value), then 0's will be shifted in, no matter what system we're on. If the sign bit is 1, some computers will shift in 1's *(arithmetic right-shift)* and some will shift in 0's *(logical right shift)*.

C guarantees no defined result if an attempt is made to left or right shift a value by an amount that is greater than or equal to the number of bits in the size of the data item (left operand). The right operand may not be negative.

Below is a function to count the number of 1-bits in the integer argument.

```
// bitcount.c

int bitCount(unsigned num) {
    int count = 0;

    while(num) {
        if (num & 1) {
            count++;
        }
        num >>= 1;
    }
    return count;
}
```

Here are several portable programs that compute the number of bits in an `int`.

```
// numbits1.c

#include <stdio.h>

int main(void) {
    int i = 0, num = 1;

    while(num) {
        num <<= 1;
        i++;
    }
    printf("%d\n", i);
    return 0;
}
```

```
// numbits2.c

#include <stdio.h>

int main(void) {
    int i;
    unsigned num = ~0;

    for (i = 0; num > 0; i++) {
        num >>= 1;
    }
    printf("5d\n", i);
    return 0;
}


// numbits3.c

#include <stdio.h>

int main(void) {
    int i;
    unsigned num = ~0;

    for (i = 1; num >>=1; i++) {
        ;
    }
    printf("%d\n", i);
    return 0;
}
```

Rotate Example

Assembler language code typically contains two rotate instructions. The rotate right (ROR) instruction shifts bits to the right. Bits shifted out at the right are shifted back in at the left. For example, the assembler instructions:

```
MOV AL, 10111011
ROR AL, 1
```

have the effect of shifting a single bit out of the right and back into the left:

```
              --------------------
=======> |                      |   ====> | |
| |           --------------------              | |
| |                                             | |
| |<=========================================| |
```

Register AL now contains the value 11011101.

The rotate left (ROL) instruction shifts bits to the left. Bits shifted out at the left are shifted back in at the right. For example, the assembler instructions:

```
MOV AL, 10000000
ROL AL, 1
```

have the effect of shifting a single bit out of the left and back into the right:

```
              --------------------
<======= |                      |   <====| |
| |           --------------------              | |
| |                                             | |
| |=========================================>| |
```

Register AL now contains the value 00000001. Note that if you have 8 rotates, you end up with the original number!

Unfortunately, C does not have a left or a right rotate operator. So let's develop a function to simulate the rotate left and rotate right statements. The function will take two arguments:

The value to be rotated (num)

The number of bits the value will be rotated by (x). If x is a positive integer, we will perform a left rotate and if x is a negative integer, we will perform a right rotate.

In order to compute the result of rotating num to the left by x bits, we will utilize the following three-step algorithm:

Extract the leftmost x bits of num.

Shift num to the left by x bits.

Put the extracted bits back into num at the right.

We will use a similar algorithm to perform a rotate right.

```c
// rotate.c

unsigned rotate(unsigned num, int x) {
    unsigned bits, result;

    if (x > 0) {
        bits = num >> (sizeof(unsigned)*8 - x);
        result = num << x | bits;
    }
    else {
        x = -x;
        bits = num << (sizeof(unsigned)*8 - x);
        result = num >> x | bits;
    }
    return result;
}
```

1. Let `b1 = b2 = 1`. Which of the following does not have the same result as the others?

a) `b1 & b2`   c) `b1 ^ b2`
b) `b1 | b2`   d) `~(~b2)`

2. Evaluate the expression: `(00001000 & 11000101) ^ (11110000)`

a) `00111101`   c) `00111101`
b) `11000000`   d) `11110000`

3. For any 8-bit integer `x`, which of the following does not result in zero?

a) `x &= (~x)`   c) `x <<= 8`
b) `x ^= x`   d) `x |= x`

4. Which of the following is true?

a) Any bit "ANDed" with 0 yields 0.
b) Any bit "ANDed" with 1 yields 1.
c) Any bit "ANDed" with 0 yields 1.
d) Any bit "ANDed" with 1 yields 0.

5. Write a single C statement to set the middle 16 bits of a 32-bit integer `num` to zero but leaves the left 8 and the right 8 bits as they originally were.

6. Write a C function with the prototype:

```
int compare(int x, int y);
```

that returns the number of corresponding bits in `x` and `y` which differ. For example, if `x = 9` and `y = 97`, the number of corresponding bits which differ is three.

```
x  =   9  =  0000 0000 0000 0000 0000 0000 1001
y  =  97  =  0000 0000 0000 0000 0000 0110 0001
```

❖ Bitwise Operator Lab

Part 1

Write a program, `bitSet.c`, which contains a function, `bitSet()`, that sets a specified number of bits in an `int` to a particular value and outputs the resultant `int` in hexadecimal notation. The function prototype follows:

```
void bitSet(int *num, int value, int start, int size);
```

The function arguments are defined as follows:

```
num        Pointer to an int in which the specified bits are to be set

value      int containing the value that the bits are to be set to,
           right justified

start      int specifying starting bit number, with the leftmost bit
           numbered 0

size       int specifying the size of the field
```

So, for example, the call:

```
bitSet(&num, 0, 2, 5);
```

would have the effect of setting the five bits contained in `num`, beginning with the third bit from the left (bit number 2), to zero.

Similarly, the call:

```
bitSet(&num, 0X55, 0, 8);
```

would set the eight leftmost bits of `num` to hexadecimal 55.

Your program should work on the data given below:

```
num         value    start    size
0x12345678  0x0      2        5
0xABCD1234  0x55     0        8
0x0000FFFF  0x17     4        9
0x76543210  0xAB     7        8
0x00002F7A  0xC4     3        10
```

Note that you may hard-code the test data into your program.

Part II
Write a program, `bitSearch.c`, which contains a function, `bitSearch()`, that looks for the occurrence of a specified pattern of bits inside an `int`. The function prototype follows:

```
int bitSearch(int source, int pattern, int n);
```

The function will search the integer `source`, starting at the leftmost bit, to see if the rightmost n bits of `pattern` occur in `source`. If `pattern` is found, then have the function return the number of the bit that pattern begins at, where the leftmost bit is bit number 0. If `pattern` is not found, then have the function return -1.

So, for example, the call:

```
index = bitSearch(0x21F41234, 0x5, 3);
```

would cause `bitSearch()` to search the number:

```
0x21F41234 (0010 0001 1111 0100 0001 0010 0011 0100)
```

for the occurrence of the three bit pattern `0x5` `(101)`. The function would return `11` to indicate that the pattern was found in the source beginning with bit number `11`.

Your program should work on the data given below:

source	pattern	n
0x21F41234	0x5	3
0x49AC12DF	0xB	5
0x6BB63221	0x3	3
0x74D85678	0x5	3
0x0001ABAB	0xF	4

Note that you may hard-code the test data in your program.

Remember that the `main()` function should appear as the first function in the program. Be sure to use function prototypes for each of the functions that are used in your program.

Output from your program should be sent to the terminal window (your screen) as well as the requested output files. Be sure to read the document on Capturing Program Output. Your full name must appear as a comment in the source file that contains `main()`. Be sure to include the output files in your zip archive.

Index

Made in the USA
Middletown, DE
26 July 2019